The Fine Delight

The Fine Delight

Postconciliar Catholic Literature

Nicholas Ripatrazone

CASCADE *Books* · Eugene, Oregon

THE FINE DELIGHT
Postconciliar Catholic Literature

Cascade Books
An Imprint of Wipf and Stock Publishers
199 W. 8th Ave., Suite 3
Eugene, OR 97401

www.wipfandstock.com

ISBN 13: 978–1-62032–172-0

Cataloging-in-Publication Data

Ripatrazone, Nicholas.

The fine delight : postconciliar Catholic literature / Nicholas Ripatrazone.

viii + 194 p. ; 23 cm. Includes bibliographical data and index.

ISBN 13: 978–1-62032–172-0

1. American literature—Catholic authors—History and criticism. 2. Catholics—United States—Intellectual life. I. Title.

PS153.C3 R90 2013

Manufactured in the U.S.A.

Contents

Acknowledgments

Sections of this book previously appeared in different forms in *Shenandoah*, *The Quarterly Conversation*, and *Pilgrim Journal*; I appreciate the support of those editors.

Many thanks to Alice Elliott Dark, whose careful mentoring helped turn an interest and concept into a coherent plan, and Rev. Patrick Madden, whose ability to wed theological and pastoral work was influential, even from a distance.

This book was written in the memory of Rev. Joseph A. Celia, campus priest of Susquehanna University.

Sincerest thanks to my parents and family, and to my wife, Jennifer, for her endless support, friendship, and love.

Permissions

Introduction

A New Language, A New Literature

"The world holds no interest for me," wrote Jesuit paleontologist Pierre Teilhard de Chardin, "unless I look forward, but when my eyes are on the future it is full of excitement."[1] Teilhard was writing to console a friend who had recently lost his mother, but those words apply to the present. Nearly fifty years after the Second Vatican Council, the International Commission on English in the Liturgy released a retranslation of the Roman Missal. Response was fractured. Parishioners scanned laminated liturgical crib sheets, relearning a language of Mass that had been habitual. Revisions such as "consubstantial" and "your Spirit" elevated the language of Mass to a higher register that neared the cadence and tenor of Latin, and forced parishioners to reflect on the context and import of their words. The future had arrived, and it sounded much like the past.

Months of garbled choral responses and confused stares are to be expected when the metaphorical language of faith changes. Most value communication through clarity and concreteness in our daily language. Leave room for cream and sugar, take the second left, wait for me at the entrance. Beyond those daily declaratives, words are attempts to clothe ambiguity. Whether by design or reaction, linguistic shorthand is used to make the divine known. Oversimplification abounds.

The experience of Latin Mass was not only a Sunday shock to the American system: the disruption was international. Congregations around the world listened to a dead tongue reborn through the ritual of Mass. For traditionalists, Latin Mass enabled believers to be placed in the presence of the divine through reverent, foreign language. The liturgical changes that followed in Vatican II were both practical and symbolic. The tongue

---

1. Chardin, *Letters*, 104.

particular to a region replaced Latin. Americans watched the Eucharist be consecrated in the same language spoken at the kitchen table. Some felt the change lessened the moment of liturgical celebration: local language seemed to only clothe the ritual, rather than sharing its skin. Others appreciated the return to a more communal Mass that closely postdated the time of Christ.

Denis Crouan's laments about French liturgy after Vatican II parallel many American critiques. Crouan argues the Council's intention was to revise the existing liturgy, not create a new rite. Parishioners need not "comprehend the whole meaning of the liturgy" because "the liturgy occupies a place beyond our normal, everyday means of comprehension."[2] It would be a "mistake" for the liturgy to be "simplified" or "explained . . . as it unfolds."[3] The Vatican II changes, for Crouan, resulted in "personalized ceremonies . . . utterly devoid of elegant expression."[4]

In late 2011 the arrival of the new Mass translation led commentator Robert Fay to wonder whether the move from Latin to the more regional Masses described by Crouan might have resulted in a profound shift in the creation of Catholic imaginative literature. Fay's thesis is enticing: if writers such as Walker Percy and Flannery O'Connor are posited as the last arresting Catholic voices, and those writers lived in a preconciliar world, Fay's perceived dearth of a present, uniquely "Catholic artistic vision"[5] might be tied to a larger decline in the Catholic aesthetic caused by the more colloquial Mass. Although Fay ends his essay on an upbeat note, wondering if the new translation might "spark a Catholic literary renaissance," his argument appears grounded in static interpretation of Catholic literature and nostalgia for a preconciliar Catholic literary world, rather than an observation of how that world has evolved.[6] Prescriptive analyses are common in Catholic literary criticism, and though they often arise from the good intention to identify and define Catholicism as a singular culture and faith, they have ironically helped marginalize a profoundly diverse and thriving aesthetic canon. Like Teilhard, Catholic literary critics should face forward; they can be informed and inspired by the past, but should not force its repetition.

2. Crouan, *Liturgy*, 20, 21.

3. Ibid., 21.

4. Ibid., 28.

5. Fay, "Catholic Writers," para. 3.

6. Ibid., para. 14.

The Fine Delight looks backward to reach forward. This book owes its title to the first line of Jesuit priest Gerard Manley Hopkins's final sonnet, "To R.B": "The fine delight that fathers thought." Hopkins's poetry was both linguistically radical and profoundly Catholic. "The fine delight" that fathered thought for Hopkins was his deep faith in Christ; the irony of the poem is that the narrator offers meticulously crafted verse to lament his "winter world" of no creative inspiration. The poem was addressed to his friend Robert Bridges, later poet laureate of England, whose agnostic beliefs were a contrast to Hopkins's faith. Bridges's posthumous collection and publication of Hopkins's poetry set the precedent for a tradition of secular writers who have adored Hopkins's idiosyncratic creativity and prosody.

Hopkins revered Christ through complicated poetry, not simple sermonizing. "To R.B." and Hopkins's own life are testaments to the eternally complicated connection between the creative act and religious faith. Ron Hansen dramatized Hopkins's biography in the novel *Exiles*, which contains a scene of the priest during a moment of recreation on a Welsh hill. Beneath the snow, the "air seemed cleansed; the leaden sky was roped with cloud; a blue bloom seemed to have spread upon the distant south."[7] Hopkins sees several sheep, and thinks that "'Shepherd' in Latin was *pastor*, and smiled as he thought of himself as twice or thrice pastoral there among the animals, in the graciousness and serenity of a school of theology."[8]

The interaction is ripe for analogy. Successful Catholic pastoral work requires inventiveness: the ability to transform concepts into analogies, analogies into practical advice and action. Although he was plagued by depression and physical maladies during his lifetime, Hopkins's poetry is uniquely pastoral in its transformative qualities. Few other poets have infused the mundane with such divinity. Hansen, though, is likely playing with the connotation of sheep as mindless followers, and Hopkins almost shares in the joke, likely aware that his personal engagement with Christ through poetic invocation made him an outsider, even among the pious.

Hopkins was not a purely devotional poet, although his predisposition toward breathless verve and exclamation might confuse the uninformed reader. His intensely personal work requires unlocking, and the key is his usage of poetry to both transform and disrupt meaning. Christ was the inciting force for Hopkins's poetry, and contemporary British idiom was

7. Hansen, *Exiles*, 20.
8. Ibid., 20–21.

an insufficient mode of expression. Extreme compression of imagery and a halting progression of adjectives and phrases cleaved his language from contemporary idiom. While the oft-anthologized "The Windhover" is appreciated for layering of image, the violence of the final stanza, "sheer plod makes plough down sillion / shine, and blue-bleak embers, ah my dear, / fall, gall themselves, and gash gold-vermillion," reveals a writer convinced that the religious sense is not compatible with complacency.

Hopkins might unsettle, but being authentically "charged with the grandeur of God" results in visceral disruption. *The Fine Delight* offers that the work of Hopkins was a precursor to the work of postconciliar Catholic writers: Catholics of varying stripes who have created personal visions of faith fueled by idiosyncratic passion rather than orthodoxy. Hopkins feared the publication and distribution of his work during his lifetime, since many peers and parishioners would find his work, like the material of "Pied Beauty," "counter, original, spare, strange." The writers profiled in *The Fine Delight* range in both subject and personal theology, with each creating imaginative work that, at some level, thrives on its implicit and explicit tensions with dogma. That tension is an archetypal characteristic of Catholic literature throughout the ages, but has been uniquely sharpened by Vatican II.

The Fine Delight hopes to reveal how tension has created moving Catholic literature, while simultaneously recognizing that what identifies or defines a work as "Catholic" is an evolving, and sometimes contradictory, set of criteria. Additionally, this book subscribes to Hopkins's notion of poetic transformation: that literature does not simply represent reality, it transforms and elevates that reality, forcing the reader to return to the natural world with renewed appreciation and sensitivity. In those ways, Catholic literature serves as a supplementary form of liturgy.

The classic works of Catholic literature are worthy of revisiting, of mining for application toward the ever-complicating present. They fully exemplify the mystery of the Catholic faith. Unfortunately, Catholic literature is often described in the past tense, and usually that past ends with Vatican II. Readers and critics need not always look backward to discover great literature in the Catholic tradition. *The Fine Delight* will offer the work of three contemporary Catholic writers whose work is particularly ripe for pastoral application and personal reflection: Ron Hansen, Andre Dubus, and Paul Mariani. These writers are also necessary axis points of perspective and style in the postconciliar literary world. The catholic appeal of these writers speaks to their Catholicism: in creating work enjoyed by both secular and religious audiences, they greatly expand the cultural reach of the faith.

Most importantly, these three Catholic writers have paid profound attention toward revealing the Word through their finely crafted words, and yet do so in a manner that does not arrive as tired proselytizing. Ron Hansen's short novel, *Mariette in Ecstasy*, is a deeply compelling story, offered to the reader in sentences wrought with the most extreme care. Hansen's narrative is built phrase by phrase, echoing the solemn progression of Mass. The white spaces of his pages occupy the silence of prayerful devotion. Hansen, a deacon in the San Jose Diocese, is a tangible example of an artist operating at the highest aesthetic level, while also presenting essential truths of the Catholic faith. Hansen identifies "churchgoing and religion" as the "origin of my vocation as a writer," crediting "Catholicism's feast for the senses, its ethical concerns, its insistence on seeing God in all things."[9] Liturgy taught Hansen that "storytelling mattered."[10]

Andre Dubus, in his essays and fiction, dramatizes the difficulty of faith-based decisions in a secular world. His characters live a hard-earned Catholicism. They are not angels, and they are rarely saints. His essays are simultaneously soft and masculine, and pinpoint the divine in the daily. Dubus makes the paradoxical genuine. He writes that the act of making sandwiches for his young daughters is sacramental: "this holding of plastic bags, of knives, of bread, of cutting board, this pushing of the chair, this spreading of mustard on bread, this trimming of liverwurst, of ham."[11] Dubus shows how a revision of perspective makes the simple spectacular.

Paul Mariani's contributions to Catholic literature include poetry and criticism. His particular attention toward the life and poetry of Gerard Manley Hopkins adds a Catholic tone of appreciation to existing scholarship. His devotion to Hopkins is almost a poetic-critical form of the Spiritual Exercises. Mariani's own poetry ponders the "sweet abyss between myself & You," the anxieties of belief during pockets of pain.[12] Mariani can be seen as a prototype of the Catholic literary critic: one who enhances understanding of misunderstood Catholic writers, but also widens his scope to find grace elsewhere.

The Fine Delight, though, does not mean to posit these three writers as the only exemplars of a literary Catholicism. Recent years have included

---

9. Hansen, *A Stay*, xii.

10. Ibid.

11. Dubus, *Meditations*, 89.

12. Mariani, *Epitaphs*, 181.

an absolute wealth of Catholic literature. *The Fine Delight* will also profile emerging and established writers offering essential, diverse representations of faith. These writers, in further fragmenting a static definition of Catholic literature, deepen the conversation about that literature. Paul Lisicky, Anthony Carelli, Joe Bonomo, Mary Biddinger, Amanda Auchter, Brian Doyle, and Kaya Oakes, among other contemporary writers, reveal a vibrant new canon. John C. Waldmeir explains that postconciliar writers "[retain] a fascination with the unique beauty and art of the Roman Church precisely because it calls them to a special kind of reverence."[13] These writers, like Hopkins, use both personal and institutional tensions to develop their individual aesthetics. The final section of *The Fine Delight* qualifies and narrows these interrogations toward the personage of the priest. Erin McGraw, John Reimringer, and Tom Bailey dramatize a changing priesthood that remains at the center of public Catholicism.

For some reading this volume, the discussions of Hansen, Dubus, and Mariani will be an introduction to essential contemporary Catholic writers. Others already familiar with the work of these writers will appreciate extended critical treatments that are long overdue. Students of literature will find useful analysis of a misunderstood literary period, and atypical considerations of writers such as Don DeLillo and Jeffrey Eugenides. Additionally, this book will offer an explicit and implicit pastoral framework toward approaching the best in contemporary Catholic literature. This book is not a pastoral guidebook; rather, it purports to offer dramatizations of faith written by artists devoted to representing complexity rather than orthodoxy. As with any useful pastoral work, the application must ultimately be personal and borne out of regional context, but *The Fine Delight* will offer many points of inspiration.

In a related vein, this volume seeks to engage the perceived separation of Catholic scholarship and personal belief. As a Catholic, I find it disingenuous to proceed further without that public confession, hoping that the reader, like a caring priest, will value good intention over perceived bias. Presupposition that the only worthwhile examinations of Catholic literature can be produced by non-Catholics, or those with only a scientific interest in religion, often leads to the oversimplification of many of the same emotional and literary elements that make Catholic literature worth reading.

Only time will show if, as Robert Fay has wondered, the new translation of Mass will lead to a fundamental shift in the language of Catholic

13. Waldmeir, *Cathedrals*, 14.

creativity: certainly the three central writers profiled in this book experienced the transition between Latin and English versions of a faith language. Literature is not meant to compete with liturgy; they are modes of celebration, different forms of religious expression. *The Fine Delight* will reveal that Catholic literature is an essential element in the faith experience, and a literature worthy of serious, and diverse, scholarship and inquiry. Catholic literature can be "the fine delight that fathers thought" in ways that are as numerous as its readers, representing a faith community that finds strength in its concurrent fragmentation and unity.

Chapter One

The Catholic Literary Paradox

CATHOLIC LITERATURE, AND CATHOLIC writers, resist definition. To be "catholic" is to be inclusive, to accept all voices, though not all writing can be considered religiously Catholic. Is a writer Catholic because of her standing within the Church: baptized, confirmed, practicing? What if she is inactive or lapsed? Is she only Catholic if she operates in fidelity with the doctrinal beliefs of the Church; are certain beliefs more important than others? Would a staunchly pro-life writer not be considered Catholic if she rejected papal infallibility? What about writers who convert to, or from, the faith? Or a writer living "culturally" as a Catholic, but not participating in the rituals of the Church? Which is more important: biography or literary content? If an atheist writes a novel about a priest, is that novel Catholic, or is it only Catholic if the characters act in accordance with Church teachings, and not leave the seminary for the secular world? When the Vatican issued a letter condemning Graham Greene's 1940 novel, *The Power and the Glory,* Greene penned a sly response to Cardinal Pizzardo in April 1954, reinforcing his allegiance to the Church. Does it make Greene any less Catholic of a writer if he elsewhere admitted to not simply adultery, but a long-term extramarital relationship? There might be no end to Catholic forgiveness, but what of literary absolution?

While these considerations do not always affect enjoyment and understanding of literary works, they are necessary and useful considerations. Father Richard John Neuhaus has used the word "paradox" to describe postconciliar Catholics in a postmodern world, and that word is especially applicable to Catholic literature. The Catholic literary paradox might be more enlightening and instructive than debilitating: as long as this discussion is used to open, rather than close, conversation and inquiry. The multiple layers of the Catholic literary paradox—that some writers are alternatively considered Catholic or not, that readers and writers pine to identify writers as Catholic who have lapsed, or reject the title, and that forces within and outside the Church have reacted against Catholic literature—help define Catholic literature.

In fact, paradoxical self-definition is an essential and endemic trait of modern Catholic artistry. Much of Flannery O'Connor's non-fiction, including her 1957 essay "The Church and the Fiction Writer," is concerned with the splintered identity of the Catholic writer. Her Southern setting and Protestant subject matter created a need for continual, forceful Catholic self-identification. Una M. Cadegan profiles novelist and reviewer Richard Sullivan, whose Catholic aesthetic created a "distinctive set of criteria for literary evaluation," including "not only the temporal and the tangible, not only the authentic rendering of social experience, but also the transcendent and the ultimate."[1] This Catholic intellectual sense might have found its origins in a reaction against the inevitable proliferation of dogmatic Catholic literature, a near subculture of "literary production, including presses, publishers, newspapers, book clubs, awards, conferences, and professional associations."[2] Although not exclusively, literature bound by preconciliar borders had the tendency to create work whose worth was "measured . . . by its literary fidelity to doctrine and dogma and its value as an evangelizing force."[3]

Consider again the writing of Gerard Manley Hopkins, a Jesuit priest who used the literary form of poetry to distill his passion for Christ. Hopkins's intense poems were not meant to sermonize, as in you *must* believe. Rather, they are testaments of *how* and *why* he believes, so that the reader might look at the world through new eyes that recognize God as the origin of all things. Hopkins's writing is transformative by being disruptive. Even poems that initially seem to carry a comforting tone, such as "Spring and Fall," refocus the reader on the complexity of existence. A linguistic innovator, Hopkins was truly a prophet of image and idea. Bernadette Waterman Ward further contextualizes this concept of transformation: she posits "Sacraments opened Hopkins to the idea that physical realities could become spiritual realities with no diminution of their physical existence . . . Without deifying the world, Hopkins could take all creation as a

1. Cadegan, "How Realistic," 46.
2. Ibid., 47.
3. Gandolfo, *Testing*, xi.

manifestation of the incarnate Christ."[4] Christ was the beginning and end, but the means was Hopkins's brilliant, though strange, practice of inscape: insular tension through formal patterns.

Yet even Hopkins, who seems like the prototypical Catholic writer, is a bundle of biographical and literary complexities. Hopkins learned from a fellow Jesuit writer that a "new sort of poetry" was being written in America, by one Walt Whitman.[5] Hopkins wrote of Whitman in an 1882 letter to Robert Bridges. Bridges had queried Hopkins about Whitman after reading Hopkins's "The Leaden Echo and the Golden Echo." Hopkins only reads several poems by Whitman but feels qualified to comment on the American's thought and prosody. Based on this small sampling, Hopkins concludes "that I always knew in my heart Walt Whitman's mind to be more like my own than any other man's living. As he is a very great scoundrel this is not a pleasant confession. And this makes me the more desirous to read him and the more determined that I will not."[6] Bridges sees rhythmic similarities between the writers. Hopkins rejects that assessment. His defense nearly reaches the incredulous, parsing poetic feet and differentiating his work because of a sprung rhythm he first observed in *Piers Ploughman* and then not again until his own usage. Hopkins is adamant that Whitman did not use that poetic move. Hopkins finds his own long lines to be "highly wrought" and "not rhythm run to seed: everything is weighed and timed."[7] Not so with Whitman: "this savagery of his art, this rhythm in its last ruggedness and decomposition into common prose."[8] Hopkins reminds Bridges that this is not an attack, but it is most certainly a moment of poetic vanity, and possibly a good bit of literary envy, though delivered with a sense of humor: even the poets' shared interest in alexandrines is coincidental, not causal. Hopkins continued the discussion a week later, adding "My de-Whitmaniser . . . was stern and a bit of a mouther."[9] Mariani thinks that "Bridges has touched on a sensitive issue, which goes deeper than mere prosody, but touches the question of selfhood and the kenotic emptying of the self [Hopkins] both desires and fears."[10] Mariani positions Whitman as a representation of Hopkins's

---

4. Ward, *World*, 132–133.

5. Mariani, *Gerard*, 157

6. Abbott, *Letters*, 155

7. Ibid., 157.

8. Ibid.

9. Ibid., 158.

10. Mariani, *Gerard*, 293.

larger anxiety, seeing the American poet as "singing not to God but rather of and for himself."[11] Certainly a world where Christ is not center would be troubling for both Hopkins the Catholic and Hopkins the poet.

The Catholic literary paradox has continued from the time of Hopkins to Vatican II. *The Moviegoer's* narrator, Binx Bolling, "dallies" with his secretaries before experiencing a life change on the cusp of Lent during his thirtieth year. But Walker Percy revels in ambiguity: in the novel's penultimate chapter, Binx's cumulative understanding of God's role in human life is ambiguous: "it is impossible to say."[12] His self-examinations seem a mix of Catholic revival and Southern-tinged guilt. Percy's own Catholic aesthetic was heavily influenced by the Protestant schema of Søren Kierkegaard. Percy's contemporary Flannery O'Connor's powerful Catholic vision was achieved through a representation of fundamentalist and Protestant characters rather than her religious peers. O'Connor noted that "the Catholic writer often finds himself writing in and for a world that is unprepared and unwilling to see the meaning of life as he sees it."[13] O'Connor used that fact to explain why she and other Catholic writers "frequently . . . may resort to violent literary means to get his vision across to a hostile audience, and the images and actions he creates may seem distorted and exaggerated to the Catholic mind."[14] While it is tempting to draw comparison to Hopkins's disruptive prosody as necessary to gain attention of his Anglican peers, Hopkins's verse was largely created for an insular audience. O'Connor very much considered herself as a literary representative of the faith, but not a dogmatist. O'Connor's usage of "violent" denotes both the often raw imagery and encounters in her short fiction, but also an echo of the need to "report the progress" of the "many rough beasts now slouching toward Bethlehem."[15] O'Connor thought the idea of a Catholic novel was "suspect," if only because that definition was more prescriptive and convenient than aesthetically accurate.[16]

The Catholic literary paradox became even more noticeable, and more intellectually profound, after Vatican II. Amy Hungerford's important volume, *Postmodern Belief: American Literature and Religion since 1960*, posits that "American writers turn to religion to imagine the purely

11. Ibid., 227.
12. Percy, *Moviegoer*, 235.
13. Ellsberg, *Flannery*, 50.
14. Ibid.
15. Ibid., 51.
16. Ibid., 95.

formal elements of language in transcendent terms."[17] Hungerford argues for a different American belief, a belief *in* meaninglessness: "belief for its own sake, or belief without content, or belief where content is the least important aspect of religious thought and practice."[18] She sees an increased scholarly focus on the literary forms and style of the Bible as allowing that text to become fodder for secular writers: "it is not what the Bible says, but what the Bible is, and how scripture sounds, that carries religiously inflected authority."[19]

Hungerford covers several writers mentioned as, in some way, Catholic, although her book's overall focus is more general. She cautions that this belief in meaninglessness is a "fundamentally Protestant way of understanding religious belief."[20] Certainly Robert Alter, in *Pen of Iron*, has documented the enduring stylistic and cultural influence of the 1611 King James translation of the Bible. Alter considers direct appropriation of biblical language, but also the biblicisms of Abraham Lincoln, Herman Melville, and William Faulkner, writers steeped in Protestant cultural tradition. Yet Hungerford offers interesting treatments of Toni Morrison, Cormac McCarthy, and Thomas Pynchon, all important American postmodernist fiction writers, whose Catholicism is particular but present, and typically only mentioned in passing. Nobel Prize winner Morrison converted to Catholicism when she was twelve. When asked if she would "rather be known as a great exponent of literature rather than as an African-American writer," Morrison responded that she, like James Joyce and Leo Tolstoy, writes out of where she comes from, and it "happens that that space for me is African-American; it could be Catholic, it could be Midwestern. I'm those things too, and they are all important."[21] Although Morrison's novels, like *Beloved*, often include Old Testament themes, she occasionally moves into Catholic territory, as in *Paradise*, and she is ever biblical in rhetoric and approach. McCarthy's wide Southwestern settings and sweeping, King James infused prose led Madison Smartt Bell to observe that McCarthy's language dresses a world where "human thought and activity seem almost completely inconsequential when projected upon the vast alien landscapes where they occur."[22] Bell, in likening

17. Hungerford, *Postmodern*, xiii.

18. Ibid., xiv.

19. Ibid., xv.

20. Ibid.

21. Denard, *Toni Morrison*, 86–87.

22. Bell, "The Man," 2.

McCarthy's voice to that of God's address to Job, arrives at a tantalizing conclusion: McCarthy's "project is unlike that of any other writer: to make artifacts composed of human language but detached from a human reference point."[23] The life and philosophy of Christ feels like it postdates the content of McCarthy's canon. Pynchon was raised Catholic, and, at least according to fellow Cornell student Jules Siegel, still "went to Mass and confessed, though to what would be a mystery," since he seemed like an overly dedicated and cautious student.[24] John Neary offers the interesting thesis that Pynchon, whose father was Protestant, "combines his mother's Catholic tradition's attraction to symbols with his father's Calvinist tradition's tendency to expose those symbols' inadequacy and hollowness."[25] When Pynchon does directly mention Catholicism, in *The Crying of Lot 49* and elsewhere, the religion is parodied into caricature, including the Vatican's ownership of manuscripts of a pornographic play. In an absurd, psychotropic world where Oedipa Maas unpacks layers of meaninglessness and confusion, the Catholic Church is a red herring, another institutional power intent on diversion.

The postconciliar writers whose literary Catholicism is muddled extends beyond the set covered in Hungerford's postmodern-focused analysis. Consider Anthony Burgess, Tom Perotta, Thomas McGuane, Tobias Wolff, Mary Karr, Mary Gordon, Richard Russo, William Kennedy, T. C. Boyle, Denis Johnson, and even Anne Rice. Add writers such as J. F. Powers, who published in both preconciliar and postconciliar times yet feels more wedded to the former. Powers's Catholic worldview was never questioned, since his subject matter was almost exclusively Midwestern priests, but his straddling of conciliar periods complicates overall identification of his work.

The fiction of Jeffrey Eugenides and Don DeLillo might be the most instructive in explicating the postconciliar Catholic literary paradox. Eugenides, raised Greek Orthodox, became interested in Catholicism during his college years, and considered converting to the religion.[26] *The Marriage Plot* (2011) includes the spiritual evolution of Mitchell Grammaticus, a Brown undergraduate who has been inching away from the Greek Orthodox faith of his youth and toward Catholicism. Mitchell admits the interest to his professor, who even acknowledges "the attraction of Catholicism"

---

23. Ibid.
24. Neary, *Like and Unlike*, 171.
25. Ibid.
26. O'Malley, "A Conversation," para. 11.

before deferring to the "schismatics."[27] Later, in explaining to others his intellectual interest in religious study, Mitchell connects the varying world religions based on the belief that "God is beyond any human concept or category."[28] Mitchell's intellectual interest evolves into personal investigation, and he begins attending a catechism class "secretly as if he were buying drugs or visiting a massage parlor."[29] Mitchell initially cites Thomas Merton as his inspiration for Catholic conversation, but the presiding priest, having "seen Mitchell's type before," likely thinks the undergraduate's religious fervor is superficial and temporary.[30] The priest gives Mitchell some readings, and Mitchell returns with questions, particularly about premarital sex, to which the priest responds that "a girl's not a watermelon you plug a hole in to see if it's sweet."[31] While busing tables, he considers the finer points of Catholic dogma, and his concerns with semantics sound influenced by Stephen Dedalus; it should be no surprise that Eugenides has admitted an affinity toward Joyce.

But it is *The Virgin Suicides*, Eugenides's darkly comic 1993 novel, that portrays Catholicism in a most thorough and fascinating manner. The novel is told through the collective perspective of a group of boys fawning over the Lisbon sisters, five sheltered daughters who ultimately commit the act mentioned in the title. Eugenides is not Catholic, but his novel is eccentrically so. When Cecilia, the youngest sister, attempts suicide in her bathtub, she is found with a "laminated picture of the Virgin Mary she held against her budding chest,"[32] the iconography contrasted with her "pagan nudity."[33] The picture is pocketed by a paramedic, and later returned to her father at the hospital. On the back of the picture appears a breathless message about sightings of the Virgin Mary, including the exhortation to call "555-MARY" for more information.[34] Mr. Lisbon, after reading the message, says "We baptized her, we confirmed her, and now she believes in this crap," referring to the almost Pentecostal connotation of religious visions and the idea of individual ecstatic experience.[35] Cecilia, pegged as

27. Eugenides, *Marriage*, 99.
28. Ibid., 137.
29. Ibid., 147–8.
30. Ibid., 148.
31. Ibid.
32. Eugenides, *Virgin*, 2.
33. Ibid., 4.
34. Ibid., 11–12.
35. Ibid., 12.

the "weird sister" by the boys, is even an outsider within her family.[36] Pious Mrs. Lisbon crumples the picture; however conservative, their Catholicism generally operates on a separate supernatural plane than the dime-store evangelizing apparent in the mass-produced icon. Mrs. Lisbon's piety is on display elsewhere; when Cecilia succeeds in her second suicide attempt, leaping onto a fence from the second story of their home, Mrs. Lisbon rejects the idea of the "heathen" practice of cremation, referencing an unnamed biblical passage "that suggested the dead will rise bodily at the Second Coming, no ashes allowed."[37] That theology is consistent with the parents' desire to control the bodies of their daughters in life. Makeup is outlawed, as well as dating boys. In fact, Cecilia's suicide occurs during the rare chaperoned party in the Lisbon basement, as if the intrusion of boys into this peculiar Catholic world has shattered its innocence. Mrs. Lisbon's religious identity occasionally appears fundamentalist. She replays religious albums on Sundays: "Beams of light pierce clouds on each cover."[38] Even the narrating boys find the music trite, imagining "pastors' families passing plates of ham" while listening to the music, not thinking that "those pious voices" could ever "churchify niches where the Lisbon girls knelt to pumice calluses on their big toes."[39]

Eugenides, no fan of melodrama, cleverly constructs the loving collective voice so that the daughters are mythologized; they might be goddesses, but they also carry a Marian tinge of purity. A photograph of Mary Lisbon blow-drying her hair makes her "head [appear] to be on fire but that is only a trick of the light," carrying the glow of a nimbus.[40] The collective perspective is actually a ruse, as the voice often lapses into omniscience. Mr. Lisbon's words about the Marian image are "his only blasphemy"; of course, the boys were not there to make such a judgment.[41] It is the local parish priest, Father Moody, who gives the boys and other outsiders salient testimony about the desiccated state of the Lisbon home, although he does not enter "the moist cave" of the girls' bathroom.[42] Eugenides offers

36. Ibid., 37.
37. Ibid., 33.
38. Ibid., 131.
39. Ibid.
40. Ibid., 3.
41. Ibid., 13.
42. Ibid., 47.

the priest choice lines: he quips that Mrs. Lisbon's religious albums are "what you might expect to hear in a Protestant household."[43]

The narrators of the novel do not attend church, and that outside perspective only increases their romanticism of these young Catholics: "five glittering daughters in their homemade dresses, all lace and ruffle, bursting with their fructifying flesh."[44] They long to enter the Lisbon home, revisiting an apocryphal account from a boy invited to dinner by the father, a teacher at the local high school. The boy recounts the grace spoken at dinner, and then his glimpse of their bedrooms: "filled with crumpled panties, of stuffed animals hugged to death by the passion of the girls, of a crucifix draped with a brassiere, of gauzy chambers of canopied beds, and of the effluvia of so many young girls becoming women together in the same cramped space."[45] Catholicism becomes a contemporary Other, a largely feminine, mysterious house that cannot be understood by the boys. Others in the community misrepresent the Lisbons' faith. A neighbor who claimed that the Lisbons "didn't have a relationship with God" is questioned by the boys, who remind him about the Marian image.[46] The man responds that "Jesus is the one she should have a picture of," revealing a Protestant distrust of Marian iconography and devotion.[47]

Cecilia's Catholicism, though, is tied to her interest in a local boy, Dominic Palazzolo. Catholicism becomes a national metonym for Italy, and when she "began slipping" into a local church to "sprinkle her forehead with holy water," it is done more out of caricatured Italian obsession rather than true piety.[48] Even the crucifix found in her room was bought "at the height of her crush."[49] Another sister, Bonnie, "fingered the rosary deep in the pocket of her corduroy skirt," her Catholicism far more private and intellectual: she writes a history paper on Simone Weil.[50] Lux, the sexually active oldest sister, appears to be the least interested in Catholicism, replacing God with Trip Fontaine, a man among boys at the high school. Lux's trysts on the roof of the Lisbon home are like symbolic gestures of escape from domestic Catholicism, and are thus in view of the collective

43. Ibid., 131.
44. Ibid., 6.
45. Ibid., 7.
46. Ibid., 16.
47. Ibid.
48. Ibid., 18.
49. Ibid.
50. Ibid., 62.

narrator. Lux's open, outdoor sexuality seems to contribute to the indoor death of the home. The previously subtle decay becomes obvious: windows filmed with such thick dirt they look curtained, sagging gutters, and even a fearful mailman, who lifts the box lid with a magazine rather than touching the metal with his hand. The girls, pulled from school, are prisoners there.

While Eugenides's novel often presents Catholicism with a parodic, exaggerated touch, his care elsewhere speaks to the import of even minor mentions. Cecilia's blood from her attempted suicide, as well as the boys' apocryphal claim of her period, sound like the blood of Christ these boys will never understand. After her suicide attempt, Cecilia eats red berries from the bushes, but sometimes only "staining her palms with the juice."[51] The only thing that draws the surviving Lisbon daughters from their musty home is an effort to save the family elm from removal by the town Parks Department. The workers, chainsaw in tow, watch the Lisbons form a ring around the tree. Their impromptu activism, colored by Eugenides's humor, even brings together the parents "in a rare display of physical affection."[52] The saving of the elm, Cecilia's favorite tree, appears nearly sacramental. Facsimiles of Cecilia's picture of the Virgin Mary begin appearing everywhere: pierced onto rose bushes, stuck in the spokes of a bicycle wheel, tucked under a windshield wiper. The collective narrators hoard the cheap imitations not for their religious import, since "the pictures were invested with significance we couldn't quite fathom," but because they think the surviving Lisbons are using them to make contact.[53] The sheer number of discovered pictures fractures the already tenuous religious connection. Are any of those iconographies holy? The boys certainly look at the Marian image with a sense of misplaced reverence.

The pictures of Mary lead to the girls' cryptic flashes of light at their window, and then the boys and girls playing albums over the telephone, all culminating with a midnight meeting in the silent Lisbon home. Lux, of course, is the one to greet the boys, and assures them that her sisters are packing for the mass elope. The plan turns out to be a ruse, and the boys make a horrifying discovery, which solidifies their role in this personal church: observers and documenters, but never participants. Yet there is complicated grace in that role: they are the keepers of the Lisbon memory, even if the boys, now men "with our thinning hair and soft bellies," are

51. Ibid., 14.
52. Ibid., 177.
53. Ibid., 183.

forever wounded by both the suicide and the mythology of those Catholic girls.[54]

For all of Pynchon's nearly-monastic reclusiveness, Morrison and McCarthy's Old Testament rhetoric, and Eugenides's surreal suburban Catholicism, Don DeLillo most fully exemplifies the Catholic literary paradox. Amy Hungerford's analysis of DeLillo is thorough and measured, leading to her thesis: DeLillo's novels "translate religious structures into literary ones without an intervening secularism . . . because they imagine language in a way that preserves a specifically Catholic understanding of transcendent experience while drifting far from Catholic traditions and themes."[55] Hungerford is careful to frame DeLillo's schema quite narrowly: he is a lapsed Catholic, formed by mid-century culture and aesthetic, whose Southern Italian Catholicism "favored popular mystical practices of Catholicism over regular attendance at Mass and reverence for the parish priest."[56] Hungerford notes rich analogous connection between the flux of liturgical language during Vatican II and DeLillo's formation of storytelling. Hungerford posits that the end of Latin Mass as a weekly, liturgical event freed that "linguistic and spiritual practice . . . for literary engagement."[57] In referencing lay perceptions of Church dogma on birth control, gay marriage, and other contentious issues, Hungerford finds DeLillo's canon dramatizing strong religious feeling without consistent acceptance of dogma. DeLillo's work, by "embodying a Catholic sacramental logic within a literary structure," shows "how one would have to think about language in order to sustain [mystical] belief while rejecting, or suspending judgment upon, the religious institutions and practices that formerly supported it."[58]

DeLillo, then, becomes a writer-priest, whose implicit training likely occurred at Cardinal Hayes High School, a school founded by Francis Cardinal Spellman, who later "became one of a minority arguing for the retention of the Latin Mass."[59] That the language of Latin Mass was only understood by the top-heavy minority of clergy and those steeped in religious education, rather than the lay majority, allows Hungerford to consider that "the barrier to understanding facilitated a mystical relation to

54. Ibid., 243.
55. Hungerford, *Postmodern*, 53.
56. Ibid., 160.
57. Ibid., 53.
58. Ibid.
59. Ibid., 62.

the language, a relation that reinforced the transubstantial, incarnational logic of other elements of the mass."[60] Hungerford expertly shows how DeLillo's central Catholic themes of "glossolalia, the Latin mass, small talk, the ritual of conversation or of the sentence . . . [create] fiction as religious meditation in which language is the final enlightenment" in *Mao II*, *The Names*, and particularly the powerful and mystical conclusion to *Underworld*.[61]

Hungerford's excellent analysis can be extended by considering one of DeLillo's earliest works, as well as a novel published after her explication. That later novel, *Point Omega* (2010), owes its title to an essential concept from Teilhard de Chardin, condensed by one of the novel's few characters into the idea of "a sublime transformation of mind and soul or some worldly convulsion."[62] The speaker is Elster, an eccentric scholar who became attracted to Teilhard's theories while an undergraduate. Elster explains that this omega point is "the final term, the last flare" of "collective human thought."[63] This ending results in a "leap out of our biology,"[64] since he wonders why "we have to be human forever?"[65] Man's ultimate goal is to return "to inorganic matter."[66]

Elster is aware that his provincial understanding of Teilhard's theory exacerbates its existing ambiguities. The ultimate problem might be that the omega point is "a case of language that's struggling toward some idea outside our experience."[67] DeLillo's short novel, which ends with Elster's daughter, Jessica, disappearing into the desert, and an epilogue set at an exhibit where *Psycho* has been extended into 24 hours, *Point Omega* almost seems like an admission of imperfection of both language and narrative. The novel's narrator, a filmmaker determined to document Elster's life in a pure, unedited state, admits that after the daughter's disappearance, the talk of an omega point "seemed so much dead echo now."[68] The omega point "has narrowed . . . to the point of a knife as it enters a body. All the man's grand themes funneled down to local grief, one body, out there

60. Ibid., 57.
61. Ibid., 75.
62. DeLillo, *Point*, 72.
63. Ibid., 51.
64. Ibid., 52.
65. Ibid., 53.
66. Ibid., 53.
67. Ibid., 72.
68. Ibid., 98.

somewhere, or not."[69] Rather than allow Jessica's disappearance, death, or discovery to complete the novel's analogical argument, DeLillo opts for the inauthenticity of modified cinema, with anonymous characters who leave, separately, into the night.

The work that complicates analyses of DeLillo is his second novel, *End Zone* (1972). A satirical take on college football culture written with unabashed appreciation for elements of the sport, *End Zone* stretches the definition of a Catholic novel. Thomas LeClair, one of the relatively few critics to devote sufficient attention to the novel, finds DeLillo creating a "displaced monotheism," with the "absolutist, monovalent assumptions and rituals of Christianity now projected upon the logos rather than flowing from the Logos."[70] LeClair, in the midst of engaging Derridean logocentric analysis, cites the novel's narrator, who finds God "incredibly outmoded," only "'three letters' in a crossword puzzle."[71] These considerations of absence versus presence cause LeClair to identify Coach Emmett Creed as a replacement for God, but that definition overemphasizes the role of Creed's logocentric ideal within the novel. As Creed's body debilitates, so do his players become more active in cosmological defining. The language and culture of these definitions reveal Catholic sensibility, either on their part or from the control of the author.

It is exactly this imperfect identification that makes *End Zone* an essential Catholic work: often literary existence on the boundaries of accepted faith offers the most nuanced and revealing representations of a belief subsumed with mystery. The novel is set at Logos College in west Texas, where "coach, warlock, and avenging patriarch" Emmett Creed has been hired to resuscitate the football program and bring recognition to the school.[72] Creed was born "in either a log cabin or a manger . . . on the banks of the Rio Grande."[73] A former fighter pilot, Creed followed his brief NFL career with a few coaching positions, and though he had gotten violent with a player, was known as someone "famous for creating order out of chaos."[74]

Creed is given wide power to create a closed system at Logos. With the recognition that "football players are simple folk," Creed cultivates a

69. Ibid.

70. LeClair, "Deconstructing," 109.

71. Ibid.

72. DeLillo, *End*, 5.

73. Ibid., 9.

74. Ibid., 10.

romantic sensibility, where players "practiced in the undulating heat with nothing to sustain us but the conviction that things here were simple."[75] Those practices were held on a field surrounded by canvas blinds, ostensibly meant to "discourage spying by future opponents," but likely to further the idea that these players were part of a grand experiment.[76] Creed watches these practices silently from above, in a tower specifically built for that purpose.

DeLillo uses Gary Harkness, an itinerant player from the Northeast, as his metafictional bullhorn. Harkness is the perfect choice. He is obsessed with God, seeking a "oneness with God or the universe" that sounds influenced by Teilhard.[77] When the Penn State freshman coach tells Gary that fans "don't go to football games to see pass patterns run by theologians," he seems disappointed, making him a good transfer choice for Logos, where players are exhorted to pray nightly.[78] Harkness is both cog and splinter in Creed's system. He "liked the idea of losing myself in an obscure part of the world"; as in *Point Omega*, DeLillo creates an idiosyncratic vision of the American southwest.[79] In fact, *End Zone* might be considered a precursor to that later novel. Gary's explanation of the geography of Logos sounds like the seclusion of that newer work: "we were in the middle of nowhere, that terrain so flat and bare, suggestive of the end of recorded time, a splendid sense of remoteness firing my soul."[80]

When Gary speaks of exile and silence, he sounds both like Stephen Dedalus and the DeLillo of interviews. Gary's physical exile "is just an extension (a packaging) . . . of being separated from whatever is left of the center of one's own history."[81] He finds "pleasure" in the "daily punishment on the field."[82] Gary's faith is private: rather than attending any variation of Mass, he lives for the afternoons of "simple calisthenics, row upon row of us, bending, breathing and stretching, instructing our collective soul in the discipline necessary to make us one body."[83] That ritual brings more thoughts in the tradition of Teilhard: "The indifferent drift of time and all

75. Ibid., 4.
76. Ibid., 9.
77. Ibid., 19.
78. Ibid.
79. Ibid., 22.
80. Ibid., 30.
81. Ibid., 31.
82. Ibid.
83. Ibid., 56.

things filled me with affection for the universe. I squatted and jumped and jumped and squatted. Life was simplified by these afternoons of opposites and affinities."[84]

Gary, though, is no monk. While catching a ball on a deep pattern route, he imagines himself "on large-screen color TV," invoking more the Sam Spence scored reels of NFL Films than any religious transcendence.[85] DeLillo's sketches of Gary and Taft Robinson, a transfer running back from Columbia, resemble the majestic renderings of athletes in motion by Thomas Eakins. Yet both Gary and Taft, essential elements of Creed's experiment, serve to undermine, and ultimately disrupt, that system. Gary's cosmological considerations are derailed by his fetish for nuclear destruction and war. He travels through the desert to audit Air Force ROTC courses with Major Staley, even playing a war game after the season ends. Gary thinks of deaths in the millions from the flick of a switch, and the subsequent inability of language to articulate widespread loss. Myna, wearing a mushroom cloud painted dress, sexualizes Gary's militaristic thoughts. Taft, a gifted athlete, star recruit, and the first black student enrolled at the college, quits the team to avoid "white father watching me run."[86] Taft's newfound asceticism causes Gary, the book's other main intellectual, to plead for Taft's return to the team: "It's football. It's *football*, Taft."[87] Taft has taken Creed's dictum of "work, pain, fury, sweat"[88] and applied them to "certain disciplines," including his independent spiritual development and a devotion to Ludwig Wittgenstein shown by a poster of the philosopher on Taft's dorm wall.[89]

Creed's patriarchal system is contingent upon two elements: the ritual and import of football language, and Creed's own identity. At a school named "Logos," students examine linguistics. Gary memorizes a new word each day and consummates his relationship with Myna amongst library stacks. And yet, as Taft later explains, their "new way of life requires a new language," and the artificer of that Word is Creed, since even the founder of the school was, quite literally, a mute.[90] Players appropriate the cadence of Creed's admonitions in triplicate: "Hit somebody, hit somebody, hit

84. Ibid.

85. Ibid., 62.

86. Ibid., 233.

87. Ibid.

88. Ibid., 237.

89. Ibid., 233.

90. Ibid., 234.

somebody" and like phrases become spiritual chants[91] Creed's hyperbole
extends beyond his creation narrative to the setting of the practice field,
where players "stood in a circle in the enormous gray morning . . . hel-
mets in hands" while "thunder moved down from the northeast."[92] Creed,
watching from above in the tower, fills the role of God. Even a player like
Taft, who criticizes Creed's methods, offers implicit acceptance of the
man's core ideals of self-sacrifice and unity.

Creed's words are few, but well-placed, and delivered with the gravity
only accumulated through reverence. As Hungerford has shown, DeLillo's
writing transposes the cadence and tenor of Latin Mass into an increasingly secular world, and *End Zone* offers another world where word and
ritual coalesce. Even if Taft concludes that Creed was "too much . . . part
Satan, part Saint Francis," the coach has succeeded in redefining the language of football on the campus.[93] As a Catholic, DeLillo knows full well
the muddle between sign and signified, and as one who has spoken of
an appreciation for the "theater" of Mass in his youth, and the Catholic
tendency to engage ambiguous ideas, DeLillo's fiction allows language to
exist in a middle ground. Language is not concrete, and it is not symbol; it
is a third mode. *End Zone* is littered with signs and representations: Taft's
posters, Professor Zapalac's posters, militaristic signs in Gary's neighborhood, and the sport platitude sign his father puts in his bedroom. DeLillo
has often mentioned his love for the physical appearance of words, how
the curve and angle of letters can deepen, or even extend, meaning. Gary
similarly realizes, after years of staring at the bedroom sign, that "meaning
faded" and "words became pictures," iconographs.[94] That appreciation of
language makes sense for a Catholic writer reared in the shadow of Latin
Mass and the transition to more colloquial English. The paradox of Latin
Mass is the paradox of sustained misunderstanding: a congregation unable to understand each reference still moves with the charge of rehearsed
action. One player on the Logos team is "memorizing Rilke's ninth Duino
Elegy in German, a language he did not understand. It was for a course
he was taking in the untellable."[95] Religion and poetic language hope to
make the metaphysical imaginable, but it is often the juxtaposition of base

91. Ibid., 10.
92. Ibid., 27.
93. Ibid., 236.
94. Ibid., 17.
95. Ibid., 64.

elements of sounds, the texture of letters, and associations that resound in the deepest way. Faith is the space between translations, the untellable.

End Zone offers the language of football as a fascinating, albeit imperfect, analogy. In a world where faith in body and subsequent transcendence of bodies leads to practical and spiritual victories, the players on the Logos College team career toward end zones real and imagined. Gary loves the apparent simplicity of football language: "When Coach says hit, we hit. It's so simple."[96] Bing Jackmin, another player, thinks Gary is wrong, claiming the players are "substandard industrial robots."[97] Gary is not deterred: "Football . . . is the one sport guided by language, by the word signal, the snap number, the color code, the play name."[98] Gary likely knows that other sports and games include similar references, but the tightness of speech to action, body to body, is unique to football language.

Taft's words to Gary late in the novel are instructive here. He promises that his isolation on campus is not to be "evasive" or meant to "[keep] traditional distances."[99] Taft exhorts: "I want you to take me literally. Everything I've said is to be taken literally."[100] Like Creed, Taft has his room, his system, "fixed up just the way I want it."[101] Taft's fate is uncertain, but Creed's system has broken down. The fissures were an inherent part of the system: when players break out in fights during practice, Creed "turned slowly to watch" rather than stopping the brawl.[102] Creed becomes sick as the season progresses, moving from his usual position in the tower to baseball benches. He loses weight, and needs a wheelchair during off-season. Gary is called from an impromptu pick-up game in the snow, where rules are stripped from the game and the players "were getting extremely basic, moving into elemental realms, seeking harmony with the weather and the earth," to a meeting with Creed.[103] Creed reiterates the need for resolve and self-discipline. He wants humility and a rejection of living for the pleasure of the senses, instead choosing the wisdom of self-immolation. The reader expects Creed's retirement to be announced, but the coach instead informs Gary that he will become captain of the team.

96. Ibid., 35.
97. Ibid.
98. Ibid., 112.
99. Ibid., 238.
100. Ibid.
101. Ibid.
102. Ibid., 61.
103. Ibid., 195.

Gary accepts the responsibility while seeing a picture of Saint Teresa of Avila on Creed's wall.

End Zone is a novel about systems of language and football that reach the finality of the work's title. The Centrex game critiques the efficacy of language, both particular to sport but also the mimetic concept of fiction. As the season progresses, the team's refined, idiosyncratic, and ritualistic language of football devolves into profanity and mumbling. The players lose their words as they lose the game. In much the same way, Creed's body, which created a patriarchal example for the players, loses its physicality and meaning. After leaving Taft's room, Gary seems destined for similar disappearance. He stops eating the next day, leading to the novel's ominous final line: "In the end they had to carry me to the infirmary and feed me through plastic tubes."[104] God, in the form of Creed, language, and ritual, has left these players, and all they can focus on is the rumor of new uniforms for the next season.

DeLillo's choice of a grave conclusion to a novel that vacillates between sarcasm and seriousness is reflected in a more recent work that exists on the periphery of Catholic literary definition. While it is not noteworthy to recognize that Salvatore Scibona is familiar with DeLillo's work, the younger writer is more than simply aware of his predecessor. From an offhand quip about DeLillo's *The Names* in a *Los Angeles Times* interview to a glowing review of DeLillo's story collection *The Angel Esmeralda*, Scibona clearly appreciates DeLillo's intellectual architecture. For Scibona, the "sinister comedian" DeLillo shows that "God or the ghost of God is haunting history."[105] Scibona emulates DeLillo's adult distance from the institutional Church, consistent with Hungerford's observations about their shared Southern Italian genealogy. Scibona recalls an anecdote from his grandmother steeped in paradox: "dispensing communion used to go much more quickly when she was young . . . because everyone was using a diaphragm! They were devout enough to deny themselves communion because they were sinning by using contraception, but they were practical enough to use contraception anyway."[106]

Regardless of Scibona's personal faith, his stated literary genealogy is steeped in Catholic writers: Flannery O'Connor, Toni Morrison, and T. S. Eliot. He speaks about O'Connor's focus on the senses in *Mystery and Manners* as creating a profound change: "when you observe the physical

---

104. Ibid., 242.
105. Scibona, Review of *The Angel*, para. 4.
106. "A Conversation," para. 49.

details of the world this way, then the present moment holds the promise of a new urgency and significance," language reminiscent of Andre Dubus's sacramental aesthetic.[107] Scibona's prose contains layers of detail without wasted words. The nexus of his achronological novel, *The End* (2008), is a carnival for the Feast of the Assumption in 1953. Scibona's descriptive style could not find a better setting.

Rocco LaGrassa, one of the novel's main characters, practices an uneven Catholicism. He is "an unremarkable Christian"[108] who "didn't follow" his priest's Latin and "wasn't paying any attention" during his youngest child's baptism.[109] He bakes "glazed sugar mounds that have the red candies on top" to obscenely mimic physical attributes of St. Agatha, but also takes Sunday morning breaks to receive Communion.[110] Other characters share his religious eccentricities. Lina Montanero was "irregular in her attendance at mass, as the Sicilians were wont to be."[111] Underground abortionist Costanza Marini "never relented in her devotion to the sacraments, but she was not a Christian."[112] Even Ciccio Mazzone, another local resident, is more attracted to the philosophical play of his Jesuit school than actual faith, concluding that if he had gained union membership "he would have lost himself in a hod or a wheelbarrow instead of in Thomas Aquinas."[113]

Ciccio's section of *The End* exists in the Joycean tradition of skepticism: he is trained to articulate rejection by those he ultimately rejects. He is confident, questioning the circular rhetoric of his Jesuit teachers. Ciccio's independence is born of his father, who "always told him to disregard every third word the Jesuits said," lest that Ciccio become "a papist knucklehead, like so many Irish and Poles."[114] For the Jesuits, the "catechism was, implicitly, out," as well as "understanding . . . clarity . . . usefulness . . . [and] declaratives."[115] Compassion was replaced with "confusion and fear": ambiguity over dogma.[116] Ciccio's complaints feel superficial, as he clearly

---

107. "Interview with Salvatore Scibona," para. 25.

108. Scibona, *The End*, 3.

109. Ibid., 5.

110. Ibid., 15.

111. Ibid., 72.

112. Ibid., 94.

113. Ibid., 211.

114. Ibid., 212–3.

115. Ibid., 213.

116. Ibid.

appreciates the intellectual play and the temporary subversion, even if he departs from the Jesuits' intended goal.

Ciccio's prototypical scene is his spring oral examination with Father Manfred. The exam is held outside at a courtyard, where yellow jackets "were dive-bombing the fruit punch" pitcher.[117] Father Manfred "was fishing them out, crushing them between his fingertips, and dropping them into a pocket in the skirt of his cassock" while Ciccio skitters through his defense.[118] The priest has an answer to every foot forward by the student, complicating analogies with asides, leaving Ciccio frustrated. Ciccio complains that the more he engages in rhetorical and theological thinking, "the more bogus everything becomes."[119] Aristotle's definition of motion has consumed them, even in this moment of relative stasis. God is an abstract, while Christ is absent. The divine is replaced with the twilight-green sky, a soft rain, and a black locust that "was dropping hundreds of tiny white blossoms onto the shoulders and the lap of the priest, who notices this and was bemused."[120] Rhetoric has replaced reverence.

Rocco, though, is the emotional core of the novel. He is a baker who closes shop on the day of the carnival, an occasion that Scibona describes equally with the fascination of an outsider and the patience of a participant. The narrator notes that "Europe was happening here," the pageantry a stark contrast to "the Protestant Jesus who went by his first name and saved souls one by one, depending on Do you believe, in your private heart, or don't you?"[121] Scibona wryly unites Rocco's profession with manna: Rocco imagines a "seething pile of shoppers . . . deep in perplexity as to why the Lord was visiting upon them this particular deprivation on this unexceptional morning."[122] Rocco had previously opened the door "every day. Without exception. The Sabbath be damned, and Christmas and Pentecost."[123] In prose that reflects Pietro DiDonato's *Christ in Concrete*, "labor coursed continually over his willing shoulders as though he had determined to build his house under a waterfall."[124] Rocco's commitment

117. Ibid., 219.
118. Ibid.
119. Ibid., 221.
120. Ibid.
121. Ibid., 34.
122. Ibid., 15.
123. Ibid., 9.
124. Ibid., 8.

is to his estranged wife and children whom he seeks, and fails to find in the novel.

Scibona effectively uses the parade for purposes of theme and plot. The Marian statue is carried down the street by "men in white robes accompanied by torchbearers who until recently had covered their heads with pointed white hoods," rehearsing the racial tension that will later disrupt the parade.[125] The Virgin is represented as plastic iconography: "smirking, her porcelain skin dark like an Arab's, the nose upturned, English, her statue dwarflike, her clothes and hands stuck with specks of diamond donated over many years by women who had had them pried from their engagement rings."[126] Congregants pin money to ribbons that hang from columns of the Virgin's stone platform. The entire parade is chaotic. A nun "scampered, her habit hovering in the infield dust" while she waves for the attention of carnival ride operators to stop the machines because "the Holy Mother was out of the church and in the street."[127] Members of the procession are nameless, defined by their attributes, including the "twelve prodigious men of early middle age" who were "slow on their feet, oxenstout, contemptuous" as they led the altar boys down the street, and the German-born bishop "in a green miter and cope, a scowling, ancient man walking with a shepherd's crook and leaning on it to balance himself."[128] Black-clothed women, "feet naked to the pebbles and the cigarette butts and the soiled napkins and the spilled pop on the pavement," pray rosaries while following the procession.[129] A band "making vehement noise" brings up the procession, leaving a "half block of empty space" that was not only "cooler," but where the tolling church bells could be best heard.[130]

It is in this empty space "which people had historically enjoined themselves from entering" that "a colored woman and a colored man were dancing."[131] Scibona's Joycean narrator describes the action with a curious mix of distance and wit: "They were clapping, [Rocco] could see, and doing a slow-stepping, herky-jerky dance, invisible, as one is in a crowd, so they surely believed, while the fevered, dissonant music kept playing.

125. Ibid., 34.
126. Ibid., 39.
127. Ibid., 38–39.
128. Ibid., 39.
129. Ibid., 40.
130. Ibid., 40.
131. Ibid., 41.

Funny."[132] When one of the dancers "smacked the lone tuba player on the back," other musicians take notice, leading Rocco to conclude that he "saw, all at once, the past . . . the present . . . and the distant future" of the dancers and their inevitable disruption.[133] The Virgin stops, the black dancers vanish, and the "parade did an unprecedented thing": the procession returns to the church.[134] "Old ladies" follow, and the men responsible for airborne entertainment "were packing the fireworks, unexploded, back into the crates."[135]

The reader forgets that only Rocco and some children, watching from above on a nearby roof, observed the entire chaos. For others, it appeared that time simply folded back on itself, and the procession rewound into church. The inciting dance was harmless, innocent jubilance, but Rocco knew that others, seeing the incomplete action, would think a "sacrilegious" had "mistaken the holy procession for a roadhouse."[136] Misunderstandings and anger would abound, and "the only part that all the versions had in common was the end—off with the lights, everybody get out, everybody go home."[137]

Scibona's novel accumulates so that its title feels less melodramatic than accurate. Bereft with paradoxes, the novel documents a particular preconciliar world of immigrant Catholic America through a postconciliar aesthetic focused on disruption and dissonance, where a man who is lost on his way to find his family is the only truthful observer of a moment of unintentional heresy. Scibona's work, like DeLillo's *End Zone*, garners its identification as a novel in the Catholic sphere through a sideways arrival, and yet that definition feels essential to the work's implicit core. For all the work's tendency to create single-note clergy like a "bumptious, shrunken, emphatic, salt white priest" with "piebald incisors" who "flexed his nostrils in spasms and allowed his saliva to collect in a froth at the edges of his lips," Scibona's work shows fascinating range within his particular Catholic aesthetic.[138]

Would *The End* ever appear on a parish reading list? It should. Yet the path toward necessary pastoral literary diversity is a long one. *The*

132. Ibid.
133. Ibid., 43.
134. Ibid.
135. Ibid.
136. Ibid., 44.
137. Ibid.
138. Ibid., 276–77.

Dogmatic Constitution on the Church, particularly the fourth chapter on the laity, offers the beginning of a pastoral framework within the scope of Vatican II. The lay and clergy "diversity of graces, of ministries and of works gathers the sons of God into one."[139] The laity have a "special vocation" to "make the Church present and fruitful in those places and circumstances" where secular life requires daily engagement.[140] To achieve this end, pastors "should recognize and promote the dignity and responsibility of the laity in the Church."[141] The result should not be administrative oversight; rather, the laity must be given "freedom and scope for acting," and given "courage" to engage in independent pastoral ministry.[142] Robert Burns sees that call leading to pastoral councils at the regional level, concurrent with the Council's refiguring the identity and conception of the priesthood, a move "from the sacral or cultic model of ministry to a more ministerial one . . . to build up and preserve the unity and love of the Christian community."[143] Waldmeir, more than Burns, engages how the laity as writer-artists participate in the paradigm shift. Waldmeir, in *Cathedrals of Bone*, remains cautious about the conciliar writers' usage of bodily analogies as remaining wedded to a hierarchical, top-heavy conception of church power and influence. Through the writing of Jesuit historian John O'Malley, Waldmeir finds promise that the rhetorical tendency of Vatican II might be identified as "[panegyric], a genre marked by the kind of discourse imaginative writers tend to employ as they develop characters and explore in their plots the ramifications of new social arrangements."[144] As for imaginative literature written during and after the conciliar time period, Waldmeir cautions that "authors do not organize their texts historically around the Council, nor do they analyze their subject matter in theological language taken exclusively from Vatican II sources . . . Rather, they dramatize the results of its rhetorical breakthrough."[145] Engaging preconciliar and postconciliar liturgies and traditions, writers "attempt both to welcome a plurality of voices and viewpoints and to regain the symbols of a unified past."[146]

139. Flannery, "Dogmatic," 390.

140. Ibid.

141. Ibid., 395.

142. Ibid.

143. Burns, *Roman*, 62.

144. Waldmeir, *Cathedrals*, 5.

145. Ibid., 5.

146. Ibid., 6.

Waldmeir finds the nexus of these tensions in the body: "desire and pain, aroma and sweat—becomes for these [Catholic] writers a source for meditating God's presence to the world . . . [and] takes shape as a sacramental reality."[147] Even the physicality of Mass—"the body sits, stands, kneels, listens, speaks, tastes and . . . touches other bodies"—contributes to Catholicism being perceived on the basis of body.[148] Paul Elie has investigated the peculiar paradox of the American Catholic writer in "The Last Catholic Writer in America." Elie wonders why, despite the apparent large population of educated Catholic readers, the communal nature of the Church, and the great traditions of previous generations, that most working contemporary Catholic writers feel "alone in the dark."[149] Elie debunks the superficial assumptions about Catholicism, particularly the expectation of community: "There is nothing more atomized than fifty suburban Catholics loping across the parking lot to fifty parked cars after Mass."[150] Elie wonders if "the authors of the best Catholic writing may not be known to us as Catholics. They may not be Catholics at all."[151] Elie's essay ultimately builds toward independence for the Catholic writer. Not an institutional independence in the sense of malleable ecumenicism, but rather of artistic autonomy. Elie is skeptical of a refined Catholic literary canon: "Catholics often make a fetish of the ideal. It seems to me that the most important thing is not to posit a shared system of values or to yearn for a Catholic community that doesn't exist."[152] Elie is hopeful, though, for the pastoral results of Catholic literature, citing that "As Catholics, we believe that we are bound together in ways that we do not realize, and that this binding is taking place in ways we cannot see."[153]

Elie's paradoxical hope is reflective of an increasing trend in Catholic literary criticism, a trend in which I admit participation. Several questions and considerations are worth noting, and *The Fine Delight* intends to continue these inquires rather than close them, in hopes that Catholic literature of the present and future will further deepen both the faith and the art produced in concert. Unlike literary criticism based on secular ideology, a Catholic literary criticism must mediate between the objectivity needed to

147. Ibid., 7.

148. Ibid., 8.

149. Elie, "The Last Catholic," 122.

150. Ibid.

151. Ibid., 127.

152. Ibid., 128.

153. Ibid.

identify work of sufficient style and earned merit, and the subjectivity of faith: the belief that reflection upon such literature has significant pastoral worth.

Similarly, what is the role of literature in the institutional Church, and in the lives of lay Catholics? In the same way that pastoral letters are not meant "to be binding in conscience" but are written rather to "awaken Americans to the problems of social justice . . . encouraging Catholics and others to become involved in the struggle for peace and human rights," so might Catholic literature be seen as another medium of faith formation and transformation.[154] Burns quotes Charles Curran's observation that the "public dialogue" element of forming these pastoral letters has set a necessary precedent for the Church.[155] Writers working in the contemporary Catholic tradition have been formed, reformed, marred, scarred, lifted, confused, and rejuvenated by the Catholic faith. Their contributions, however paradoxical and contradictory, are impossible to ignore in the literary, pastoral, and religious senses. Mary Gordon's words about moral fiction are equally applicable to the range and depth of contemporary Catholic literature: "Serious fiction is uniquely qualified to combat the sound bite. It says to us that the truth of human beings is often more complicated than we think. What we might like to call the truth is often made up of several truths, including the first thing we thought, its opposite, and something in between."[156] Those paradoxes enhance, and not devalue, the Catholic literary aesthetic.

And that aesthetic is wide. Catholic readers and critics desire to identify particular writers on the fringe of Catholicism as Catholic because they want the best of the word's secular connotation to apply to art of the faith. Catholic writers after Vatican II did not become more Catholic, nor did they only, as Ross Labrie has posited, channel tension between hierarchy and laity into realizing "their inherited, and largely Protestant, American individualism."[157] They have negotiated the personal and the communal, and have made individual choices in the shadow of liturgical tradition and the Church. For some writers, Catholicism is artifice more than faith belief. Yet others have created literature while believing in far more than the meaninglessness posited in Hungerford's analysis. Here are three such writers.

154. Burns, *Roman*, 114.

155. Ibid., 115.

156. Gordon, "Moral," para. 20.

157. Labrie, *The Catholic*, 9.

Chapter Two

Literary Mysticism

The Fiction and Essays of Ron Hansen

RON HANSEN DESCENDS FROM two literary origins: John Gardner and William Gass. Gardner, a cultural Protestant who once quipped that he was "the last person on earth who still believes in the almighty Zeus" and Gass, an avowed atheist, might seem unusual exemplars for a staunch Catholic like Hansen.[1] Yet Gardner and Gass framed the moral and stylistic discussions regarding American fiction, and the teaching of that fiction, during the 1970s and 80s, conversations that both directly and indirectly influenced Hansen's development as a writer.

Gardner and Gass have a complicated history. Gardner devotes four full pages within his 1978 polemic *On Moral Fiction* to rebuking William Gass's theories, criticizing him as one of the contemporary writers who concentrates "on language for its own sake . . . [rather] than with creating fictional worlds."[2] Gardner attacks Gass's theories of the conceptual nature of words, and claims that despite Gass's consideration of characters as "verbal structures," Gass's own early fiction contains "magnificently vivid characters and scenes."[3] Only when Gass shifts from creating the fictional dream to writing "fiction designed to prove a theory" does he regress to "mere language—puns, rhymes, tortuously constructed barrages of verbiage with the words so crushed together that they do indeed become

---

1. Swindell, "Our Best," 39.
2. Gardner, *Moral*, 71.
3. Ibid., 68.

opaque as stones."[4] Gardner's problem with Gass's style is that it echoes a larger motif in contemporary fiction, "texture over structure," and this again reveals Gardner's major thesis: "the mistake is a matter of morality, at least in the sense that it shows, on the writer's part, a lack of concern."[5]

In another, less antagonistic work, *The Art of Fiction*, Gardner devotes nearly three pages to Gass's novella "The Pedersen Kid," a work he considers "a more or less perfect example of the [novella] form."[6] His praise should not be surprising. Gardner published the story in a 1961 issue of his literary magazine, *MSS*. The novella's action "is a continuous stream moving through a series of climaxes, focused throughout on a single character, young Jorge."[7] These climaxes are "increasingly powerful," complemented with "suggestions of mystic ritual."[8] Gardner notes "how thoroughly realistic all this is, for all its symbolic freighting . . . nearly every detail works symbolically as well as literally."[9] Gardner's discussion of Gass's trademark syntactic meanderings is nearly mute; rather, Gardner's focus is on the mystical structure of the work. The spare analysis begs expansion: others have appropriated Gass's seemingly sparse prose for ideological purposes, but the novella is rich and layered enough to be read on its own merits, as a self-contained whole. "The Pedersen Kid," though authored by Gass, is a near-perfect presentation of Gardner's poetics.

Mariette in Ecstasy, Hansen's 1991 novel, would pass the litmus test of both Gass and Gardner. Hansen admits reading "just about everything [Gass] has written, often over and over again," calling him "sentence by sentence . . . [possibly] the finest descriptive writer in America."[10] Yet Hansen agrees with Gardner that Gass found it "hard . . . to commit to the fakery of storytelling" because "many of his plots, as in 'The Pedersen Kid,' deliberately go nowhere."[11]

Perhaps no living writer was more instrumental in defining Hansen's view of fiction than Gardner. For Hansen, Gardner was part mentor, part icon. In the preface to his essay-eulogy, "The Wizard: Remembering John Gardner," Hansen shares that, when feeling the desire to stop

4. Ibid.
5. Ibid., 69.
6. Gardner, *Art*, 179.
7. Ibid., 180.
8. Ibid.
9. Ibid., 181.
10. Ron Hansen, 2012.
11. Ibid.

a day's writing, he wonders: "What would John Gardner do?"[12] Hansen first discovered Gardner's work while a student at the fabled Iowa Writers Workshop, where he included Gardner's name in a litany of postmodern writers. Hansen's essay might be misconstrued as feeding the Gardner literary legend, but he paints an even, realistic impression of the complicated teacher, classifying *On Moral Fiction* as "jeremiad."[13]

Gardner was an immediate supporter of Hansen's published work and manuscripts in progress. He showered praise and recruited Hansen to join him at the annual Bread Loaf Conference. Hansen explains: "at a critical period in my life, he had faith not just in what I'd done but what I would do and his friendship and esteem made me feel as if I'd been accepted into a highly selective fraternity."[14] Short of Gerard Manley Hopkins, no other writer receives similar praise in *A Stay Against Confusion* or within Hansen's interviews. And yet Gardner was a study in opposites: his critical writing railed against the same experimentation and metafiction he produced within his own creative work. Hansen does not share Gardner's polarization, but Hansen's tension between preconciliar experiences and postconciliar writing can be likened to Gardner's wranglings.

Hansen finds his origin as a writer within the preconciliar world. In the Latin Mass of his Omaha youth, "liturgical rites were grand theater . . . filled with magisterial ceremony, great varieties of mystery and symbol, and a haunting Gregorian chant that sounded good even if poorly sung."[15] The theater trope is useful: priests performed Mass to an audience that was observant rather than participatory. Speaking about the genesis of his "vocation" as a writer, Hansen reflects on his perception of Mass through the lens of one concerned with storytelling: "Each Mass was a narrative steeped in meaning and metaphor, helping the faithful to not only remember the past but to make it present here and now."[16] Hansen found narratives "all over the place, in the paintings, statues, Stations of the Cross," and felt that Mass "increased my reverence for narrative. Story wasn't just revered or sanctified; it was understood that it was an element that ought to be incorporated fully into your life."[17]

12. Hansen, *A Stay*, 57.

13. Ibid., 60.

14. "Interview with Ron Hansen," para. 13.

15. Hansen, *A Stay*, xii.

16. Ibid.

17. Brown, "Participating," 39.

Another essay, "Eucharist," is a fine meditation on reception of the Host. Hansen cleverly distills his memory of his first Communion Mass through "Kodachrome snapshots . . . [showing] our hands folded and fingers steepled, our faces solemn," adding a pastel tinge to the recollections.[18] Hansen easily settles into the reverence of a child participating in this preconciliar procession, and his details complete the picture. The priest, a monsignor, wears "gold-embroidered white vestments," and resembles the "destroying God of Abraham" as he offers Communion in Latin.[19] Later, as an altar boy, Hansen experienced the Latin more often, though "large parts of the history and lore of the sacrament were going way over my head."[20] It was a pleasant, and perhaps necessary, confusion, since he felt "privileged to be there and observe up close the mystery in which Christ's body and blood were somehow actually confected from ordinary bread and wine."[21] A similar experience is reflected during a Christmas pageant of his youth, when, as a result of a mistake, Hansen is the only student in his class without a role. He is then assigned the part of Luke the evangelist, the narrator of the tale, and a curious experience occurs. Hansen plays the role of conduit, "reciting sentences I didn't fully understand," filled with "fascinating and archaic words."[22] It was the first time Hansen realized "the power that majestic language had for an audience."[23]

Hansen has attended daily Mass for much of his life. He was a teenager during the Vatican II liturgical shift, and found that the new translation made Mass "more like a supper than a sacrifice."[24] The solemnity might be lessened, but the new translation "puts more responsibility on the parishioners to actually know what is going on and to participate."[25] Hansen has voiced misgivings about the most recent retranslation. He laments that his years spent on the Translations and Revisions Committee of the International Commission on English in the Liturgy "[working] on getting the theology and sense of the Latin exactly right while also creating prayers that were beautiful, even poetic" seems to have been ignored, as

18. Hansen, *A Stay*, 232.

19. Ibid.

20. Hansen, *A Stay*, 241.

21. Ibid.

22. Ibid., 18–19.

23. Ibid., 19.

24. Frykholm, "The Risks," 24.

25. Ibid.

those "translations have been jettisoned," instead releasing "prayers that are not just unlovely but ungrammatical."[26]

Hansen finds freedom in his cradle Catholicism, noting "faith that has settled into a person is not restrictive but liberating."[27] Literary converts "sometimes go too far in condemning others or insisting on perfect orthodoxy," whereas those "who grow up with a religious faith and are settled into it realize that there's more openness and pliability and solace in it than it might appear to those on the outside looking in."[28] Hansen accepts that "All the mysteries don't have to be solved for me."[29] His sentiment does not equal lax theology, or fictional theory. Hansen is clear that he devalues Christian fiction that is merely "evangelization or testimony" because "that's not how Jesus himself would have told the story."[30] He worries that "if you don't have an altar call at the end [of Christian fiction], people think it has failed," much preferring a more gradual approach."[31]

Although Hansen's origins as a storyteller are clearly connected to his Catholic faith and culture, his earliest novels were not explicitly Catholic. *Desperadoes*, a "highfalutin Western," was followed by *The Assassination of Jesse James by the Coward Robert Ford*, another historical novel.[32] Hansen notes general biblical themes in the background of those works, but concludes "there comes a time when we find the need and the confidence to face the great issues of God and faith and right conduct more directly."[33] Hansen's phrasing is an act of humility, and yet also a pronouncement of responsibility. Gardner's more altruistic arguments for moral fiction are reflected in this statement, one that positions Hansen as a writer aware of his literary-pastoral role. It is telling that he does not use the modifier "Catholic," nor does he reference any dogmatic points. Additionally, his mention of "right conduct" speaks to Gardner's earlier contentions against Gass regarding fiction's role as an opportunity to dramatize the world. Neither Gardner nor Hansen would support a prescriptive fiction, but both support a sense of moral honesty.

26. Ron Hansen, 2012.
27. Brown, "Participating," 41.
28. Ibid.
29. Ibid., 44.
30. Ibid.
31. Frykholm, "The Risks," 25.
32. Hansen, *A Stay*, 5
33. Ibid., 4.

Waldmeir considers *Mariette in Ecstasy* a work that challenges the critical sense that "pre- and postconciliar writing divides neatly, if not exclusively, between contrasting calls for, on the one hand, a 'vertical' connection between the individual and God and, on the other, a more horizontal union between God and the wider nexus of social interactions."[34] Despite its representative importance to his overall thesis, Waldmeir only devotes a few pages to the novel. Ross Labrie's *The Catholic Imagination in American Literature,* published six years after the release of Hansen's novel, does not include a single mention of the work. Waldmeir's decision is not to a fault, but Hansen's novel is worthy of more sustained analysis and mining as an essential postconciliar Catholic imaginative work.

Hansen realized *Mariette in Ecstasy* was an unusual follow-up to his earlier writing, but "knew the book would get published somewhere, even if it were a small press,"[35] noting there is "room for Catholic fiction intended for smaller audiences."[36] He explained that "each book teaches its writer how it ought to be written, and that may leave some worthy manuscripts hunting in vain for an audience, but it doesn't necessarily diminish their worth."[37] Still, he was "worried that the book would be misunderstood by reviewers and that I would be ridiculed in academe."[38]

Hansen's initial idea for the novel came from seeing "photographs of the convent in Lisieux where Saint Thérèse and her sisters were cloistered."[39] One particular photo showed Thérèse "smiling at the camera as she did laundry," while another included her "performing in a convent play with her veil off and her long hair loose."[40] The images gave him "an intimate glimpse of that secret life," and he wondered, "why aren't there novels like that?"[41]

His process began with scenes based on the photographs of Saint Thérèse, as well as his own Catholic schooling. He "laid each scene on the floor until I found a rhythm, and then I developed a chronology based on the pre–Vatican II feast days" because he "liked the idea of liturgical

34. Waldmeir, *Cathedrals,* 25.
35. Hansen, *A Stay,* 9.
36. "Interview with Ron Hansen," para. 11.
37. Ibid.
38. Nelson, "Stewards," 82.
39. "Interview with Ron Hansen," para. 3.
40. Ibid.
41. Ibid.

timelessness and the dreaminess of the present tense,"[42] which Thomas Wendorf finds "bestows on images and actions a greater immediacy and palpability."[43] "Cribbing and stealing from hundreds of sources," Hansen soon allowed his research "to be distorted and transmuted by figurative language, forgetfulness, or by the personalities of the fictional characters."[44] The result is a work that feels heavy in deliberate and necessary craft, extending even to the sentence and phrasal level, where Hansen "was aiming for some of the qualities of prose poetry with an impressionistic, cinematic approach that edits a lot out that the reader is forced to fill in, thereby becoming a co-creator."[45]

The actual text and content of *Mariette in Ecstasy* is the perfect marriage between Gass's distrust of language and the fictional dream, and Gardner's hope for a moral fiction communicated through experimental narrative. Certainly *Mariette in Ecstasy* is not as typographically innovative as Gass's *Willie Masters' Lonesome Wife*, nor does it exist in the absurdity of Gardner's *Grendel*, but the result is an authentically postmodern text with a firm control over pagination and the concept of book art. Set in 1906 in upstate New York, the work exists within a particular historical space and place, allowing Hansen to negotiate time and idea for fictional effect.

The first page of the novel is the "Directoire des Religieuses du Couvent de Notre-Dame des Afflictions," a list of women housed at the novel's main setting. The left column is populated with names, with the word "Sister" repeated until the word loses its efficacy, like the need for these women to cast aside certain emotions. The women's diverse responsibilities include "Equerry," "Extern Farmer," and "Winemaker." Several novices are present, and one very important postulant, Mariette. The list immediately establishes the rigidity of the order, not to mention the depersonalization of the Sisters: these women have become their habitual responsibilities. The ages range from 81 to 17, with Mariette the youngest.

This initial list is followed by a schedule, deemed the "Winter Life of the Sisters of the Crucifixion." Not only are these women framed by their actions, but their life is regimented in the strident sense of "Winter." They "rise in silence" at 2 a.m., and their day consists largely of prayer, work, and classes, until "we all go to bed" in the early evening. There is a slot

---

42. Ibid., para. 6.
43. Wendorf, "Body," 45.
44. Hansen, *A Stay*, 9.
45. "Interview with Ron Hansen," para. 9.

for recreation, which is portrayed later in the novel as Sisters frolicking in high grass, pointing to birds and laughing; one sister is "jumping and shrieking joyously" while playing badminton.[46] The text proper begins afterward, and Hansen's arrangement of run-on sentences has the visual appearance of poetry. Place and weather are immediately established, as is the community nature of the convent, with a mention of the nondescript "thirty nuns" engaged in chant.[47] Hansen's initial focus is on the nonhuman elements of this location, documenting movement in recursive syntax: "Wind, and a nighthawk teetering on it"; "Cattails sway and unsway"; "Grape leaves rattle and settle again."[48] Hansen's penchant for opposition continues elsewhere, as "wings batter and bluster" and "tree branches nod and subside."[49] Mother Céline, the prioress and older sister of postulant Mariette, is the first individual introduced, head downward as she moves with grace. Hansen's admitted influence from photography and film might be supplemented by engravings, as his sentences have visual texture with a shade of ambiguity: "Wide plank floors walked soft and smooth as soap."[50]

The convent's church is fifty years old, and the daily life has likely changed little since the original dedication. Sisters cook and sew in preparation for the reception Mass of Mariette, scheduled on August 15, the Solemnity of the Assumption of the Blessed Virgin Mary. Although the women form a collective whole, Hansen imbues individual, and often opposing, personalities. Sister Sabine, who "strolls" to the Guernsey cows she milks, allows her hands to "ride their caramel hides" before smelling her palms and smiling.[51] Sister Aimée "hates the morning."[52] Yet these women swallow any discomfort. Punishment is silent but sharp: one sister late to prayer "prostrates herself facedown on the floor until her shame has passed."[53] Another sister suffering through menstrual cramps must do the same, "as if she's been nailed facedown on a crucifix."[54] The other sisters step over her, but Mariette joins her on the ground.

46. Hansen, *Mariette*, 53.
47. Ibid., 3.
48. Ibid.
49. Ibid., 5.
50. Ibid., 4.
51. Ibid., 5.
52. Ibid.
53. Ibid., 8.
54. Ibid., 66.

Paradoxically, the same convent culture meant to displace vanity creates preoccupation with the corporeal, reinforcing Waldmeir's analyses of postconciliar literature. Mother Saint-Raphaël's body defines her: though she is "hugely overweight," her legs are "slight as a goat's."[55] Rosebush cuttings are "tightly sashed below the great green-veined bowls of her breasts," and the mortification has produced "skin that is scarlet with infection."[56] She accepts the pain in silence. Carla A. Arnell finds a consistent trope of pain throughout the novel, extending to Céline's later cancer, and reaching its spiritual apex in Mariette's mysterious bleeding.

Men are absent from this world. Although novices "[pluck] tan feathers from twenty wild quail shot by a Catholic men's club," those men only shoot the game, but do not consume it.[57] The only man ancillary to this community is Reverend Henri Marriott, whose "soft white hair is harrowed and wild," complemented by a food-stained beard.[58] Marriott celebrates Mass for the order. His celibacy yokes him with the Sisters, and his masculinity is not Hansen's true choice of juxtaposition within the novel. The work's distinct variable is young Mariette, seventeen, the daughter of a local doctor, Claude Baptiste. Baptiste is a skeptic, the only practitioner for forty miles, and unhappy to have lost Céline, his other, Vassar-educated daughter to the order. He does not attend Mariette's procession through town, and he spends the High Mass in her honor "standing in misery by the first station, where Christ was condemned, his forearms over his hot suit and vest, his eyes as red as noise."[59] Mariette's family is wealthy, and as part of her vow of poverty, she must decide to "whom her jewelry and porcelains and laces and gowns ought to go."[60] Her family's wealth is in contrast with her lodging at the convent, where her nine-by-nine "cell" is described in detail: "Whitewash has been painted over the plaster walls but the joints and high ceiling planks are shellacked oak and mahogany."[61] White dominates the room, blanching the cotton sheets and an aged armoire. The only color in the room comes from "a hideous Spanish cross and a painted Christ that is all red meat and agony."[62]

55. Ibid., 5.
56. Ibid., 6.
57. Ibid., 11.
58. Ibid., 6.
59. Ibid., 15.
60. Ibid., 8.
61. Ibid., 23.
62. Ibid.

There will be not even "a scrap of mirror" in her cell at the convent, but a floor mirror stands in her bedroom at home.[63] She disrobes in front of that mirror, "pretty and naked and seventeen," the litany of conjunctions connecting her beauty, sexuality, and youth.[64] That trinity becomes of particular concern for Mariette upon her arrival at the convent, yet Hansen already establishes her attractiveness. She "pouts" her lips and "esteems her full-breasts as she has seen men esteem them."[65] Mariette "haunts" her skin rather than touching it, leading into a pronouncement: *Even this I give You.*[66] Young Mariette is offering her body to Christ, and that offering is charged with sensuality.

Mariette is to be wed to Christ; she even wears her mother's dress of "white Holland cloth and watered silk."[67] Each postulant receives similar treatment, including a procession through town, but Hansen is careful to only represent Mariette's entrance, thus making her seem special. She is special, but she is also an immediate target, unwelcomed by Mother Saint-Raphaël, whose "frowning pink face [was] all puckers and creases."[68] Though she "stares at the too-pretty postulant" with the gaze of judgment, she is somehow powerless, "weeping with happiness" at Mariette's engagement with the High Mass.[69] Later, when weeding around a garden bench, Mariette pricks her hand with a thorn and begins to bleed. Saint-Raphaël "puts spit on her forefinger and softly caresses the blood from the wound" but "there's such an odd confusion of feelings in the grandmotherly face that Mariette hesitantly wrests her hand away."[70] Saint-Raphaël tells Mariette to not "misinterpret simple tenderness," following with an admonition: "There's a great deal about you that troubles me."[71]

Hansen resists the lesser religious novelist's urge to canonize Mariette through idolatry. In the tradition of Graham Greene's troubled whisky priest in *The Power and the Glory*, Mariette feels perpetually unworthy; she explains her name's pronunciation as "Mar-iette, like a flaw."[72] The

63. Ibid.
64. Ibid., 9.
65. Ibid.
66. Ibid.
67. Ibid., 12.
68. Ibid., 13.
69. Ibid.
70. Ibid., 65.
71. Ibid.
72. Ibid., 15.

often envious sisters always catch Mariette's missteps, including when she "tightens her throat on the higher notes and slightly mispronounces the Latin *c*."[73] Their envy inevitably returns to Mariette's appearance, and the reason becomes clear: Mariette's ecstatic moments, her mysterious connections to Christ, often intersect with indirect or direct representations of her palpable sexuality. Hansen introduces the conjunction with a most curious anecdote. Four years old, Mariette stared at a painted crucifix in her mother's room and "touched his pink mouth, the pink rent in his side, and then she touched her own mouth. She touched underneath her skirt."[74] The sexuality is less pornographic than exploratory, but the connection remains. During her first night at the convent, Mariette experiences a moment of frozen ecstasy: naked, "kneeling on the floor," she "yields up one hand and then the other just as if she were being nailed like Christ to a tree."[75]

The austerity of his surrounding descriptions makes Hansen's representation of Mariette that much more complicated. The aforementioned ecstasy occurs in the haustus room where, just outside, Sister Agnès collects clothes to launder. The text breaks during Mariette's ecstasy, and then refocuses on the next page, where Agnès has entered the room; the doors in the convent are never to be fully shut. Mariette's embarrassment adds credibility to her ecstasy. Yet Mariette has not been sheltered from sexuality, or sex; it is important to allow those words to exist independently, and they do in the novel. When Agnès ties a scarf around Mariette's hair, the action enters the postulant's memory as "a fruit picker [did] after having intimacies with a foreman in tree shade."[76] Agnès passes a warning from the prioress about flirtations with the priest, not to mention "particular affection for some of her sisters."[77]

One capable of particular affection is Sister Hermance. "Sweet," but also "fat" and "toad-eyed," she "trundles" forward, and speaks behind a cupped palm.[78] In their first conversation, Mariette says she will "try to be irresistible."[79] Her words are not meant to be seductive, as she is referring to an equally prideful pursuit of sainthood, but Mariette's affect on others

---

73. Ibid., 13.
74. Ibid., 16.
75. Ibid.
76. Ibid., 18.
77. Ibid.
78. Ibid., 19.
79. Ibid.

is never bound to intention. It is Hermance who first brings Mariette to her cell and explains how Mariette should arrange her things, concluding with a suggestion to banish the personal pronoun from her vocabulary and thoughts: "Everything in this room is *ours*. Even you, you are ours now."[80] Later, while Mariette plants seeds in the garden, Hermance's gaze overwhelms the narration. She stands behind Mariette and seems to modulate the description: "Killdeer kite down and dally above Mariette, as if suddenly interested. Turtledoves watch from the telephone wire," all leading Hermance to again elevate Mariette: "*We will have a bounty. Everything she touches will grow. Dirt puts itself in her hands.*"[81] Hermance could have easily replaced the feminine pronoun with Christ; in fact, her prioress would likely demand it. She later concludes Mariette has "powers."[82]

Hansen uses the texture of touch elsewhere to add further nuance to the atmosphere of the novel. On Ash Wednesday, a day when the priest's smudge of dust has a grating acoustic sense, the concept of touch is apparent, as one sister is "drawling four fingers along the white wall" before entering Mariette's empty cell, "her callused hands softly touching down on the furniture."[83] She "is pleased to smooth the grey blanket" and "tips a water pitcher" before "[opening] the armoire and [pressing] her face to Mariette's habits, inhaling the delicious perfume that exudes from them."[84] The sister's touch leads to her discovery of a dislodged floor plank, where she finds Mariette's writings in which the postulant voices intense desire for the presence of Christ, and her uneasiness with all the attention.

After Mariette's stigmata becomes public knowledge, Sister Hermance is on night watch in the postulant's room, and acts as part nurse, part admirer. Again, the prose carries the moment, as Hermance unwraps the cloth from Mariette's hand and submerges it in water, where "Blood seeps silkily from the hand wound, turning and rumpling underwater until it gradually untangles into nothing more than color."[85] She continues to appreciate Mariette, who sleeps in front of her. Hermance's words are whispers, but they are heavy: "You have turned your face from me too often. You have been frightened by my affection."[86] Hermance then licks

80. Ibid., 24.
81. Ibid., 52.
82. Ibid., 79.
83. Ibid., 161.
84. Ibid.
85. Ibid., 120.
86. Ibid., 121.

the blood from Mariette's wound, saying "I have tasted you, See," and that she has "loved you more than myself," calling Mariette a "sacrament."[87] Waldmeir notes that "in no way do [her action's] lesbian overtones deter from the remarkable conclusion" of Hermance identifying Mariette as sacramental.[88]

Hermance is not the only sister smitten with Mariette. Sister Emmanuelle hides behind another sister so that she might "discreetly adore the new postulant in her simple night-black habit and scarf."[89] The narrative again settles into the subjective perspective, as the lines "She's as soft and kind as silk. She's as pretty as affection" belong to Emmanuelle.[90] Emmanuelle has knitted an embroidered handkerchief for Mariette, the result of "hours of needlepoint."[91] Emmanuelle "flushes pink" at Mariette's smile.[92] Sister Saint-Denis says that Mariette "is Christian perfection" and "lovely in every way."[93] Sister Philomène calls Mariette her "particular friend" and "a saint."[94] The narrator almost joins the appreciation; a marked difference exists between the gray, spare description of the first pages, and how everything appears perfumed after Mariette's arrival: "Warm water that smells like grapefruits is sheeting grayly on the rollers as it presses from the wet linen."[95] Mariette shares with Philomène how she would "[whip] herself with knotted apron strings" and "[rebuke] temptations against chastity by lying naked on thorns."[96]

A scene steeped in sensuality occurs when several sisters adapt *The Song of Songs* into a playlet. Mariette stars, "her great dark mane of hair in massacre like the siren pictures of Sheba."[97] Her habit is off, and she has "shockingly dressed her soft-nakedness in a string necklace of white buttons that are meant to seem pearls and red taffeta robe that is like a bloodstain on linen."[98] Sister Geneviève plays the bridegroom, and speaks the

87. Ibid.

88. Waldmeir, *Cathedrals*, 29.

89. Hansen, *Mariette*, 57.

90. Ibid.

91. Ibid.

92. Ibid.

93. Ibid., 68.

94. Ibid., 60, 62.

95. Ibid., 60.

96. Ibid., 61.

97. Ibid., 82.

98. Ibid., 83.

language of lust: "You ravish my heart . . . How delicious is your love . . . Your lips, my promised one, distilled wild honey."[99] Mariette's monologue concludes with "Let my Beloved come into his garden, let him taste its precious fruits."[100] Sister Philomène, who "impishly [smiled]" earlier, knows that "We shouldn't be doing this."[101] Hermance, whose affection for Mariette has already been clearly established, loves the performance.

The sexual metaphors of the scene are apparent, particularly through the play on entrance. Sister Pauline narrates that "she hears her Beloved knocking," to which Sister Léocadie, in the audience, responds "Oh, go ahead . . . Just let him in and get on with it."[102] Philomène covers her ears, but Hermance "squeals with joy."[103] Mariette's later lines continue the metaphor: "When at last I opened to my Beloved, he had departed and disappeared . . . I sought him but did not find him. I called to him but he did not answer me."[104] The entire play is lighthearted, drenched in the small audience's sarcasm, but the import is complicated: Mariette's performative language mirrors her words used in her letters to describe Christ.

Mariette's arrival takes a toll on all inhabitants of the convent. Horses "shamble lazily" and sisters pray the Angelus "while slouching tiredly."[105] "Each" of the other novices "hates" Mariette as she reads from her formation essay: "we see how important it is for God to be away from us and be the one we pine for but cannot have, for desiring God invigorates us."[106] During a scene of evening conference, all sisters consider their sins, both in silence and communally. Mariette follows the lead of others, and vocally airs her sins, but her peers, "sitting in jury" behind her, offer a litany of complaints about her: "distracting . . . a daily temptation . . . [has] provoked me."[107] Nothing compares to the words of Mother Saint-Raphaël, which astonish the others. She accuses Mariette of pride, calling her a "princess of vanities" who has "sought our admiration and attention . . . for being pretty and fetching and young."[108] Mariette is "slack in her work and

99. Ibid.
100. Ibid.
101. Ibid., 82–83.
102. Ibid., 84.
103. Ibid.
104. Ibid.
105. Ibid., 66.
106. Ibid., 60–61.
107. Ibid., 88.
108. Ibid.

lax in her conscience," as well as a "temptation" and "pet" to the novices and sisters.[109] Mother Saint-Raphaël saves her strongest admonitions for last, labeling Mariette "a snare and a worldliness to me and a terrible impediment to the peace and interests of the Holy Spirit."[110] The indictment is damning, and Saint-Raphaël offers pointed advice to Mariette: "ask for some sign that you truly have a religious calling . . . meditate upon the sorrows of Our Lord. Especially His agony in the garden, His scourging at the pillar, His being crowned with a garland of thorns."[111]

That dramatic scene occurs at the midway point of the novel, and though Hansen has slowly been building the emotions of this world, the second-half of the novel arrives at a breakneck pace, with plotting the envy of most thrillers. Mariette leaves the makeshift tribunal and prays in her room. She continues her silent meditation, "a book without words or pictures," until she is asked to bring hot tea to her sick sister, the prioress.[112] Carla A. Arnell's thorough analysis of Céline's physicality as a contrast to Mariette's pinpoints these as causal events. Céline descends quickly into sickness, with "cracked, parched lips and a trace of sour yellow; a forehead as hot, perhaps, as candle wax; frail eyelids that are redly lettered with tiny capillaries; green veins that tree and knot under the skin of her hands."[113] A nearly cartographical investigation of a sick body, sketched with the same manner of documentation Hansen previously used to establish setting. Céline admits she has been stealing and reading the letters intended for the priest.

Stern Mother Céline commands respect, but is still Mariette's sister. She asks: "Are you and Father still on good terms?"[114] The question might be one practiced for any postulant, but the concern is voiced because of their father's unhappiness with Céline's commitment to the order. Céline shares information that, taken together with Claude Baptiste's later actions, cement him as the foil of the novel. The doctor has written a letter identifying Mariette as "too high-strung" for convent life, relying on gossip about Mariette's "trances, hallucinations, unnatural piety" and more.[115] Céline proceeds in a professional manner, distilling her advice to Mariette

109. Ibid.

110. Ibid.

111. Ibid., 88–89.

112. Ibid., 89.

113. Ibid., 91.

114. Ibid., 30.

115. Ibid., 31.

into one sentence: "Don't try to be exceptional; simply be a good nun."[116] Céline explains that her coldness is necessary: "I have many sisters in my family now."[117]

The scenes of recreation between the sisters momentarily ease the narrative's tension, but also allow Hansen to further humanize the women primarily known for their rejection of individuality. The novices have a "secret place" up in the bell tower, where they are "bad."[118] They talk about old boyfriends, and "what we miss. Whiskers. Dancing. Everything."[119] They recall watching a girl and a soldier have a picnic before kissing, and then almost becoming intimate. Mariette, playfully but also "tauntingly," wonders if she was the girl.[120]

Mariette is certainly the "gossip of the summer," and her beauty results in constant warnings, including a handsigned admonition to not tempt Father Marriott.[121] Marriott is an open-minded ally: he asks Mariette to document her visions in writing, and to circumvent the prioress in the sharing of those narratives. Her first letter identifies the priest as "my dearest and only father on earth now," and includes specific instructions given to her by Christ.[122] The letter, and the first part of the novel, ends with words she claims come directly from Christ:

> *You will have no solace or pity . . . You will be tortured by gross outrages and mistreatments, but no one will believe you. You will be punished and humbled and greatly confused . . . God will seem dead and indifferent . . . you will seek me fruitlessly and without avail for I shall hide in noise and shadows and I shall seem to withdraw when you need me most . . . And yet you will believe, Mariette, but as if you did not believe; you will always hope, but as if you did not hope; you will love your Savior, but as if you did not love him, because in this time your true feelings will fail you, you will be tired of life and afraid of death, and you will not even have the relief of being able to weep.*[123]

116. Ibid.
117. Ibid., 33.
118. Ibid., 34, 35.
119. Ibid., 35.
120. Ibid., 36.
121. Ibid., 37.
122. Ibid., 42.
123. Ibid., 43–44.

These words arrive before Mariette's stigmata, and their typology is reminiscent of Isaiah's prefiguring of Christ. The predictions of rejection are to be expected; more surprising is how Christ will hide from Mariette and reject her calls for help. The oppositions that follow offer a paradoxical claim, and speak to a curious prison of suffering. Mariette will suffer personally and communally, dividing her body into two selves. In later letters, Mariette continues her pleas: "*And where is Jesus? He comes no more when I call to him.*"[124] The letters end up in Céline's desk drawer rather than the priest's home. After confession, he asks if she has been writing down her thoughts; Mariette "turns to him in surprise but doesn't say," knowing it was likely that her sister had stolen the correspondence.[125] The physicality of their suffering yokes the sisters even more than their shared blood. Mariette seeks pain as penance, submerging her hands in hot water because she "wanted to hurt."[126] During her sister's sickness, she stands naked in her cell, wire wrapped around her torso: "One upper thigh is blackly streaked with blood that is seeping from the rabbit wire that is tied just below her sex."[127]

Hansen often precedes one of Mariette's ecstatic moments by a description tinged with sexuality, or a highly sensual representation of body. While scrubbing refectory tables, Mariette's skirt is pinned up to her thighs, and "faint brown hairs stir on her calves as she moves."[128] Soon afterward she stops cleaning, joins her hands, and her "wet blue eyes are overawed as she stares ahead at a wall and she seems to be listening to something just above her."[129] Stigmatic experiences soon follow, consistent with the blurred delirium of her ecstasy. Swift pain precipitates "reddened palms," and Mariette's speech is strange: "What a great favor Christ shall be giving me!"[130] Similar exclamation occurs when Mariette speaks to Sister Catherine about her youth with the prioress, then Annie Baptiste. They prayed and spoke of Christ, and though Mariette reflects in metaphor, the approach is telling: "With Annie I first found myself before Jesus crucified . . . Such blood flowed from his hands and head!"[131] Catherine

124. Ibid., 72.
125. Ibid., 82.
126. Ibid., 70.
127. Ibid., 103.
128. Ibid., 62.
129. Ibid.
130. Ibid., 73.
131. Ibid., 74.

later defends Mariette as "passionate . . . perhaps too proud [but] *not* hysterical."[132] The testimony appears in one of the transcribed interviews peppered through the text. Hansen's usage of the decidedly postmodern interruption of embedded interviews "surprised" him, noting he "knew it as a cinematic device to make narratives more economical."[133]

Claude Baptiste returns to the narrative, and Hansen has a special role for his worldly skepticism. Baptiste greets his daughters with their birth names, and tells them about the external world: his patients, the Panama Canal construction, baseball, and the New York governor race. Mariette remains silent during his talk, and though she "truly loves and misses him," simply looking at him "gives her pain, for he is so frontally there, so forceful and huge and masculine."[134] After Mariette says she is enjoying the convent, he prods: "You like it well or just a little?"[135] Mariette thinks "*Every knife in his house has a keen edge.*"[136]

Baptiste's next arrival is the result of Hansen's clever plotting, and another example of Hansen's ability to create a thoroughly dramatic scene. Céline's sickness requires her father's care, and he is again steeped in foreign masculinity: "Farm mud crumbles from his high boots and messily scatters across the floor planks as he walks. Although he has dressed in European elegance and bathed himself in perfumes of musk and civet, he carries in his clothes from his morning rounds an odor of illness that is still so offensive that Sister Aimée has cupped a palm over her nose and Sister Philomène inches back her chair half a foot."[137] He is the perfect foil here: calculating, male, and secular. Mariette watches him as she would "a magician," though her description undercuts his iconic presentation: "he has changed into a too-heavy man with a glossy mustache and unhealthy white nails."[138] His "unclean palms" are fitted beneath "Annie's jaw," an example of Hansen's subtle shifting of monikers, and then proceeds to "daintily" untie her nightgown to check her breasts.[139]

Claude Baptiste's ownership of his daughter's body exists as long as he will live: as the only doctor in the area, he is her examiner and keeper,

132. Ibid., 75.

133. "Interview with Ron Hansen," para. 4.

134. Hansen, *Mariette*, 78.

135. Ibid.

136. Ibid.

137. Ibid., 95.

138. Ibid., 96.

139. Ibid., 96–97.

despite all of her power and success within the order. His entire professional life has been devoted to observation, diagnosis, and monitoring, and his daughters receive his sharpest inquiries. Mariette "remembers how his hard white shirt cuffs would often be brownly spotted with some patient's blood."[140] His request for the other sisters to leave during the examination is rejected, so he allows Mariette to remain. He "turns away" only when Mariette raises Céline's nightgown to collect her urine in a brandy glass.[141] Baptiste's gaze remains on Mariette, and she "feels his eyes like hands. Enjoying her. She knows their slow travel and caress."[142] Waldmeir quotes similar phrasing to suggest a history of sexual abuse from Baptiste. It is difficult to arrive at another conclusion, and nudges toward another possibility: might Baptiste be a tangible version of the devil so often alluded to within the novel? After Céline's death, he "goes up to the oaken grille and hangs on it with all his fingers for a half hour or more."[143] The image is in contrast with the village women "slumped" in pews, and the grave diggers palming their hats.[144] Baptiste might be hanging on the grille for support, but he is also hanging and remaining onto his control of his younger daughter.

Shortly after the prioress was diagnosed with cancer, Mariette experiences her second stigmata-like experience, preceded by the "blood-red light" of a December sun during the feast day for Saint Lucy, patron saint of the blind.[145] There is no blood, only a stinging palm, but she is "hoarding" the pain like a bad but necessary gift.[146] The arrival of the pain causes the text to again refer to Annie as Céline, who falls from her rapidly worsening condition. In a strange prefiguring of her later stigmata, Mariette "sees that Sister Philomène's hands are red with blood" from helping Céline.[147]

The cycle of traumatic event or sexual representation followed by stigmatic action continues after Céline's funeral. Father Marriott sees Mariette "intently staring at the crucifix above the high altar, her hands spread wide as if she were nailed just as Christ was."[148] Blood "scribbles down her

140. Ibid., 125.
141. Ibid., 97.
142. Ibid.
143. Ibid., 104.
144. Ibid.
145. Ibid., 99.
146. Ibid.
147. Ibid., 101.
148. Ibid., 107.

wrists and ankles and scrawls like red handwriting on the floor."[149] Arnell finds the occurrence as another representation of Mariette's "twin desire for artistic expression and affliction."[150] Hansen's predilection for the nearly pictographic results in a text constructed with Gass's interrogation of the page as lexical boundary. Boxes enclose words, lists populate pages. Hansen's other narrative mentor, John Gardner, who claimed that Gass's own fiction transcended the cold experimentation of his theories, was likely referring to the strangely emotional undercurrent of "The Pedersen Kid." In *Mariette in Ecstasy*, Hansen manages to reach sentiment while maintaining artifice, even reveling in the disconnect between linguistic and story truths. Mariette, her body as a physical and metaphysical canvas, is an active participant in this art.

Part 3 continues Hansen's subject-verb-object constructions of single-sentence representations of place: trees creak, winds flute, smoke flails, gusts zing, leaves scutter, and windowpanes yelp. Mariette enters the priest's home with wounds on her feet, leaving red prints on the floor. She "smiles crazily" and says "Oh, look at what Jesus has done to me!"[151] Mariette's wounds go public: she is placed in the infirmary, where the bleeding continues, though there is no reddening around the wounds. Hansen uses "weeping" to describe the "pinkish serum and blood" that escapes from the wounds.[152] Father Marriott is an early believer, quoting Luke 1:38: "Behold the handmaid of the Lord."[153]

Mother Saint-Raphaël becomes the prioress upon Céline's passing, and soon writes a letter to Mother Superior of the order, voicing skepticism about Mariette's stigmata. She also reads a statement of her concerns to the congregated sisters. Her overall topic is stigmata, but she transitions to Mariette. She is guarded, promising to disqualify Mariette from the order if the postulant is found to be lying, but Saint-Raphaël also strikes a more even tone, wondering "if these indeed are preternatural gifts from God, then in His giving them to one of ours in the cloister He has gone to great effort to keep the stigmata hidden from the world."[154] The statement of a pragmatist, not a true skeptic.

---

149. Ibid.
150. Arnell, "Wild Writing," 194.
151. Hansen, *Mariette*, 112.
152. Ibid., 116.
153. Ibid., 117.
154. Ibid., 133.

Mariette is closely monitored, though she sneaks out for Mass, noting that she has "work to do."[155] Although the sisters have made Mariette "the topic here," her connection becomes strongest with Father Marriott, who has been selected to undertake an investigation.[156] The priest mentions that four scriptorium books read by Mariette were of particular interest to him, including texts about the seventeenth-century Ursuline convent group possessions, a medical text, a compendium of saints, and a text documenting stigmatics.

The reader is left to make the implicit connections, as anatomy, possession, and sainthood are all elements of Mariette's experience. The final text, titled *Le stigmatization, l'extase divine, les miracles de Lourdes: Response aux libres penseurs*, is of primary concern. Jennifer Stevens contextualizes the late nineteenth-century text: "[with] the rapid advance of science and the growing sophistication of medicine, the phenomenon of stigmata became a focus of interest for both doctors and psychologists."[157] Louise Lateu was profiled in the text by physician Antoine Imbert-Goubeyre, who "produced the first data on stigmatics, listing all known cases century by century."[158] Despite the fact that prior to the nineteenth century, "stigmatization was common grounds for beatification," none of Imbert-Goubeyre's twenty-nine stigmatics became a saint, "suggesting that the church had started to draw up a set of criteria for sainthood that would be able to stand the scrutiny of an increasingly scientific age."[159] Imbert-Goubeyre's approach was not without criticism, even from a potentially accepting audience as the Paulist Fathers, who, in a contemporary issue of *Catholic World*, conclude the physician is "somewhat too strong in his own faith for the purpose which he has in hand."[160] Imbert-Goubeyre operated from a Catholic-centric schema, largely devoid of scientific doubt, relying "on the authority of the church . . . worthless for those who pose, whether sincerely or not, as unbelievers."[161]

Arnell finds a French Catholic precursor for Mariette's character, quoting Richard D. E. Burton's study of "women and the culture of suffering in France," where religious women "willingly assumed, and even

155. Ibid., 123.
156. Ibid., 124.
157. Stevens, *The Historical*, 162.
158. Ibid.
159. Ibid.
160. "Talk About," 570.
161. Ibid.

actively sought out, pain, suffering, illness, and ultimately, death in order to redeem them."[162] Arnell places Mariette within this historical and literary tradition of women whose "suffering has redemptive potential, not just for the sufferer but also for all of humanity."[163]

Arnell also suggests another, more curious prototype for Mariette: "a modern female version of the medieval 'wild man,' a stock romance character whose wildness disrupts and challenges conventional society."[164] Her sketch is based on Hansen's deliberate representation of "nature's wild beauty to defamiliarize the ordinary world and dilate the reader's conventional perspective, making readers more receptive to the supernatural mystery of Mariette's pleasurable pain."[165] Doctor Baptiste plays a role in representing the "secular society" that is the equivalent of the "aristocratic court" in the medieval romance tradition.[166]

Unlike Baptiste, Father Marriott's queries arrive with the tone of a hopeful supporter. Mariette "is all inwardness and certainty," saying she is "Worried . . . Humbled. Embarrassed," as well as confused by the bleeding.[167] Father Marriott asks for an explanation of Mariette's ecstatic moments, and she settles into a full-page reverie. She feels "possessed by Jesus."[168] The priest's response might appear pointed, but his wording is harmless: "Isn't it possible for me to believe you had formulated that answer in your head before visiting me here? You could have *borrowed*, for example, from the books you have been reading."[169] He is not questioning Mariette's ecstasy, rather, the origin of the language she uses to describe and frame that experience. Mariette does not feel threatened, and she continues, describing the Jesus of her ecstasy as being "horrible with blood," and yet his pain was less from the physicality and permanence of the crucifixion, and more "his human sense of failure, injustice, and loneliness."[170] Mariette claims that Christ gave her his wounds because she requested to share in his suffering, and that he actually suggested she speak to the priest about the experience. Father Marriott is flattered by the thought of reach-

---

162. Arnell, "Wild Writing," 183.

163. Ibid.

164. Ibid., 182.

165. Ibid., 183.

166. Ibid., 185.

167. Hansen, *Mariette*, 126.

168. Ibid., 128.

169. Ibid., 129.

170. Ibid.

ing the mind of the divine. Mariette concludes her testimony with a self-effacing statement: "And now I wonder if I haven't made it all up in some way, or if it's even possible."[171] Father Marriott, on cue, says he believes her. Mariette is devilishly clever, and Hansen again refuses to explain. Readers are tempted to disbelieve her at points, but does the capacity, and potential talent for duplicity, equal evil? The written testimonies of her fellow sisters are almost evenly split between jealousy and reverence. Hansen presents them paragraph-by-paragraph, without attribution of origin. Father Marriott, in reporting his experiences to a colleague, admits that "*We mortals have such a great hunger for supernatural things,*" particularly the religious, as they are "*bored and dull and tired of each other, and we have such a yearning for some sign from God that this matters.*"[172] He does not perceive Mariette's sexuality, rather noting her avoidance of any touch. He does wonder, though, if she is merely "*trying to entertain.*"[173]

Consistent with his postmodern usage of texts within texts, and layers of narrative perspective and efficacy, Hansen avoids answering the reader's ultimate question: were the stigmata real, or imagined by Mariette's fervent belief? A selection read during one of Mariette's first dinners at the convent was the *Lectio Divina* from Dame Julian's *Revelations of Divine Love*. One sentence is telling: "Some time earlier [Dame Julian] had asked three gifts from God: one, to understand his passion; two, to suffer physically while still a young woman of thirty; and, finally, to have as God's gift three wounds."[174] The narrator reveals no reaction on Mariette's part.

Mystery abounds, but Hansen truly stacks the literary deck on one side. During the January feast day of Saint Agnes, virgin martyr and patron of rape victims, Mariette awakens to see her cell door open. She hears "hitched breathing," and though it is dark, "she knows there are four there," and feels herself "being seen and changed and imagined."[175] Her blanket is pulled away, and she is too frightened to move. She is "fiercely pressed down to the palliasse and miseried by hands. Even her mouth is covered."[176] She is powerless against the "harsh kisses and pressures and hate and insistence."[177] The assault continues as "Hands haul her night-

171. Ibid., 130.
172. Ibid., 148.
173. Ibid.
174. Ibid., 25.
175. Ibid., 143.
176. Ibid.
177. Ibid.

gown as high as her thighs" and her knees are parted.[178] The attack ends, and she later opens her eyes to an empty room, unsure if she was dreaming, yet leaning toward the reality of the rape. The imagined identity of these four assailants is never revealed.

The incident, real or imagined, is incredibly troubling. Was it an attempt to deflower Mariette, and thus disqualify her from the order? Was it an attack from the devil? A later confrontation is violent but not sexual, as the sound of "heavy furniture" and "hoarse breathing and heaves and hard, masculine effort" come from Mariette's cell.[179] One of the sisters even identifies the event as a night-battle with the devil, noting that afterward, Mariette was free of blood, "but her face was horrible. She'd lost every trace of beauty."[180] Hansen entertains the presence of physical evil in the novel, including a rushed confession from an anonymous sister. Father Marriott notes that each "sentence slightly changes in tone," but he is unable to identify the speaker. Her claims include initial collusion with Mariette, alleged theft of "chemicals and instruments" to induce bleeding as part of her "cruel deception."[181] The priest's thoughts stray to Mariette's smile while being blessed, and her "pretty form as she kneels at his prie-dieu."[182] He is noticeably affected by the thoughts, his hands "cold," his face "white," and he composes himself to turn the inquiries toward the unnamed sister.[183] She "hisses" a retort: "She's in your dreams, isn't she, priest."[184] Her timing is perfect despite the cover of the purple curtain. Father Marriott also receives a letter from "A Worried Priest" that warns him to avoid Mariette's duplicity and refuse her Holy Communion. In later testimony, the priest says the devil sent him the letter.

Odd occurrences continue. Out in the snow-covered grass, Mariette sees "a boy in a green mackinaw coat surging through the high snow at the pasture fence fifty yards away," waving frantically with both hands.[185] He shouts "phrases that a hard wind tears apart" before she reenters the priory.[186] A curious incident; even more curious is the connection to Gass's

178. Ibid.
179. Ibid., 151.
180. Ibid., 152.
181. Ibid., 153.
182. Ibid.
183. Ibid.
184. Ibid.
185. Ibid., 146.
186. Ibid.

novella, "The Pedersen Kid," already presented as a favorite of both Hansen and Gardner. The fragmented tale starts with a boy, having escaped his home after a man stuffed his family into the cellar, found stranded during a Midwest snowstorm. The novella ends with a nightmarish trek toward the boy's home. The boy's testimony of what happened to his family includes a cryptic reference to the likely perpetrator: "The green mackinaw. The black stocking cap. The yellow gloves. The gun."[187] Mystery through fragmentation. Hansen is certainly using the trope of snow to sketch Mariette's iconography: she "is just beside Mother Céline's fresh grave and starkly black against the white stage of the snow and the green curtain of pine woods, but glamorously alone and forlorn like a pretty girl about to sing" before she "lifts her hands as if she's written on the palms."[188] Even scenes bereft of snow have the feeling of a painting: "Sheep whose wool is tan as slush herd against the flitched boards of a fodder shed until Sister Saint-Luc walks out with a great load of cornstalks, a blood cross on her forehead."[189]

The intensity of the narrative continues when Sister Honoré corners Mariette in her room, demanding to see her wounds. She "throws a hand over Mariette's mouth and tilts her back against the writing desk as she tears at the windings of bloodstained cloth on the postulant's hands, whispering that she'll put a stop to this foolishness, that she's sick of Mariette playing the saint when half the convent knows she's lying."[190] As part of later testimony, Honoré says a naked Mariette showed no wounds, mentioning that she "felt awkward and lewd," but "proud that I have exposed her and changed some people's minds."[191] She misunderstands the exposure, expecting the wounds to remain, though the wounds of stigmatics usually disappear. Honoré, along with seven other sisters, sign a letter to demand Father Marriott *treat this hoax with the thoroughness and gravity it warrants.*[192]

Mariette's ecstatic moments are often preceded by particularly corporeal representations of Christ, and Hansen's prose hugs each contour: she "kneels below a horrid crucifixion that she hates, Christ's flesh-painted head like a block of woe, his black hair sleek as enamel and his black beard

187. Gass, *In the Heart*, 14.
188. Hansen, *Mariette*, 166.
189. Ibid., 170.
190. Ibid., 154.
191. Ibid., 155.
192. Ibid., 161.

like ironweed, his round eyes bleary with pity and failure, and his frail form softly breasted and feminine and redly willowed in blood."[193] She feels Christ's presence "flow down from her head like holy oil and thrill her skin like terror," and sees him as "good friend and father and husband to her . . . wholly loving her common humanness."[194] The narrative fully inhabits Mariette at these moments, and they reinforce the conclusion that this experience is fully authentic: "She feels her feet twisted behind her as both [wrists] are transfixed with nails and the agony of both soles is as though she's stood in the rage of orange, glowing embers."[195] Christ might be father and husband to Mariette, but her union with the divine is reaching a shared body.

After one of Mariette's particularly violent moments of ecstasy, Mother Saint-Raphaël asks if she has "any idea how disruptive you've been?"[196] The gossip has disrupted their silence, the gifts from the villagers have disrupted their poverty, and the inquiries have disrupted their "rule of enclosure."[197] Yet Saint-Raphaël feels guilty about her necessary role: she asks Mariette to stop the experience, but to also "heal me of the hate and envy I have for you."[198] That hate translates into real punishment, with Mariette being taken from her already spartan cell to a four-by-six storage closet, "now empty save for a holy water stoup and a palliasse rolled up underneath a simple wooden cross."[199] This is a jail, and Mariette is in the corner, "undressed still and kneeling on the hard floor like the night terror in a child's closet, her wild brown hair all thrash and storm, her hands hidden behind her back, her stare as serious as torture."[200] Her public penance includes lying facedown on the floor of the dining hall, and then on a carpet near the church's nave. Yet she has become iconographic: "She is the stillness that ends their prayers. She is as present to them as God."[201]

"Mariette in ecstasy": the novel's title begins one of the final dramatic scenes. Several sisters gather "to confirm their witness" as they try "to share in the Christ [Mariette] is seeing as she stares at a spot just above their

193. Ibid., 157.
194. Ibid., 158.
195. Ibid.
196. Ibid., 160.
197. Ibid.
198. Ibid.
199. Ibid., 164.
200. Ibid., 165.
201. Ibid.

heads."[202] She watches Christ sing in choir, and then "He holds my hand in his and we two walk down the hallway to his house inside ours. Which is his heart."[203] The prioress is also in the audience, but she does not stop the show. Mariette continues: "We are alone. We touch each other, but he withdraws. 'You are unclean,' he says, and I am ashamed because I see that it's true. Every sin I have committed is written in ink on my skin. Christ tells me to undress. And then he gently washes me with his hands. With holy water from great earthen jugs heated by the sun."[204] Each of Christ's words "penetrates me as softly as water entering a sponge," and though it feels like a long time has passed, she keeps time by "the choir singing the verses and responsories for Lauds."[205] She concludes her ecstasy on its highest dramatic note: "he gives me food as I have never eaten. And fine wine from a jeweled chalice. When he tells me to sleep, I do so at once, and he holds me. And I share in him as if he's inside me. And he is."[206] The prioress "harshly slaps Mariette's face" before storming out of the room.[207] Yet the integrity of Hansen's narrators complicates the prioress's reaction: she assumes a sexual connotation, yet the union Mariette is describing might be more Eucharistic. Body becomes body.

Another public ecstasy results in metonymic reactions: "Hands touch down in the blood covenant" followed by "Hurrying sandals in the hallway."[208] The sisters carry Mariette's blood like a sacramental mark. Her disruptions require difficult decisions, and though this is a community of women, it is men who are instrumental in the final moments. They are a study in contrasts. Father Marriott is "as absent as an overcoat hung on a chair," while Doctor Baptiste's "wreath of dark hair" was held by "a floral pomade."[209] Arnell finds that the doctor's "elegant apparel and perfumed smells reflect his efforts to distance himself from his patients' suffering," which now represent his skepticism toward his daughter's supernatural experiences.[210] Mother Saint-Raphaël is the only woman present. She explains the situation: "We have been like a household with a hundred opin-

---

202. Ibid., 166.
203. Ibid., 167.
204. Ibid.
205. Ibid., 168.
206. Ibid.
207. Ibid.
208. Ibid., 170.
209. Ibid., 171.
210. Arnell, "Wild Writing," 186.

ions about an illness but no certainty. We need the verdict of a doctor."[211] Science must extinguish all natural possibilities before a miracle could be considered. Father Marriott's words are much more optimistic: "We are only here to see," and though Hansen continues his statement, those preceding words are set aside before the identifying tag.[212] Marriott certainly wants to "see," as in bear witness to the miracle he so clearly supports.

Mariette must undress for the examination, and while the priest turns to give her privacy, her father "skeptically peers" while washing his hands.[213] Naked, she tells him "*Je vous en prie*" : at your service.[214] Her father "stares at her and dries his palms," the actions deliberately lengthening the moment.[215] He begins by "stroking the rib just beneath her left breast," concluding there is no wound, no scarring.[216] There are no wounds on her palms either, though Mariette says "Christ took back the wounds."[217]

Doctor Baptiste desires tangible evidence of the divine. While the priest finds the lack of wounds miraculous, Baptiste is "frank and unimpressed, as firm and practical as a clock," concluding "You all have been duped."[218] Hansen has shared an anecdote about "a priest friend who points out that the opposite of faith is not doubt but certainty. I think God intended that—it is a way of making us creative instead of smug in our belief."[219] For Hansen, God desires a dynamic Catholic faith; not one where belief is rewritten on whim, but where Catholics are creative in building and sharing that faith. In the pastoral sense, this penultimate sequence of the novel presents the drama of a provincial dilemma projected against the entire world of faith. *Mariette in Ecstasy* dramatizes the result when God enters human midst in a visceral manner, and shows that many, including those most traditionally pious, are unprepared for tangible confrontation.

After the doctor leaves, the prioress admits her doubt "was simply political."[220] It is her decision to remove Mariette from the convent. Although the buildup has been slow, the expulsion is swift, and Mariette is

---

211. Hansen, *Mariette*, 171.

212. Ibid., 172.

213. Ibid.

214. Ibid.

215. Ibid.

216. Ibid.

217. Ibid., 173.

218. Ibid.

219. Frykholm, "The Risks," 27.

220. Hansen, *Mariette*, 174.

soon "bleakly tottering through the churned slush and mud of the village, her hair in torrents, wintry rain like tines on her face, the white Holland cloth soaked through and hedged with stains."[221] Her expulsion is a tragic conclusion for a figure that has already suffered so much, and introduces the novel's final act. Mariette is back home, though the novel's timeline is still structured by feast days. It is a domestic life, controlled by the father of her childhood, as she appears comparatively small and docile in his "darkpaneled den," his masculinity signified by "Whiskey . . . in a square crystal decanter."[222] The narrative jumps to 1912. Mariette is still home, in a housedress, tutoring French to a high school student. It is the December feast day of St. Lucy, and snowing, "White flakes are fluttering through the trees like torn paper."[223] She feels a sudden, unexplained pain, which Waldmeir sees as the final implication "that we are to accept the stigmata as genuine."[224] The narrative jumps five more years, where her father "tilts heavily in his wheelchair in the shaded garden yard, his dinner napkin still tucked in his high starched collar."[225] He says they will "be having to-matoes soon," the casual speech of a married couple.[226] Mariette responds with silence, as she "whispers the *Nunc Dimittis* of Compline."[227]

The next section is dated 1929, on the feast day of Saint Thérèse of Lisieux, Hansen's original photographic inspiration for Mariette. Now forty, Mariette stands in front of the same bedroom floor mirror, and her esteeming is delivered in the exact same language as years earlier. She has not wavered. The novel ends with a letter composed by Mariette on Easter Vigil in 1937. Hansen wrote the letter while taking a Christology class at Santa Clara University, as he completed a Masters degree in Spiritu-ality. Mariette writes that she has been mocked by the Devil, who *"tells me the years since age seventeen have been a great abeyance."*[228] She says that *"Christ still sends me roses"* and, echoing the words, of Mother Saint-Raphaël, *"We try to be formed and held and kept by him, but instead he offers us freedom."*[229] The final phrase of the book comes from the course's

221. Ibid., 176.
222. Ibid.
223. Ibid.
224. Waldmeir, *Cathedrals*, 27.
225. Hansen, *Mariette*, 177.
226. Ibid.
227. Ibid., 178.
228. Ibid., 179.
229. Ibid.

professor, Rev. Francis Smith SJ, who, when "counseling a young woman about a religious vocation," said that "Maybe God is saying, 'Surprise me.'"[230] Hansen "instantly" knew it would be the book's final line, and "just had to write to that point."[231] The narration is a sequence of surprises and shocks, a useful interrogation of complacent faith. Hansen implicitly posits the absurdity of a Catholic worldview built upon miracle that is often prescriptive rather than understanding. The expulsion of Mariette from the convent is not the true evil present in the book; far more troubling, in the Catholic sense, is the assumption that God only touches us from afar, and will never again walk in our midst.

Mariette in Ecstasy pastorally fits Hansen's perspective of Catholic writing as geared toward the inquisitive rather than the final, reflecting Mary Gordon's call for moral complexity in fiction rather than dogma. Hansen finds the publication element of writing as an opportunity for "self-disclosure and communion with others."[232] This form of public authorial confession, whether explicit or implicit, often results in readers "[questioning] and [illuminating] their own lives."[233] For Hansen, the deep reflections spurred by fiction might lead readers to "become aware of a horizon beyond which abides the One who is the creator and context of our existence."[234] This desire for a communally spiritual literary experience might be connected to Hansen's laments of lay participation in the preconciliar church of his youth, where the "laity were little more than an afterthought" in the Mass.[235] Hansen offers the anecdote of a "parishioner strolling around the church lighting votive candles, oblivious to the Consecration even as the shaken bells heralded it."[236] He follows with a litany of how the laity were not allowed to participate in word or in touch, with the wine never passing unordained lips, and women only allowed beyond the altar railing "for chores like cleaning and lily arranging."[237]

Hansen's Catholic writing, particularly *Mariette in Ecstasy*, might be seen as a postconciliar method to regain lay participation in the mechanisms of the Church. If Vatican II increased lay participation in the

---

230. "Interview with Ron Hansen," para. 7.

231. Ibid.

232. Hansen, *A Stay*, xvi.

233. Ibid., xvi.

234. Ibid., xvi–xvii.

235. Ibid., 259.

236. Ibid.

237. Ibid., 259.

celebration of Mass, likewise Hansen's postconciliar imaginative writing extends the spirit of liturgy beyond the space and place of Mass; never replacing it, but supplementing it, offering further complexity toward the end of deeper and sustained reflection. Hansen's fiction has always lauded the priesthood without resorting to type or sentimentality; from his story "My Communist" to *Exiles*, his novelistic biography of Gerard Manley Hopkins, Hansen has dramatized the priesthood as sacrament in motion, a necessary pastoral salve for the secular world. Hansen has certainly seen his own writing and faith practice as intertwined, dual purposes for pastoral ends. Hansen entered the permanent diaconate in 2007. He had previously been a "lector, Eucharistic minister, and spiritual director."[238] He explains that "an outsider would probably suspect that being 'clergy' would cramp a fiction writer's style or imprison him within a limited scope of pious subjects, but I have found the calling to be liberating because it intimately presents to me the lives of so many striving, ordinary, crazy, hopeful, sinful, fractured people who are, even at their worst, deeply loved by God. And if they are loved by God, I need to honor them with my writing."[239]

Mariette in Ecstasy interrogates the language of Catholic faith and theology, yet these inquiries are faithful acts, prayers in prose. Sister Agnès tells Mariette about the advice of the prioress; that "Jesus Christ ought to be their grandest passion, just as . . . God's holy will, ought to be their only desire."[240] Hansen's novel refigures our religious conceptions of "passion" and "desire," but without the goal of undermining the spiritual, or the dogmatic, foundation. The book is an investigation into dogmatic definition and theology in the general Joycean tradition, but without the spite of that earlier writer.

Mariette in Ecstasy also offers the dramatization of a potential saint. For some Christians, the second coming of Christ is a most frightening concept: certainly the New Testament dramatizes rejection and persecution before acceptance and reverence. The Christ of Mark's Gospel makes difficult familial choices in the service of his greater calling; he disrupts in order to reveal. Hansen explains the role of Catholic writers in similar terms. They "have as our model storyteller the Jesus who came to be among sinners and in that immersion heal them" using parables "to

238. "Interview with Ron Hansen," para. 16.

239. Ibid.

240. Hansen, *Mariette*, 18.

convey a radically new sense of what God is like."[241] Mother Céline's words ring true: "You aren't understandable . . . You may be a saint. Saints are like that, I think. Elusive. Other. Upsetting."[242] The paradox of revering Christ, and yet not being able to recognize his Second Coming in form and function, is not lost on Hansen, who uses the static setting of daily addresses for Mother Saint-Raphaël to say that "We know there *are* miracles in the gospels, but we show them disrespect if we dispose ourselves to believe in the simply fabulous."[243] She concludes that "sainthood has little to do with the preternatural but a great deal to do with the simple day-to-day practice of the Christian virtues."[244] She must be aware that this statement is incorrect, or at least disingenuous, as the Christian who prays or does alms daily will not, considering the strict requirements, ever be canonized a saint. Arnell finds Saint-Raphaël's "clean and clear" theology a necessary glue for the order, yet uses her character to "suggest that a narrow focus on prosaics can foreclose the kind of openness to the mysterious that is necessary for access to the divine."[245] *Mariette in Ecstasy* dramatizes "the paradox of Christ as both wild and civilizing . . . an agent of disruption."[246]

Yet Saint-Raphaël's admonitions are part self-serving, part necessary reminders. She is not surrounded by saints; she is surrounded by women who "stand at their windows in knitted black sweaters and watch as a cruel wind sharks what it can," who chase a spider across a page of ecclesiastical history.[247] This visually vanilla world is necessary to make Mariette's experiences all the more shocking, as her public blood shatters their monochrome setting. Mother Saint-Raphaël's fears come true, as crowds wait outside the church, pining for a view of the famed Mariette, who "cries with shame as she receives the Host, then stands and hides her face in her bandaged hands."[248] Mother Saint-Raphaël says "Skeptics will always prevail. God gives us just enough to seek him, and never enough to fully find him. To do more would inhibit our freedom, and our freedom is very dear to God."[249] The sister's criticisms are applicable to her own self.

241. Ron Hansen, 2012.

242. Hansen, *Mariette*, 92.

243. Ibid., 133.

244. Ibid.

245. Arnell, "Wild Writing," 188.

246. Ibid., 198.

247. Hansen, *Mariette*, 135.

248. Ibid., 137.

249. Ibid., 174.

Mariette rejects allegorical reading, but does carry Marian traits. She dreams of being pregnant, and her "breasts ache with milk."[250] She holds "the infant Christ to them and he smiles as he feeds on her."[251] These are maternal, not sexual images; they are nearly Eucharistic. Yet there are sexual elements of the novel, even if many commentators use the comparatively euphemistic "sensual." Mariette's love for Christ "is not ethereal or idolized but, quite explicitly, sexual" and it continues "until it consumes her in the physical onset of stigmata."[252] The sexuality of the novel firms it as a postconciliar work, the "apposite example . . . [compared to] the theological proclivities of the popular *Baltimore Catechism*, which began by defining God as 'perfect Spirit,' without body."[253] Waldmeir also finds a particularly postconciliar role of the body in supporting that the "distinguishing feature of Catholic sacramentality has been the notion that sacraments not only represent God's presence, they also effect that presence."[254] Hansen's novel dramatizes what happens when a community devoted to Christ meets him in the flesh.

To be fair, that arrival is foreign, visceral, and sexual. So why do some insightful critics like Carla Arnell describe Mariette's experience as sensuous rather than sexual? Arnell's analysis moves in an interesting direction, finding the sexuality of the book elsewhere: "in [a] depiction of Céline's suffering body, images of sickness, sexuality, and sensuousness overlap in a surprising way, with the words 'shameless' and 'slatternly' conjuring up the bed of a whore as much as a sick nun."[255] A smart analysis, but one that redefines sexuality in the novel as clearly something problematic and violent, as in the fact that the "illness functions as a force of nature that rapes Céline, leaving her exposed and vulnerable."[256]

Sexuality in *Mariette in Ecstasy*, and the novel as a whole, is best served existing within ambiguity, and as Wendorf suggests, thus creates a unique pastoral document: "Revealing the incompatibility of reductive medicine and faith and the elusiveness of certainty for science and theology alike . . . [the novel offers] a kind of reconciliation of conflicting voices—that human life and all of creation is grounded in mystery that is

---

250. Ibid., 100.

251. Ibid., 100–101.

252. Waldmeir, *Cathedrals*, 27–28.

253. Ibid., 28.

254. Ibid., 29.

255. Arnell, "Wild Writing," 193.

256. Ibid.

not so much science's enemy as freedom's charitable friend."[257] "Freedom" is the same word Hansen uses to explain the ultimate appeal of Catholicism: "seeing God in all things, and in its acceptance of sinfulness and the regular, even hourly, need for conversion."[258] In fact, this freedom, for Hansen, is nearly on par with the love of God; perhaps they are the same. After *Mariette in Ecstasy*, Hansen has never shied from voicing his perceived pastoral responsibilities as a Catholic writer: "I want people to notice God's actions in their lives and in the lives of others and to have sympathy for other people. I want them to see that there is something going on here that matters."[259] That recognition is accomplished by "slowly draw[ing] the reader into a deeper understanding."[260] If Hansen believes that "religion is a lot roomier than people think when they are looking at it from the outside,"[261] it follows that he finds fiction's possibility for moral instruction to exist in "empirical experience of the road not taken."[262]

Hansen's Catholic aesthetic paradoxically interrogates language and narrative in the tradition of Gass, but in the ethical service of Gardner, and requires the recognition of a third, equally important influence: Gerard Manley Hopkins. Hansen found Hopkins's ascetiscm a counter to Gardner's lifestyle, and whereas Gardner spoke of believing in the Walt Disney type of magic in fiction, Hopkins preferred the authentic supernatural possible through Christ. Although Hansen was first attracted to Hopkins's language, that diction opened toward the shared religious sensibilities that Hansen has crafted in his own postconciliar manner.

Hansen even appears to sneak a reference to Hopkins within *Mariette in Ecstasy*. It is difficult to not see shades of "The Windhover" in this excerpt: "A peregrine falcon is suspended on the air, hunting some hidden prey, and suddenly twists into a dive of such speed that Mariette loses track of it until the falcon has flared high up into the sky again."[263] Hopkins's essential "Pied Beauty" reads like inspiration for Hansen's representation of setting. Arnell finds his "natural world [as] one in which beauty exists side by side with ugliness."[264] Though Arnell describes Hansen's

257. Wendorf, "Body," 56.

258. Ron Hansen, 2012.

259. Nelson, "Stewards," 25.

260. Ibid.

261. Ibid., 27.

262. Ron Hansen, 2012.

263. Hansen, *Mariette*, 35.

264. Arnell, "Wild Writing," 189.

approach, she could just as easily be summarizing the canon of Hopkins: "[through] this interplay of worlds—convent, secular household, and wilderness—Hansen seems to suggest that the world is odder and more mysterious than humans know."[265]

Hansen's interest in Hopkins evolved into his 2008 novel, *Exiles*, that concurrently dramatizes Hopkins's life as a Jesuit and the wreck of the *Deutschland*, a steamship headed for New York. Although rich at the sentence level, the novel is more linguistically traditional than *Mariette in Ecstasy*. Still, the work is a progressive historical novel. Hansen notes that the novel is a dramatization of Hopkins's journals and letters. Hopkins is an appropriate subject, since his aesthetic dialectic resides in the paradox of his Jesuit asceticism and poetic dynamism.

Hansen's narrator sounds like a biographer, as Hopkins's daily actions are delivered with elegiac sentiment. Hansen gives the same treatment to the passengers of the *Deutschland*, focusing on the five nuns who would become the emotional core of Hopkins's famed sequential poem on the loss. Hansen evades sentimentality in *Exiles* because the reader knows both Hopkins and the nuns will reach tragic ends. That the ending is revealed early allows Hansen to channel Hopkins without fear: "There were fields of shorn barley or wheat, now blond and fallowed with winter, Jersey cattle sedately chewing silage in their pens, their hides ruffed like hackles in the cold, sodden, pillowy gray quilts of cloud hanging so close they seemed just out of reach of her hand."[266] Although the narrator is not Hopkins, he shares an ardent desire for natural cataloging, exactly the same consumption of surroundings that Hopkins used to ground his more conceptual thoughts.

Hopkins's sexuality, which has become of concern for queer theorists in recent decades, is engaged tangentially in the work. At St. Beuno's, where Hopkins studied theology, the Rector's mantra is "*nunquam duo, semper tres:* never two, always three," so that the men would be discouraged from fostering "particular friendships."[267] Hopkins must follow the rule while going on a trip with a fellow student, "the big, bluff, confident manly sport that Hopkins found attractive."[268] When the omniscient narrator reflects on Hopkins's personal journals and writings, there "was no mention of

265. Ibid., 190.
266. Hansen, *Exiles*, 37.
267. Ibid., 11.
268. Ibid.

a girlfriend," and a similar bachelor life was cultivated at Oxford, which Hopkins "would imitate."[269]

Hopkins's sexuality, however hidden, contributes to his identity as an "exile." So does his Catholicism: he converted in 1866, to the ire of his Anglican peers. Even his mother "would pass along to him whatever unsavory gossip she heard about the church . . . and the only time she or her husband ever visited him as a Jesuit was when he lay dying in Dublin in 1889."[270] He is not the only one, as Sister Aurea, one of the casualties of the *Deutschland* wreck, says "Christ was an exile, too."[271]

The end to *Exiles* has been foreshadowed from the first pages, but Hansen pauses: "Imagine it otherwise."[272] What if Hopkins survived his "winter world," and could write and teach beyond his previous near-punishment of grading thousands of elementary Latin papers? What if Mariette was able to remain in the convent, and serve as a model of piety to the others? *Mariette in Ecstasy* and *Exiles* exist to further those questions, and fit Ross Labrie's observation of authentic Catholic works that "often end with a lingering, unresolved complexity—even if the moral foundations of the universe have been made adequately clear to the reader."[273] Hansen's writing offers the possibility that disruption might be the best pastoral, and fictional, model. Hansen's blurring of saints and sinners occurs outside ecclesiastical walls, but with equal complexity, in the writing of Andre Dubus.

269. Ibid., 87.
270. Ibid., 92.
271. Ibid., 72.
272. Ibid., 195.
273. Labrie, *The Catholic*, 18–19.

Chapter Three

A Literary Sacrament

The Fiction and Essays of Andre Dubus

Stephen Minot, reviewing Andre Dubus's *Separate Flights* for *Ploughshares* in 1976, wondered if there was room in that decade for a writer with no interest in trickery or stylistic innovation. Minot's question was borne out of John Barth's seminal essay, "The Literature of Exhaustion," but his broader concern would be echoed most convincingly by the fiction debates between John Gardner and William Gass that extended into the next decade. Ron Hansen was the literary progeny of that unlikely duo, and Dubus is a distant relative. Minot's review arrives at an appreciation for Dubus's style, refining his earlier simplification to a recognition that Dubus preferred complexity of emotion and conflict over syntactic play. Hansen's short fiction, collected in *Nebraska* and *She Loves Me Not*, includes both traditional and experimental narratives. Dubus's interest in story, as well as Catholicism, focused on an interrogation of dogma rather than form.

Dubus tried to receive Communion daily, even after a selfless act left him paralyzed from the waist down in 1986. That physical trauma metaphorically reveals, and perhaps intensified, his passion for the body of Christ. Hansen's essential symbol is the suffering Christ; Dubus's central symbol is the rejuvenating power of the Eucharist. Dubus needed "God manifested as Christ, who ate and drank and shat and suffered, and laughed. So I can dance with Him as the leaf dances in the breeze under the sun."[1] In his essays, fiction, and interviews, Dubus yoked the sacred and

---

1. Dubus, *Meditations*, 87.

the profane, finding that delineations between the two were manmade. In "Sorrowful Mysteries," the main character's girlfriend is introduced within such a litany: "She likes dancing, rhythm and blues, jazz, gin, beer, Pall Malls, peppery food, and passionate kissing, with no fondling. She receives Communion every morning, wears a gold Sacred Heart medal on a gold chain around her neck."[2] Dubus finds no need to explain the proximity of sexuality and faith; his characters are very much of the world. Dubus was concerned with the person of Christ far more than a conceptual God, and the Eucharist enabled him, and often his characters, to befriend Christ, to receive grace within a violent present.

In 1977, nearly a decade before his injury, Dubus already viewed the body as a temporary, broken vessel. Sacraments "soothe our passage" through life, particularly his morning Eucharist, "the taste of forgiveness and of love that affirmed, perhaps celebrated, my being alive, my being mortal."[3] Without the "touch" of the Eucharist, "God is a monologue, an idea, a philosophy; he must touch and be touched, the tongue on flesh."[4] For Dubus, Communion was communal: he needed to experience Christ without "thinking" or "talking," rather a silent, intimate moment, paradoxically shared with others.[5]

Dubus was aware of these paradoxes of his faith. Dubus's son, Andre, writes in his memoir *Townie* about how his estranged father would bring the children to Mass, a matinee show, and dinner each Sunday. Dubus was "one of the only men in church not wearing a jacket or tie" and he "refused" to tithe, asking "You think Jesus ever wore a fucking tie? Did Jesus spend money on *buildings*?"[6] Several commentators have noted Dubus's disdain for ecclesiastical authority, a skepticism dramatized in his fiction. In "All the Time in the World," LuAnn Arceneaux "overlooked what was bureaucratic or picayune about the Church" because of the saving power of the Eucharist.[7] Luke Ripley, the frank narrator of "A Father's Story," explains why he does not tithe: "I don't feel right about giving money for buildings, places. This starts with the Pope, and I cannot respect one of them till he sells his house and everything in it, and that church too, and

2. Dubus, *Selected*, 393.

3. Dubus, *Broken*, 77.

4. Ibid.

5. Ibid., 78.

6. Dubus III, *Townie*, 56.

7. Dubus, *Dancing*, 90.

uses the money to feed the poor."[8] Luke prefers the parish of his friend, Father Paul. That church "is made of wood, and has a simple altar and crucifix, and no padding on the kneelers," a construction more in line with his vision of Christ, who made "no mention . . . of maintaining buildings, much less erecting them of stone or brick, and decorating them with pieces of metal and mineral."[9] Yet neither Luke, nor Dubus, means to oversimplify. Rather than tithing, Luke donates to Franciscans running a shelter in New York City, though he realizes that giving money is easy: "Being a real Catholic is too hard; if I were one, I would do with my house and barn what I want the Pope to do with his."[10] This true Catholicism is "too hard" for even some of his fictional priests, like Father Joe in "Adultery," who leaves the priesthood because of his desire for women. While a priest, Joe was already parsing theology with desire, and one of his qualifications helps explain the idiosyncratic tendencies of other Dubus characters: "it was not God he loved, it was Christ: God in the flesh that each morning he touched and ate, making his willful and faithful connection with what he could neither touch nor see."[11]

Yet Dubus's most poetic paradox might be that although he is a writer who has garnered secular critical praise for his willingness to remain within the real, to refuse to blink when relationships descend into violence, adultery, and hopelessness, he held a mystical conception of Christ. Dubus found that mystics "transcend all that drowns me," and are able to "remain in harmony with the earth and their fellow human beings, and, yet, are above it all as they enjoy union with God."[12] Dubus's literary mysticism is more grounded in the prosaic than Hansen's, yet his characters' Catholicism sometimes creates moments of heightened lyricism. In "Sorrowful Mysteries," Gerry Fontenot lies in bed, praying the rosary while thinking of Sonny Broussard, a black man sentenced to death by the electric chair for raping a white woman. Sonny has become a point of prayer for Gerry, and Dubus cleverly replaces the prayerful repetition of the name of Christ with the vulgarities associated with Sonny. The community is angry and wants revenge, but "every night Gerry prays for [Sonny's] soul."[13] Though it "is a Thursday, a day for the Joyful Mysteries," Gerry looks toward the

8. Dubus, *Selected*, 456.

9. Ibid.

10. Ibid., 457.

11. Ibid., 443.

12. Kennedy, *Andre*, 128.

13. Ibid.

corner streetlight and considers the Sorrowful Mysteries.[14] Sonny becomes a type of Christ, "on his knees in the Garden of Olives," his "face is lifted to the sky": "Tied to a pillar and shirtless, he is silent under the whip; thorns pierce his head, and the fathers of Gerry's friends strike his face, their wives watch as he climbs the long hill, cross on his shoulder, then he is lying on it, the men with hammers are carpenters in khakis, squatting above him, sweat running down their faces to drip on cigarettes between their lips, heads cocked away from smoke; they swing the hammers in unison, and drive nails through wrists and crossed feet."[15] The moment and setting of Gerry's prayer allows him to amalgamate the Passion narrative with an empathetic, imagined event. Dubus stresses bodily and emotional pain, as well as the rejection of a man's community. The imagined scene transitions from Calvary to Sonny's final moments before execution, though the crowd has a different role in the event. In the analogical Christ scene, the crowd is active in the violent punishment; in the prison they are talking and "smoking and drinking and knitting . . . clapping a hand on a neighbor's shoulder, a thigh" while an "electric chair waits" for Sonny.[16] They jeer rather than strike, while the prison guards, stand-ins for the Romans, strap Sonny into the chair. Gerry "shuts his eyes, and tries to feel the chair, the straps" as he attempts to feel "so hated that the people who surround him wait for the very throes and stench of his death."[17] This is no distant prayer: Gerry becomes Sonny, "he is in the electric chair."[18]

This ability to "become" Sonny, who in turn is an imperfect symbol of the suffering Christ, speaks to how wide Dubus defines the Eucharistic act. Paul J. Contino's fine analysis of Dubus's "Eucharistic imagination" explains how, in Dubus's personal essays and for many of his characters, receipt of the Host makes them feel whole: "The kenotic gift *of* the Eucharist undergirds the human offering of kenotic attentiveness *to* the Eucharist, and thus allows a human participation in the sacrificial love which the Eucharist represents."[19] The Eucharist also creates unity with other parishioners and Catholics, as well as a reminder that sacraments are constant and universal. In "Out of the Snow," LuAnn Arceneaux had learned that there were seven sacraments in the Catholic Church, "all but

14. Ibid., 391.
15. Ibid.
16. Ibid.
17. Ibid.
18. Ibid.
19. Contino, "Andre," 54.

one administered by a priest," and yet "being a mother had taught her that sacraments were her work, and their number was infinite," a phrase Dubus repeats in his non-fiction.[20] The sacrament of marriage is thus used as the transition from official sacraments to the unofficial sacraments of parenting and daily life, which seem to both outnumber and outweigh the official within Dubus's work.

Dubus's personal theology of the sacramental is best explicated in "Sacraments," an essay that begins with a sentence so syntactically jumbled that it sounds like the writer's thoughts permeate the page without filter: "A sacrament is physical, and within it is God's love; as a sandwich is physical, and nutritious and pleasurable, and within it is love, if someone makes it for you and gives it to you with love; even harried or tired or impatient love, but with love's direction and concern, love's again and again wavering and distorted focus on goodness; then God's love too is in the sandwich."[21] Clearly Dubus considers love the essential sacramental ingredient, and he defines the authentic human action of love as arising from the same wellspring as God's love. The coexistence of the divine and the mundane, the sandwich, at first sounds tongue-in-cheek, but Dubus was aware of the bread metaphor, and later in the essay makes it clear that the transforming love of making the sandwich is analogous to the preparation of Host for Mass. Dubus admits that preparing sandwiches in a wheelchair "is not physically difficult" within his small kitchen, but "it can be a spiritual trial."[22]

Dubus establishes his interpretation of Catholic theology at the beginning of his individual works, and "Sacraments" is no exception. He acknowledges a set amount of sacraments in the capitalized Catholic Church, but he personally revises the definition: "no, I say, for the church is catholic, the world is catholic, and there are seven times seventy sacraments, to infinity."[23] He follows with an ethereal description of the weather while sitting at his Massachusetts desk, implicitly suggesting that God is found in that natural world, and resists codification. While it "is good to be baptized, to confess and to be reconciled, to receive Communion, to be confirmed, to be ordained a priest, to marry, or to be anointed with the sacrament of healing," Dubus concludes "it is limiting to believe that

20. Dubus, *Dancing*, 181.
21. Dubus, *Meditations*, 85.
22. Ibid., 89.
23. Ibid., 86.

sacraments occur only in churches."[24] His postconciliar sentiment does not reject the machinations of the Church in sustaining and sharing the Holy Spirit, but it does decenter that institution, finding the love of God as capable in the hands of laity as in the religious.

Dubus's meditations complicate the traditional definition of a Catholic writer. His Catholicism can be intensely personal, wholly independent of the traditional Christian community; he claims that, even when unable to attend daily Mass, he is "still receiving Communion, because I desire it; and because God is in me, as He is in the light, the earth, the leaf."[25] Yet it would be incorrect to label Dubus as merely a "spiritual writer." The actual Eucharist, taken at Mass, gives him "joy and strength," while the "Communion of desire" is an intellectual, rather than sensual, experience.[26] This desire to live a sacramental life of the "senses" is centered with the Eucharist, but extends to the sandwiches he makes for his daughters. An earlier essay, "On Charon's Wharf," engages both concepts. He believes that the Eucharist, which he describes as "the touch," redefines death and earthly life, and that he "can [also] do this in an ordinary kitchen with an ordinary woman and five eggs."[27] He prepares and cooks the eggs while the woman sets the table. They then eat, and, sitting together, "have become extraordinary: we are not simply eating; we are pausing in the march to perform an act together; we are in love; and the meal offered and received is a sacrament which says: I know you will die; I am sharing food with you; it is all I can do, and it is everything."[28] This domestic sacrament is less about undermining ecclesiastical power and more about identifying love as the ultimate sacramental element. In doing so, Dubus allows further flexibility of definition, finding sex and sexuality as possibly sacramental "if our souls are as naked as our bodies, if our souls are in harmony with our bodies, and through our bodies are embracing each other in love and fear and trembling."[29]

For Dubus, an equally profound sacramental moment was the last day of his father's life, when "he was thirsty and he asked me to crush some ice and feed it to him."[30] Fatherhood is one of Dubus's essential tropes,

---

24. Ibid.
25. Ibid.
26. Ibid., 87.
27. Dubus, *Broken*, 79.
28. Ibid.
29. Dubus, *Meditations*, 91.
30. Ibid., 95.

traversing the Catholic and secular spheres of his fiction and non-fiction. "Digging" establishes Dubus's youthful perceptions of his father and establishes norms of masculinity that resound in his other works, as well as informing *Townie*, the memoir of his son, Andre Dubus III. The thin, sixteen year-old Dubus is a stark contrast to his "ruddy, broad-chested father" who wanted him to work in the summer.[31] Young Dubus is not interested, but his father is work incarnate, employed as a surveyor for the same company since college. He keeps "a twenty-two caliber pistol for cottonmouths" holstered on his belt.[32] He is an archetypal male for his son: quiet at home, where he smokes and reads detective fiction and "books about golf."[33] Dubus listens to his father speak rather than conversing with him, fearing "his voice, suddenly and harshly rising."[34] His father rarely yelled, yet the "fear" of his booming voice "was part of my love for him."[35]

The relationship between Dubus and his father, then, feels comfortably preconciliar: he is shy with the older man, but their silence goes deeper. Their activities of hunting, fishing, and watching professional wrestling and minor-league baseball are moments of shared participation rather than emotional connection. Although Dubus describes these moments with sentiment, he admits being "ashamed" that words, and therefore direct emotions, never deepened their relationship.[36] This introduction is essential to the core of "Digging": Dubus digging trenches for a contractor. His father passes his son to the foreman, saying "Make a man of him."[37] The phrase feels less melodramatic than consistent with the preconciliar masculinity of French Catholic Louisiana. Dubus is surrounded by black workers, and as he does in other essays, recognizes the racial injustices inherent in these grown men making cents more than him an hour.

The sacramentality of "Digging" occurs on multiple levels. In the same way Dubus found the divine in the careful, habitual actions of making sandwiches, so do the hours "under the hot sun . . . raising the pickax and swinging it down, raising it and swinging, again and again till the earth was loose" amount to a reforming of surrounding and self.[38] Yet he

31. Ibid., 19.
32. Ibid., 20.
33. Ibid.
34. Ibid.
35. Ibid.
36. Ibid., 22.
37. Ibid., 24.
38. Ibid., 25.

does not feel like a man, the strength absent in his body, as well as "in my soul."[39] Exhausted, he is unable to continue. The pickax, "this thing of wood and steel that was melting me," becomes his cross.[40] He is only body, "sick, hot, tired, and hurting flesh," and not soul, feeling "a very small piece of despair."[41]

The noon whistle blows, and Dubus joins the black workers in the shade, but becomes sick and sleeps until lunch ends. Dubus is saved from further pain by his father, who returns to the worksite and takes him to buy a hat rather than bringing him home. His father questions why Dubus did not ask for help, but Dubus had long ago learned that "I could not tell a man what I felt, if I believed what I felt was unmanly."[42] He spends the rest of the day working under that pith helmet, before returning home, where "women proudly greeted me when I walked into the house."[43] They are worried about him, but he returns to work the next day, and the succeeding days. Dubus is careful to stress the monotony of that work, as well as the communality with the black men. "Someone" told the workers the trench was finished, and Dubus wonders, "Who dug out that last bit of dirt?"[44]

The question is naïve, but also prescient: Dubus has made the action of work a sacrament, a sequence of moments profoundly important to his young self, and yet no one had "blown a bugle" to celebrate their accomplishment.[45] Dubus ends the essay by thanking his father for not taking him home, for instead "tenderly" helping him stay at the job rather than "nestled in the love " of his mother and sister, only "yearning to be someone I respected . . . a man among men."[46] The ending is complicated: Dubus does not subvert these conceptions of masculinity, but rather offers a more compassionate road toward them, and identifies that route as the sacramental love of his father.

This complicated love for his father makes their final moments together so moving. In fact, Dubus, then a Marine captain, found sacraments aplenty during these strained moments: the love of family and

---

39. Ibid.
40. Ibid.
41. Ibid., 26.
42. Ibid., 27.
43. Ibid., 30.
44. Ibid., 31.
45. Ibid.
46. Ibid., 32.

friends collected during his father's final days, as well as the often ignored sacraments "from those who flew the plane and worked aboard it and maintained it and controlled its comings and goings; and from the major who gave me emergency leave, and the gunnery sergeant who did my work while I was gone."[47] Dubus realized none of these things in the moment, instead thinking he "was a son flying alone."[48]

His father's body is now frail, and in asking for help his father is reversing the roles so carefully dramatized in "Digging." The father requests ice for his dry mouth, and Dubus describes the simple preparation with sacramental love. In "Digging," Dubus realized he would have never become a man if he had stayed in his fan-cooled home, his father "peering" at him, and yet he realizes that his father was always watching, in the metaphysical sense.[49] He now understands that his father was watching "to see if I could go out into the world, and live in it without him."[50] Dubus confides to his sister that the next day he would finally speak the words he has felt but never voiced: that he loves his father.

The essay ends with Dubus learning that his father has died before dawn, leaving Dubus not with sadness, but the recognition that for much of his life he "did not understand love . . . and the sacraments that make it tactile."[51] He ends the essay with a Catholic observation of the divine in the everyday: "I had not lived enough and lost enough to enable me to know the holiness of working with meat and mustard and bread; of moving on wheels or wings or by foot from one place to another; of holding a telephone and speaking into it and listening to a voice; of pounding ice with wood and spooning the shards onto a dry tongue; of lighting a cigarette and placing it between the fingers of a man trying to enjoy tobacco and bourbon and his family as he dies."[52] Dubus's words carry weight because they are prefaced by the writer's recognition of his imperfections. Thomas Kennedy notes that parenthood "is not a static condition in Dubus's fiction," and that malleability extends to his essays.[53] Kennedy and Contino both see Dubus using fatherhood as emotional and spiritual proving ground. In his essays, Dubus is clearly aware of the complexity and importance of

47. Ibid., 98.
48. Ibid., 96.
49. Ibid., 32.
50. Ibid., 98.
51. Ibid., 99.
52. Ibid.
53. Kennedy, *Andre*, 70.

fatherhood, and is unafraid to voice his own personal shortcomings: "In my life, I have been too much a father in an empty house; and since the vocation of fatherhood includes living with the mother, this is the deepest shame of my life, and its abiding regret."[54]

Dubus's son, the novelist Andre Dubus III, offers further insights into these concerns in *Townie*, a searing memoir of street violence, family dysfunction, and the cathartic nature of storytelling. The memoir's first scene reveals that Andre shares his father's worries of youthful masculinity voiced in "Digging." The elder Dubus suggests, during one of the few times a month he sees his children, that they go running together. Andre is unprepared; he only owns "a pair of Dingo boots," and needs to borrow his sister's sneakers.[55] The sneakers are far too small, and though his feet are cramped, Andre does not tell his father. He savors the moment of running with his father on the older man's birthday, but his body strains: "my mouth and throat were thick and tasted like salt, my thighs hurt almost as much as my feet, and even though I was pumping my arms and legs as fast as I could I seemed to be barely moving."[56] Like the elder Dubus in that Louisiana trench, Andre's body and soul are changing under this strain. Only at the end of the run does Andre admit, feet swollen and toes split, that the sneakers belonged to his sister. His father, squatting beside him, comes "tenderly" like his own father, and Andre ends the scene with similar recognition: "I couldn't remember ever feeling so good. About life. About me. About what else might lie ahead if you were just willing to take some pain, some punishment."[57]

Townie documents the same paradoxes apparent in Dubus's fiction: good men, and sometimes good fathers, making bad decisions. When Andre describes his father as "waiting for me at the top [of the hill], running in place, his beard glistening in the dappled light," he is aware that this construction of a father is the result of a son longing for a more tangible, constant emotional connection.[58] Yet *Townie* evolves to an even more complex emotional place: young Andre, with no father at home, begins lifting and training, obsessed with becoming strong. The perils of that mindset become clear when Andre's sister Suzanne is raped in Boston, and Andre, after phoning his absent and now horrified father, feels "dark

54. Dubus, *Meditations*, 93.

55. Dubus III, *Townie*, 3.

56. Ibid., 6–7.

57. Ibid., 8.

58. Ibid., 7.

joy spreading through my chest at having just done that to him, the one who should've been here all along, the one who should never have left us in the first place."[59]

Andre's raging anger reaches a punching bag, never the faces of the rapists, and that is the sum realization of *Townie*: the masculine desire for revenge is often based more in pride than justice. Years later, Andre sees his wife's open New Testament, and looks toward its Matthean call to "*Love one another*" as a "possible reprieve" for his life steeped in violence.[60] The process is slow, but is concurrent with Andre's renewed perception of fatherhood. *Townie* is far too complex to be simply an indictment of an imperfect father. The final quarter of the memoir shows how after his accident, Dubus inverted the importance of writing and spending time with his children, recognizing that "now was the time to do things together."[61]

Dubus's ultimate contribution to Catholic literature is a similar willingness to be emotionally honest, to allow faith and theology to exist within his fiction without becoming the dogmatic structure. His son Andre noticed this, writing that whenever he read his father's work he grasped "a vision that was both bleak and redemptive . . . a deeply compelling blend of the profane and the sacred, like a drunk confessing his sins to a good priest only to go out and commit them once more but this time not as unconsciously, not as cruelly, and not as if that would forever be his fate."[62] His perceptions become more accurate the deeper one revisits his father's canon: Dubus was a Catholic writer who saw faith as a continuous action, likely realizing that fair-weather believers thought allegiance to God on a Sunday would lead to bliss for the rest of the week.

Here Dubus does not exactly depart from Hansen, but operates within a different schema. Hansen is a postconciliar writer whose main Catholic subject matter has been historical; his mode has been largely postmodern at the language level. Hansen's paradox is that he writes about religious men and women, priests and nuns, living within the sometimes sinful, often fragmented halls of their faith. He interrogates the visceral intersection of faith and reality; Mariette, in body, offers empirical evidence of Christ to a community that is confounded by real texture. Hansen's decentering narrative, ranging from layers of detail and metaphor to pictographic representations of place contributes to the revision. Dubus

59. Ibid., 122.
60. Ibid., 346.
61. Ibid., 362.
62. Ibid., 361.

writes about married men and women, often adulterous, who sometimes identify as deeply Catholic, and sometimes exist as culturally Catholic. Although both writers are concerned with the Catholic body, Hansen is concerned with the physical intersection of the person of Christ with the divinity of Christ. Christ is essential to Dubus, but particularly his presence in the Eucharist. The result is that Dubus, the more "realistic" writer, becomes more mystical through his analogical modes.

In "Out Like a Lamb," Dubus writes about living cheaply on a seventy-acre property in New Hampshire. As part of the rental agreement, Dubus must ensure the farmer's sheep do not escape the fence. Dubus thinks back to a youthful, romanticized idea of Christ "holding a lamb in his arms," meant to symbolize that humans "were sweet and lovable sheep."[63] After living on the farm for several weeks, Dubus realizes the analogy more likely meant that humans "were stupid helpless brutes, and without constant watching we would foolishly destroy ourselves."[64] Dubus's tongue only sounds half in his cheek. The bulk of his writing reveals a belief, at least on the page, that men are decidedly imperfect, and that only receipt and contemplation of the Eucharist can save them. Robert P. Lewis finds, again, the body as the nexus of these imperfections. The "curse" and "blessing" of bodiliness creates, in Dubus's fiction, "two contrasting modes of ritual response to this elemental sorrow."[65] Lewis delineates between these modes in the following manner: "The Faustian response is spiritualistic, individualistic, onanistic, unforgivingly perfectionist, mute, and, all too often 'male': the Eucharistic is fleshly, communal, festive, tolerant of human frailty, conversational, and, typically, 'female.'"[66]

Although Dubus dramatizes these dualities within a postconciliar world, his beliefs were born in a preconciliar one. In 1948, a young Dubus goes to a minor league baseball game, where an outfielder shows his teammates "a condom from his wallet."[67] As with some of his more youthful narrators, Dubus reacts with learned disgust at this symbol of sexuality, the "awful solemnity of mortal sin."[68] The observation occurs in passing, but as will be seen with the poetry of Paul Mariani, Dubus threads the Catholic experience in a layered, referential manner. That same outfielder

63. Dubus, *Broken*, 4.
64. Ibid.
65. Lewis, "Bodliness," 36.
66. Ibid., 37.
67. Dubus, *Broken*, 16.
68. Ibid.

"was dating a young Catholic woman, who later would go to Lourdes for an incurable illness."[69] Dubus thankfully resists the urge to give more importance to the anecdote, instead ending the memory in ambiguity: "that afternoon I was only confused and frightened, a boy who had opened the wrong door, the wrong drawer."[70]

Dubus uses Catholicism to qualify his regional identity as a southern writer. Only when Dubus joined the Marines in 1958 did he meet "real southerners, drawling Protestants."[71] His preconciliar Catholic identity was formed at a Christian Brothers school from third grade through the end of high school. Education came through stories "to show and dramatize morality," from the mouths of brothers who were French and Mexican, not southerners.[72] The diversity and ethical depth of this education is reflected in Dubus's personal literary theology. Dubus shows his lay Catholic characters attending Mass, but these characters often live morally outside of that dogmatic world. Although he is specifically discussing Dubus's theme of parenthood, Thomas Kennedy's observation is equally applicable here: the spiritual evolution of Dubus's characters "might be seen as a growth to this 'weakness' [of love], to the openness of heart that, in weighing love against principle, chooses the former, although without releasing the latter."[73] Kennedy finds this to be the "moral paradox of the contemporary Catholic portrayed by Dubus, the encompassment into a single tension of the heart of the law of the Old Testament and the love of the New."[74]

Although these transformations often occur in bedrooms and kitchens, at work or at baseball fields, they find their origin in the celebration of Mass, and Dubus is one of the most thorough postconciliar writers of that experience. Yet some typically supportive commentators like Robert P. Lewis find the "peremptory affirmations" of Dubus's devotional essays "slip[ping] too readily into the idiom of Sunday Supplement inspiration."[75] That comment comes more from the tonal expectations of the critic rather than the authentic experiences of the writer, and speaks to the continuous need for Catholic literary critics to apologize for the more devotional

69. Ibid.

70. Ibid.

71. Ibid., 91.

72. Ibid., 90.

73. Kennedy, *Andre*, 77.

74. Ibid.

75. Lewis, "Anamnesis," 148.

aspects of Catholic literature. Lewis's comment is admittedly focused on short pieces such as "Girls," originally published in *Portland Magazine*, the journal of a Catholic university. Dubus waxes poetic about an altar girl who becomes fodder for Marian meditation and appreciation. Yet Dubus was clearly aware both of his form and audience. When Lewis claims that Dubus "approaches theological notions like a Hemingway hero, on the pulse of sensation and with an implicit disdain for either mediating structures of thought or for conceptual speculation," the criticism sounds more like a preference for form than an observation of content.[76] To reverse Lewis's argument using his own examples from Dubus's fiction, Dubus made little pretense toward sustained theological consideration because he was more interested in representing the immediate mystery of Catholic ritual in domestic, daily life.

Dubus begins "Bodily Mysteries" by noting how the "struggle" of each day "confined to a wheelchair"[77] is made easier by "physical contact with God" through the Eucharist.[78] As he watches the priest consecrate the Eucharist, Dubus feels that he "was no longer a broken body, alone in my chair. I was me, all of me, in wholeness of spirit."[79] This sense of wholeness is consistent with a sense of oneness with the parish community, with time, with God. Dubus seems genuinely in awe that "flawed and foolish me" can have this experience.[80]

Dubus documents daily Mass, where he sees "the same people, as in a neighborhood bar."[81] Once, when a small funeral is being held, Dubus wonders if he should leave, but the priest says he should stay and receive, since they are a "community."[82] He no longer worries about attending those types of services, thinking that it is "good for us strangers to be here as witnesses to death and life"; in fact, they are no longer strangers in that church, they are "peaceable."[83] Although never one for ornamentation of design, Dubus found the physical layout of his church as essential to this uniting "with the mortality of our bodies, with the immortality of our

---

76. Ibid., 252.
77. Dubus, *Meditations*, 100.
78. Ibid., 101.
79. Ibid.
80. Ibid., 102.
81. Ibid., 131.
82. Ibid., 132.
83. Ibid., 133.

souls."[84] He considers the role of the priest, concluding that "liking him is not important"; if most Catholics go to Mass "to take part in ritual, and to eat the body of Christ," the concern must be with the priest as a representation of Christ, not as a human personality.[85]

When Mass ends, the parishioners "tell each other good-bye" but do not say the words, instead they "wave" and "nod."[86] "Earthly time is upon us again; we enter it, and go to our cars," another sense that Dubus found power in the solemnity of place and service.[87] Dubus's post-Mass ritual was idiosyncratic, and speaks to his recognition that sacrament occurs beyond church walls, and often in strange ways. Self-aware of his movements in the parking lot while in his wheelchair, Dubus waits for people to leave before wheeling around the lot, singing, quipping that although the priest might hear, he "must be merciful about things more serious than someone singing off-key."[88] Dubus leaves the lot for the street, where he passes people entering the church for a support group meeting, and then sees a seemingly unwell man rush toward the church, raise his middle finger, and scream the accompanying vulgarity. Dubus, rather than feeling repulsed by the action, is fascinated. He considers the moment: "the roofs of the church and rectory, and the alcoholics talking and smoking, and me singing and sweating in the wheelchair, and the man in the suit and tie, with his finger up as far as he could reach."[89] His conclusion is curiously apt: "On that morning under a blue November sky, it was beautiful to see and hear such belief: Fuck *God*."[90] Yet, in the theological world of Dubus's essays, the man's heresy must be contextualized in the world of the Eucharist, which "fills the church" and moves beyond its walls, even filling that man.[91]

Although they might seem overdrawn, Lewis's previous criticisms of Dubus's tendency toward Catholic devotional writing in his essays were a step in a larger arc and argument: that the essayistic language of Dubus "forecloses on the tensions between the sacred and the secular which

---

84. Ibid.
85. Ibid., 135.
86. Ibid., 133.
87. Ibid., 134.
88. Ibid., 138.
89. Ibid., 141.
90. Ibid.
91. Ibid., 145.

his characters struggle to negotiate despite their religious observance."[92] Representations of Mass and worship are certainly more complex and diverse in Dubus's fiction. In "Voices from the Moon," young and religious Richie Stowe struggles to understand a newfound, convoluted addition to his family dynamic—his father's decision to marry his brother's ex-wife—while simultaneously discovering his own sexuality. Richie's faith is filled with awe and reverence, and its overly sentimental moments are forgivable because of the stress of his family situation, as he realizes "it will be very hard to be a Catholic in our house."[93]

The conclusion is connected to Richie's imagistic and associative brand of Catholicism, consistent with other younger religious characters in Dubus's fiction. Upon seeing the "suffering head of Christ" in a church crucifix, Richie thinks of a different type of imagined pain: "his father and Brenda naked in her bed . . . her moans, her cries, seeming more in pain than pleasure."[94] Those images "collided with his prayers."[95] With a similar heightened tone, the story's third-person, subjective narrator shows Richie, "nearly breathless," and "Father Oberti's face was upturned and transformed" while consecrating the Eucharist.[96] In an apparent contradiction, Richie likens the priest's expression to that of "men or women [in movies] gazing at a lover" before concluding that they "were not at all the same."[97]

The contradiction is grounded in the word "longing," which the narrator better refines as Richie's "longing to consume Christ, to be consumed through Him into the priesthood, to stand some morning purified and adoring in white vestments, and to watch his hands holding bread, then God."[98] Richie's swell of faith, as described by the narrator, goes from the "descent of the chalice" to a later, more prosaic representation of the father "in white shirt and black pants."[99] The modulation is consistent with Dubus's theology: solemnity during Mass, reality afterward.

The ensuing conversation appears in direct dialogue. Richie worries that his family is living in sin, but the "calm and gentle" priest stresses love

92. Lewis, "Anamnesis," 252.
93. Dubus, *Selected*, 289.
94. Ibid., 289.
95. Ibid.
96. Ibid., 291.
97. Ibid.
98. Ibid., 292.
99. Ibid.

over judgment, acknowledging that while Richie "will have some embarrassment" and "pain," he is a "strong boy," and ready for the tests of faith.[100] The plea is heartfelt, devoid of dogma and instruction, and ends with advice: "Go play baseball, and live your life."[101] Dubus immediately juxtaposes the grandeur of this Mass scene with another, connected longing. Richie sees Melissa Donnelly "in the shadows under the arch of maples."[102] Their conversation includes talk of God, and Richie's explanations of why he goes to daily Mass. The narrator describes their flirtations with the same tone as Richie's awe for the mystery of Mass. She calls Richie "Father Stowe"[103] before kissing him; later in the novella he remembers "her scents and the taste of her mouth," and, while hoping she comes to see him play softball, he "tried to taste her" again, implicitly reflecting the shared orality between kissing and receipt of the Eucharist.[104]

Richie's preconciliar faith leads him to make polar decisions, and he worries that "to receive Christ he could not love Melissa."[105] When the novella ends, he seems to choose Melissa over the priesthood, as his sentimental Catholic perception has evolved from the priest's consecration to a more holistic, cosmological sense of love: "He saw in the stars the eyes of God too, and was grateful for them, as he was for the night and the girl he loved."[106]

The domestic issues in "The Pretty Girl" are markedly more intense and violent. Polly is raped by her ex, Ray, whose coarse masculinity is immediately established in the short novella's opening line: "I don't know how I feel till I hold that steel."[107] The surge of strength caused by weightlifting becomes parallel with Roy's sexualization and violence. Polly realizes that men "need mischief and will even pretend a twelve-ounce can of beer is wicked if that will make them feel collusive while drinking it."[108] Dubus manages to show Polly's comparative good nature without allowing her to descend into type. She attends Mass weekly "but did not receive

100. Ibid.
101. Ibid., 294.
102. Ibid., 294–295.
103. Ibid., 298.
104. Ibid., 313.
105. Ibid., 338.
106. Ibid., 358.
107. Ibid., 65.
108. Ibid., 83.

communion because she had not been in the state of grace for a long time."[109] Polly slept with another man during the final months of her marriage, and the worry over that sin also causes her to not seek confession. For Polly, there is a distinct difference between recognizing something is wrong as "defined" by the Church, and her lack of regret; the result is that simply attending Mass becomes the "one religious act she could perform" without doctrinal guilt.[110]

Dubus, through Polly, reveals how Mass attendance is never simple. Polly "liked entering the church where the large doors closed behind her."[111] She might feel out of place, wishing that "being a Catholic were as easy for her" as it was for her sister, Margaret, but the subjective narration is clearly one of awe rather than fear.[112] The ceiling, windows, walls, altar, cross, pew, kneeler, and other physical attributes of the church are described in detail, before Dubus reiterates Polly's simultaneous sense of identification and detachment through his usage of plural pronouns: "she rose and sang with the others, listened to her voice among theirs, read the Confiteor aloud with them, felt forgiven."[113]

Polly's state is nearly hypnotic, as "her mind was suspended" in Mass, though she "did not pray with concentration," but rather a nearly ecstatic state.[114] The narration becomes less subjective and absolutely attuned to her psyche as she watches the parishioners receive the Eucharist of which she is unable to share. The description of these people as "they chewed or dissolved the host in their mouths" is focused on appearance, on body.[115] These bodies, though, have transformed as Polly "tenderly watched": "no face was pretty or plain, handsome or homely."[116] Polly feels "merciful" toward the strangers, her family, and herself; as "she moved with them in the day" at the conclusion of Mass, it is clear that Polly has experienced some personal sacrament, some metaphysical extension of the Eucharistic moment.[117]

109. Ibid., 87.
110. Ibid., 88.
111. Ibid.
112. Ibid., 86.
113. Ibid., 88.
114. Ibid.
115. Ibid., 89.
116. Ibid.
117. Ibid.

The conscience of LuAnn Arceneaux, the narrator of "All the Time in the World," was "set free by the mores of her contemporaries and the efficacy of the pill," so she does not share Polly's reservations about receiving the Eucharist.[118] Like Polly, LuAnn felt "at home . . . among strangers" at Mass, and it was only in that place that "she was all of herself, and only herself, forgiven and loved."[119] Dubus contextualizes LuAnn as living at a "time in America when courting had given way to passion."[120] His word choice here is telling: the sexual act led to revelations of selves, and these revelations left lovers "frightened or appalled," open and naked to a severe world.[121] After several lovers, LuAnn realizes that this passion is within her, not external; she loves with body and not soul, and it is nearly heartbreaking to hear her subjectively narrated laments: "with each man . . . the drumroll of pregnancy would terrify him; that even the gentlest . . . would gratefully drive her to an abortion clinic and tenderly hold her hand while she opened her legs."[122]

Dubus allows the connotations of passion to coalesce in a later section of the story. LuAnn realizes that "the hot purity of her passion kept her in the Church."[123] The statement initially sounds odd, but, as with many of Dubus's characters and contemporary Catholics, an unpacking of their personal theologies creates fascinating results, and is consistent with Lucy Ferriss's observation that "no woman [in Dubus's fiction] ever attempts to construct a dialogue with the divine or to carry on a spiritual life outside the symbolic dimensions of sexual or maternal love."[124] LuAnn sees her sexual passion as being absolutely "with her flesh," and because of that, she felt the actions "did not need absolving by a priest."[125] LuAnn's musings might sound like convenient personal theology, but she is clearly a character attracted to, and grounded in, the metaphysics of Catholic ritual. For "perhaps six minutes" after receiving the Eucharist, she feels "in harmony with the entire and timeless universe."[126] LuAnn's predilection toward the more supernatural elements of faith is reflected in "The Tim-

118. Dubus, *Dancing*, 85.
119. Ibid., 84.
120. Ibid.
121. Ibid.
122. Ibid., 88.
123. Ibid., 90.
124. Ferriss, "Never," 41.
125. Dubus, *Dancing*, 90.
126. Ibid., 91.

ing of Sin," when she responds to a question about her belief in the devil with an anecdote: "I don't know. I believe in possessions, and exorcisms. I don't know if there's a devil . . . when I was at BU, somebody in our group started this: if you said the Lord's Prayer backward, the devil would appear. There were probably only two of us who even believed in God. Me, and one of the guys. We laughed, we snorted coke, we drank tequila, but no one would say that prayer backward. I wouldn't right now. I don't know if there's a devil, and I'll stay with that."[127] Polly and LuAnn are not the only female characters concerned with doctrinal procedure. In "Bless Me, Father," Jackie, though having once "indulged in heavy petting,"[128] remained in "the state of grace," still receiving Communion "to the sound of guitars" at collegiate Folk Mass.[129] Jackie's language is repeated by Juanita Creehan, the main character of "Waiting," who whispered "petting" "through lattice and veil" because it was the language used by priests, both during confession and "Saturday morning catechism classes."[130] Nuns use the same language, but Juanita makes a distinction: some "priests looked as if they had petted" but not the nuns, so the "word seemed strange on their tongues."[131]

Jackie's perceived sins pale in comparison to her father's adultery. Jackie is unsure of her father's Catholicism: he attends Mass, but "stayed in the pew" while she received at Easter.[132] When Jackie confronts him about the affair, he reaffirms his faith, but offers a convoluted explanation of the affair and the aftermath. While it was a "mistake" to sleep with the other woman, he "felt just as sinful about leaving her."[133] The father says directly what other characters merely show in Dubus's fiction: that adultery is a "sweet lie, sometimes a happy lie, but a lie."[134] That honesty is followed by more truth consistent with Dubus's perception of men: "I don't know one man who's faithful. Not in here anyway," her father says, while pointing to his forehead.[135] The story ends in similar ambiguity. Although the father has ended the affair, his tone regarding the action leaves Jackie feeling empty.

127. Ibid., 155–6.
128. Dubus, *Times*, 62.
129. Ibid., 61.
130. Dubus, *Selected*, 44.
131. Ibid.
132. Dubus, *Times*, 64.
133. Ibid., 66.
134. Ibid.
135. Ibid., 67.

The father's secular confession to Jackie is an example of how liberally Dubus's characters treat this essential sacrament. In "The Timing of Sin," LuAnn Arceneaux mentions needing to go to Saturday confession as a habitual practice, ensuring that she is "always being forgiven."[136] The other woman, Marsha, is assured that the confession is "a very simple language," but LuAnn speaks in general terms: "I'll say I placed myself in the occasion of sin."[137] Marsha's naïve questions include querying LuAnn's required penance, which she assures does not result in being "on my knees for hours"; instead, she will be told "to spend a few minutes with God."[138] LuAnn adds that "I'll be talking to you, too," an attempt at levity that merely shows her low trust in the sanctity of the sacrament.[139]

Dubus's characters are often superficially Catholic, or practice highly idiosyncratic personal theology. Regardless of their true intentions, there is no shortage of lapsed or wavering Catholics in Dubus's fiction. Juanita, the character who used the word *petting* in the confessional because it "was a vague word and kept her secrets," stops going to confession during her junior year of high school, after having sex with her boyfriend.[140] Juanita's drift from the Church feels more connected with her emerging sexuality than any considered rejection of doctrine, though other characters lapse for more concrete reasons. Dubus resists making these characters into parables, or crafting stories where their renewals of faith are the end result. In "Separate Flights," Beth Harrison has been having an affair with Robert Carini, and thinks of him while lying in bed next to her husband. She fantasizes each night until "her passion took her nowhere, returned her from nowhere."[141] She longs to be "able to sin"; the power and freedom to choose sin is more important than Robert, than any man.[142]

Curiously, Beth still feels fractured guilt, because "in order to sin you had to depart from something you believed in," and Beth had "stopped" being Catholic "as unconsciously as your face tans in summer and pales in winter."[143] Her loss of faith was not reactive; rather, "it had been largely

---

136. Dubus, *Dancing*, 167.
137. Ibid.
138. Ibid.
139. Ibid.
140. Dubus, *Selected*, 44.
141. Dubus, *Finding*, 178.
142. Ibid.
143. Ibid., 179.

a matter of sleeping late on Sunday mornings."[144] Now, years later, her agnosticism is apathetic: "it didn't seem to matter" if God existed.[145] The divine was never a topic of conversation with her husband.

Beth's apathy differs from most Dubus characters, who are more active in the machinations of the Church, even if they are in doctrinal or cultural disagreement on particular points. Naval officer Gerry Fontenot, the epistolary narrator of "Deaths at Sea," quips that God is not concerned with the sex lives of sailors. Gerry's narration is a useful representation of how Dubus develops the connection between cultural Catholicism and family life. He shares that he and his wife are "the only practicing Catholics . . . who don't even use rhythm and are still childless, while the others have babies year after year and are in despair and moving closer to a time when they will leave the Church."[146] The distant narrator of "Rose," though not Catholic, speaks with similar pessimism about Rose and Jim Callahan: "Devout Catholics, she told me. By that, she did not mean they strived to live in imitation of Christ. She meant they did not practice artificial birth control, but rhythm, and after their third year of marriage they had three children. They left the Church then. That is, they stopped attending Sunday Mass and receiving Communion."[147] The narrator continues his commentary, and were it not for his consistently overarching tone, he might be construed as a convenient mouthpiece for a sometimes skeptical writer: "There is too much history, too much philosophy involved, for the matter of faith to rest finally and solely on the issue of contraceptives. That was long ago, and now my Catholic friends tell me the priests no longer concern themselves with birth control."[148] The narrator of "Rose" can speak these observations without the need for personal qualification, and therefore they carry less dramatic resonation than similar observations by Catholic characters.

If the lapsed state of Dubus's characters offers a useful window into postconciliar discontent, perhaps the most telling representation of faith in his fiction is consistent moral ambiguity and complexity. "If They Knew Yvonne" is steeped in preconciliar Catholicism that offers insight into the cultural layover beyond Vatican II. The story begins with the narrator's memory of his eighth grade spent, like Dubus, at a Christian Brothers

144. Ibid.
145. Ibid.
146. Dubus, *Last*, 8.
147. Dubus, *Selected*, 213.
148. Ibid.

school. One brother gives each student a picture of Thomas Aquinas, "seated, leaning back against one angel whose hands grip his shoulders," looking like "a tired boxer between rounds."[149] Harry's simile is not surprising, but even more important is the mention of the apocryphal tale that a woman was sent to tempt Aquinas in his room, but he resisted her, and was followed by angels who "encircled his waist with a cord, and squeezed all concupiscence from his body so he would never be tempted again."[150]

That *Baltimore Catechism* style melodrama is followed by a recanting of the Decalogue, with particular focus, as in the Aquinas picture, on sexual sins. Appropriate to their age, the discussion is focused on the evils of masturbation. Suggestions for resisting the temptation include never being alone, completing chores and playing sports to "use up your energy," Marian devotion, and most importantly, receipt of the Eucharist.[151] The brother leaves them with unusual advice: "you'd actually be doing someone a favor if you killed him when he had just received the Eucharist."[152] The narrator appropriates this melodrama when recounting his first sexual sin, when it felt like "everyone on earth and in heaven had watched" his private act.[153] His guilt during the next few days reaches an apex when he confesses the sin, and then prays the rosary. He, like his family, are devoted preconciliar Catholics: they fast from midnight until Communion, attend weekly Mass, and live with the guilt of transgressions.

Dubus, as he does in the majority of his fiction, imbues a particularly American tinge to the family's Catholicism. The narrator's fourteenth summer consisted of "baseball in the mornings, and friends and movies and some days of peace, of hope—then back to the confessional where the smell of sweat hung in the air like spewed-out sin."[154] Thoughts of sexuality begin at home, where his college-bound sister Janet and her "smooth brown legs" offer a glimpse into young relationships, and the discovery of condoms near cigarettes in his parent's bedroom leads the two into a doctrinal discussion.[155] The conversation between the siblings is unsurprisingly one-sided. Janet asks her brother if he is surprised to learn that his parents still have sex, and attempts to educate his perception through

149. Ibid., 174.
150. Ibid., 174.
151. Ibid., 175.
152. Ibid.
153. Ibid., 176.
154. Ibid., 177.
155. Ibid., 176.

postconciliar theology: "Do you know that some people—theologians—believe a mortal sin is as rare as a capital crime? That most things we do aren't really evil?"[156] The narrator's response is concrete: "They must not be Catholics," showing how sin, rather than faith, is used as the basis of his religious self-definition.[157] The narrator knows that his Episcopalian father calls the crucifix in their bedroom a "graven image,"[158] but his sister says the boy should not think of their father as "a Protestant who had led Mother away from the Church."[159]

Dubus cleverly portrays the preconciliar, image-based personal theology of these characters. His sister trusts in words—"several times she used the word love"—but the boy reacts and reflects in imagery, thinking of finding "a condom lying in the dust of a country road; a line of black ants was crawling into it."[160] Words might work on one level, but images are reoccurring, and even a few years later, "having done it again after receiving Communion that very morning," the narrator reacts impulsively.[161] After an impromptu confession over the phone to his priest, he returns home in a fury, leading to another image, this one of self-violence: a rejection of the sexual, bodily self.

The background of "If They Knew Yvonne" is necessary before the introduction of the titular character, also Catholic-schooled but not "bothered as much as I was" by the education.[162] From "petting" to "a clothed pantomime of lovemaking," Yvonne and Harry are intimate, leading him to "proudly" go to confession.[163] The narrator doubts the thoroughness of Yvonne's own confessions; she is portrayed as the pursuer, and when the narrator stops one of her advances, they enter into a dogmatic dialogue reminiscent of Harry's earlier conversation with Janet. Yvonne pushes him with questions, asking why they should "draw the line at climax?"[164] Henry asks her to see the argument to its natural end—loss of her virginity—but she admits fear.

156. Ibid., 179.

157. Ibid.

158. Ibid., 178–9.

159. Ibid., 180.

160. Ibid.

161. Ibid.

162. Ibid., 182.

163. Ibid.

164. Ibid., 184.

That hesitance disappears as Dubus settles into the lyricism reserved for religious or sexual ecstasy. They drive "out to a country road, over a vibrating wooden bridge, the bayou beneath us dark as earth on that moonless night, on through black trees until I found a dirt road into the woods."[165] Harry's caution returns upon "seeing her trusting face and shockingly white body," but realizes that the "Brothers hadn't prepared me for this."[166] The sexual theology of instruction was focused on lust, however temporary. That love does not last beyond a few months of sex. Harry notices her physical and social imperfections, and Yvonne shares his boredom with the relationship. Harry's first confession in five months is imperfect: he perceives his sex as "a man's sin," but Father Broussard is less romantic, chastising Harry for "[stealing]" sexual intercourse, "given by God to married couples," for mere "physical pleasure."[167] Harry exits the confessional feeling "unforgiven" because of their differing perceptions.[168] The same divergence occurs when Harry returns to his older, more personal sexual sin. Father Broussard says he has "countermanded God's law"; Harry stops receiving Communion.[169]

Janet's divorce and return home moves the story toward its final act. Their mother's worry that Janet will not be able to marry again in the Church is assuaged in a surprising way: Janet reveals that they never had a religious wedding. Other than the time of her own affair during the doomed marriage, Janet received the Eucharist, justifying the action because the Church is not very "smart" about sex.[170] She explains that "the Eucharist is the sacrament of love and I needed it very badly those five years and nobody can keep me away."[171] Janet, again, finds the blame for unhealthy perceptions about sex with the Church: "too many of those celibates teach sex the way it is for them. They make it introverted, so you come out of their schools believing sex is something between you and yourself, or between you and God. Instead of between you and other people."[172]

165. Ibid., 185.
166. Ibid.
167. Ibid., 189.
168. Ibid.
169. Ibid., 190.
170. Ibid., 193.
171. Ibid.
172. Ibid.

The story's penultimate scene is Harry's long-delayed confession, now with Father Grassi, introduced earlier as the more forgiving and approachable priest. Grassi jokes with Harry; he is a priest far less concerned with doctrine than reconciliation. They have a dialogue rather than an interrogation, and Harry explains that his understanding of sin was formed by the Christian Brothers, who "concentrated too much on the body."[173] Harry revisits his first experience with Yvonne, and the priest quips whether Harry wanted to "mutilate yourself with a can opener."[174] Grassi ends on a more serious note, but one that is also more realistic than the previous priest. He shares John 17:15: "I do not pray that You take them out of the world, but that You keep them from evil."[175] Although the scene ends with the priest's recommendation for penance, the intimation is that Harry feels both forgiven and comforted.

"If They Knew Yvonne" might be the test case for Anita Gandolfo's assessment of Dubus. His characters, according to Gandolfo, are "concerned with the sacramental life in a manner more consonant with the 1940's than the 1980's."[176] The "peculiar version of Catholicism" present in Dubus's work is, for Gandolfo, "a religious expression limited solely to the world of innocence."[177] This preconciliar innocence of faith meets the postconciliar reality of sexuality in Dubus's work. That tension is equally apparent in Hansen's *Mariette in Ecstasy*: a postmodern, postconciliar work about a preconciliar world. Both Dubus and Hansen use the conciliar period as a literary axis point. Raised in preconciliar times, but adults in a postconciliar Church, both writers dramatize lay and religious Catholics metaphorically straddling that hopeful conciliar line bordered on both sides by provincial realities.

Dubus's postconciliar narratives interrogate Father Grassi's Johannine quotation. Dubus does not shield his characters from the evils of this world. In "Out of the Snow," LuAnn Arceneaux returns, fighting for her life during a dramatic home invasion. Her words after the attack feel applicable to much of Dubus: "If evil can walk through the door, and there's a place deep in our hearts that knows how to look at its face, and beat it till it's broken and bleeding, till it crawls away. And we do this with rapture."[178]

173. Ibid., 195.

174. Ibid.

175. Ibid., 196.

176. Gandolfo, *Testing*, 148.

177. Ibid.

178. Dubus, *Dancing*, 193.

Nor does Dubus posit simple faith as a way to erase or evade that evil. Catholicism is a salve, but a complicated one, and his characters sometimes reject the same tenets that might help them. The result, for some commentators, might be a fictional world where fidelity to doctrine is low, but his fiction exudes realism, a curious contradiction to the criticism that his essays sometimes lapse into the devotional. The realism of Dubus's fiction builds from domestic settings to the uneven relationships borne from those close quarters. Assumed relationships crack under pressure, as in "Miranda Over the Valley." Eighteen year-old Miranda is pregnant, and afraid. Added to the equation is a sense of sterile procedure to the medical element of the experience. She visits a gynecologist who asks if she plans to keep the baby. Joy is replaced by procedure. Miranda's twenty dollar check completes the transactional procedure, and she exits the office to Halloween: "dusk had descended and where groups of small witches, skeletons, devils, and ghosts in sheets moved past her."[179] The holiday setting reinforces Miranda's newfound feeling of difference, and she is "numb, stationary" while handing out candy.[180] She calls her boyfriend, Michaelis, and asks him to choose a "trick or treat," with the "trick" being her pregnancy.[181] He responds to her nervous humor with talk of marriage.

Miranda's parents are generally supportive. Miranda's father tells her not to worry, that they are simply "good kids" who got "into a little trouble."[182] Her father's understanding is based on pointed assumptions. When Miranda corrects his statement that they do whatever is best for the two of them with "and the baby," he responds with condescension: "Come on, sweetheart. That's not a baby. It's just something you're piping blood into."[183] Her father's cold skepticism becomes rhetorical compassion; when Miranda assures that she can have and support the baby even with Michaelis's pursuit of a law degree, her father responds: "I know you can work. That's not the point. The point is, why suffer?"[184] He offers another beer to Michaelis in the midst of his plea to Miranda.

Her mother is even less reserved. She stresses that marriage is "work," and that some years were like "standing in the rain."[185] She then

179. Dubus, *Selected*, 3–4.
180. Ibid., 4.
181. Ibid., 5.
182. Ibid., 7.
183. Ibid., 9.
184. Ibid.
185. Ibid., 10.

admits that "relationships" with other men "helped" her survive her own marriage, and punctuates her confession with a smack of the table.[186] Her husband's expression is not shown to the reader, but her own, at least to Miranda, showed "a coaxing trick that she did not want to understand."[187] Her parents' suggestions to wait for marriage and finish school would be reasonable, if not for her current situation, and what Miranda would have to decide in order for them to become a possibility. She is nervous, but the best Michaelis can offer is a shrug.

Most noticeably absent from "Miranda Over the Valley" is any discussion of Catholicism. Their silence does not equal disbelief, but the absence of any theology in a story whose axis is an ethical decision is surprising for Dubus. The parents' suggestion of abortion is pragmatic, not emotional. That comparatively lesser sexual transgressions create the profluence in other stories further reveals the preconciliar mark on Dubus's canon. Sin is most evil when it can be held and tasted, and Miranda's unborn child remains mysterious.

Miranda's decision to get an abortion, as well as the moments prefacing the procedure, occur off the page. The reader is placed months later, when Miranda feels not "remorse," but a sensation of "dying."[188] An unsuccessful relationship with another man is followed by a brief return to Michaelis, but the aftermath of the abortion has emotionally wounded her. In the final line of the story, Miranda leaves Michaelis "lying naked in the dark."[189] She is perhaps Dubus's most solemn and incomplete character: he leaves her wounded, without any sense of completion. Even Polly in "The Pretty Girl" achieves some measure of personal justice, despite the cost, whereas Miranda is permanently scathed.

No story better examples how Dubus dramatized the morality and immorality of his Catholic characters than "A Father's Story," perhaps Dubus's most anthologized work, and the one, not surprisingly, open to the most interpretations. The tale is used to critique Dubus's literary fidelity to Catholicism and to uphold his dedication to the trope of fatherhood. Since the work has become convenient fodder for theory or ideology, it is worth returning to at the sentence level to assess where critical response ends and critical rewriting begins.

186. Ibid.
187. Ibid.
188. Ibid., 12.
189. Ibid., 19.

The dramatic nexus of "A Father's Story" is a decision made by Luke Ripley, obliquely referenced in "Voices From the Moon," and a first person narrator comfortable speaking to the reader. The story's structure stresses the narrator's personal approach toward Catholicism. Since "A Father's Story" is the most critically received work of Dubus's canon, it might be useful to begin backwards: from the criticism to the text, from that central action outward. Anita Gandolfo offers a damning assessment of Luke's decision. Her criticism should not be rejected out of turn, since most of her observations about Dubus are quite perceptive. Yet her reading of "A Father's Story," and her general comments about Dubus's work, are ultimately dismissive, regardless of how well-argued. Consistent with the "peculiar vision of Catholicism" she has found in Dubus's fiction, she finds Luke's actions reflective of a Catholic moral rewriting that "reveals his indebtedness to the Sentimental Love Ethic for his definition of love."[190] Gandolfo continues: "Amazingly, Dubus presents Luke's abandonment of the man in the road . . . and protection of his daughter as virtuous."[191] Gandolfo's criticism stems from her claim that the "moral center of Dubus' fiction . . . is the isolated individual self."[192] She finds "no indication" that Dubus intended Luke to be "an unreliable narrator," as well as "no suggestion that he wants to shock the reader by the fact of Luke's having abandoned a possibly still living man and gone to Mass in order to obliterate evidence of the accident."[193] She adds that Dubus's canon has prepared, or almost prefigured, Luke's actions: "love between fathers and daughters is a strong theme in Dubus' work, suggesting that indeed he expects readers to admire this father for having saved his daughter the ordeal of a police inquiry."[194]

In Gandolfo's assessment, Luke's "extreme actions" are presented without flinching, and that presentation shows the writer's implicit approval.[195] Dubus's work "presages the primary distortion of individualism—Catholicism formulated with no operative paradigm, no shared meanings."[196] That Gandolfo ends her section on Dubus with brief biographical references to his children, marriages, and Marine background

190. Gandolfo, *Testing*, 149.
191. Ibid., 150.
192. Ibid., 150–1.
193. Ibid., 150.
194. Ibid.
195. Ibid., 151.
196. Ibid.

to explain his "process of privatization" speaks to the possibility that un-comfort with the ethics of his characters has resulted in a prescribed type of reading.[197]

Gandolfo's reaction is not so much incorrect than misapplied. Dubus himself, in an interview with Bonnie Lyons and Bill Oliver, admits Luke's central decision was immoral. Yet that is not the point of the story. "A Father's Story" is Dubus at his narratalogical finest, and a useful example of how misapplied Catholic literary criticism can reduce the standing of a deserving work. The story begins with a phrase that teaches the reader how to understand the entire narrative: "My name is Luke Ripley, and here is what I call my life."[198] The sentence's construction accomplishes, as Gandolfo surmises, an individualistic Catholic worldview, yet does so with a secondary distance. As a narrator, this is what Luke *calls* his life, not what his life *is*; consideration of a few sentences or paragraphs of Dubus's tale reveals a speaker comfortable with tongue-in-cheek commentary, and it is exactly that levity that creates the dramatic gravity of his discovery and subsequent decision. Luke's choice of "calls" is both idiom and cipher.

Gandolfo's reading sounds like "A Father's Story" has been digested as a third-person narrated work. Luke's absolute control of the narrative information forces the reader to not only trust in his words, but leave the story with that trust tempered, and perhaps strained. He begins by identifying his life by the stabled horses he owns, a barn, and his property, but qualifies that "I call it my life because it looks like it is, and people I know call it that, but it's a life I can get away from when I hunt and fish" and listen to opera.[199] The first paragraph of the story already establishes a sense of escapism, a desire to be more than the tangible, perceivable elements of his life. Luke even admits that his "real life is the one nobody talks about anymore" except for his friend, Father Paul LeBoeuf.[200]

Father Paul is Dubus's most nuanced fictional representation of a priest, as compared to Joe in "Adultery," whose former priesthood was used for metaphorical purposes. Luke sees Paul as "another old buck," a "ruddy" faced man he can hunt and fish with; they have dinner together each Wednesday night.[201] Luke and Paul are frank with each other. Luke prefers giving money to a shelter and bread line in New York City rather

197. Ibid.
198. Dubus, *Selected*, 455.
199. Ibid.
200. Ibid.
201. Ibid.

than tithing his local St. John's; Paul teases him about it and "wants to know how much because he believes I'm generous and good, and he is wrong about that."[202] Luke refuses to answer, saying "I can't let my left hand know what my right is doing."[203]

Father Paul also came to dinner when Luke was still married to his wife, Gloria, and was the first to comfort him when she left. Luke thinks that Paul "was doing his work but coming as a friend too, and I thought what good work he had. I have no calling."[204] His keeping of horses is his calling "in that other life," but not his real, internal one.[205] Luke's consistent redefinition of self and identity speaks to the malleability of narrative truth in "A Father's Story." His willingness to shift between real and public life, past and present, reveals an awareness of how his Catholic identity is fractured by the complications of reality rather than dogma, of practice versus theology.

Luke feels that his private life "can be seen in miniature in that struggle in the dark of morning" before sunrise.[206] Luke makes the bed and boils water for coffee, and all the while he "talk[s]" to God, wherein he "offer[s] him my day, every act of my body and spirit, my thoughts and moods, as a prayer of thanksgiving."[207] Such offertory was a "habit" when Luke was in Catholic school, but has now become a "ritual."[208] This ritual occurs in silence, and is done with attentiveness, because "I never feel certain that I'll be here watching birds eating at tomorrow's daylight."[209]

Luke remembers a statement by Father Paul one night: "Belief is believing in God; faith is believing that God believes in you."[210] The sentiment and grammatical construction of the phrase might invite Gandolfo's earlier criticism: that Luke, and other characters within Dubus's fiction, are more concerned with localizing themselves in relation to God rather than revering and humbling themselves before him. Yet Paul's statement was likely spoken for good theological reason: Luke is a character who recognizes his imperfections, and has his own form of devotion. Dubus's

202. Ibid., 457.
203. Ibid.
204. Ibid., 458.
205. Ibid.
206. Ibid.
207. Ibid.
208. Ibid.
209. Ibid., 459.
210. Ibid., 461.

choice of the word "talk" rather than "pray" to God in the morning reveals that Luke has a particular conception of his relationship with the divine.

Even a statement like "at St. John's, Father Paul and five or six regulars and I celebrate the Mass" speaks to the importance of lay participation, of the unity of this community.[211] Luke admits that, while "looking at Father Paul and the altar, and uttering prayers," he is often "distracted by scrambled eggs, horses, the weather, and memories and daydreams that have nothing to do with the sacrament I am about to receive."[212] That Eucharist is another part of his Catholic ritual, a ritual that "allows those who cannot will themselves out of the secular to perform the spiritual."[213] His distractions are replaced with a feeling of "excitement" and "certainty" after receipt of the Eucharist; Luke knows, though, that afterward "the mystery ends" in an immediate sense, and he returns "to the life people see."[214]

That life, in the familial sense, is a lonely one. Only his daughter Jennifer visits, and Luke worries "about her the way fathers worry about daughters but not sons."[215] Luke struggles to understand womanhood; seeing his daughter makes him long for Gloria. He laments that "ritual" might have "healed" the marriage, using the same language that he does for Mass.[216] And yet perhaps the closest shared action of ritual, their practice of the rhythm method, caused strain to their marriage, "so angered and oppressed by our passion that we could see no further than our loins."[217] Some days they could reject the church's ban on contraception, but would always dispose of the remaining condoms before they again "submitted to the calendar."[218]

Gloria is no longer Catholic, and the children only attended Mass when they visited Luke. Jennifer is an agnostic, but it is her "womanhood that renders me awkward"; Luke has no intentions of converting anyone.[219] Contemporary female sexuality is the center of his inability to understand Jennifer's womanhood. Luke is "certain . . . that she has very happily not

211. Ibid., 460.
212. Ibid.
213. Ibid., 461.
214. Ibid.
215. Ibid.
216. Ibid., 463.
217. Ibid.
218. Ibid., 464.
219. Ibid., 465.

been a virgin for years," and he is more bothered by his certainty of that truth than the truth itself.[220]

That discussion of Jennifer's sexuality, the core of her womanhood that Luke does not understand, immediately precedes the second hand report of her accident. As Luke controlled the integrity of the narrative material at the start of the story, so does he largely share Jennifer's memory as embedded information rather than direct dialogue, thus allowing his first person voice to further shade the truth. Luke is awakened from a sleep that had started while "listening to the wind in the trees,"[221] the same wind he imagined had "swayed and shook [trees] as if they might leap from the earth" during Jennifer's drive back from a New Hampshire beach.[222] Luke, in nearly an attempt to assure the reader of the testimony's veracity, says he "can see" and "feel" the scene. He becomes so embedded in the scene that he is able to focus on individual sounds: empty beer bottles clinking together, wind through an open window, Jennifer singing to a cassette tape.

Jennifer makes her confession with the only direct dialogue of the scene besides her saying "Dad": "I hit somebody. With the *car*."[223] She hit the man at the crest of a hill, and sped from the accident. The dark, confused scene is imagined by Luke in his bed before Jennifer arrives, since it was her knock on the door that pulled him out of the "dream."[224] Dubus is far too cautious a writer for narrative laziness. The ambiguity is profound. Luke, through the sacramental love that had been built with patience in the first half of the story, was able to live the dramatic moment with Jennifer. Whether or not this dream was merely a reflection of her later story is not important. Luke, in fact, admits the confusion. Her story was told "not as I tell it now, for that was later as again and again we relived it in the kitchen or living room" and then on the trails or in the pasture.[225] Narrative and chronology are malleable in "A Father's Story," yet Dubus does not resort to psychic reasons for Luke's ability to imagine his daughter's accident. The closest symbol of transition he offers is the wind Luke "heard in my sleep," that ended when Jennifer closed her window.[226] There is no clear explanation because this story exists entirely in the narrative world of

220. Ibid., 465.
221. Ibid.
222. Ibid., 466.
223. Ibid., 467.
224. Ibid.
225. Ibid.
226. Ibid.

Luke Ripley, a world where he controls the representation of his life, even when that life is blurred beyond recognition.

Luke rushes out in the pickup and drives to the scene of the accident. His prayers become pessimistic, but he concludes that if the man "were dead, they would not get Jennifer."[227] The wind continues to haunt the night, as weeds are "whipping, a mad dance with the trees above them"; the force even lifts Luke's strides.[228] Luke discovers the man face down and still in the grass, and he then feels God "in the wind and the sky moving past the stars and the moon and the fields around me, but only watching me as He might have watched Cain or Job. I did not know which."[229] Luke's discovery of the man evolves from inanimate language, including seeing first his shirt and describing the man as "long" rather than "tall," to more intimate language of body as he searches for a pulse.[230]

Luke prays for the man's soul, and is forced to confront his own existing sins: not asking Father Paul to offer the last rites, and not calling for an ambulance. When Luke "stood and turned into the wind" to leave the scene, he is either metaphorically facing the God he has tested and perhaps rejected through action, or he is confronting the same elements of the night that seemed to make the country wild with sin earlier.[231] That wind still moves when Luke returns to the house, where Jennifer says "I thought you'd call the police," but Luke has not.[232] Her actions at the house—"capping the rye and putting it away, filling the ice tray, washing the glasses, emptying the ashtray, sponging the table"—reveal a desire to erase the past through a domestic present.[233]

The next morning, Jennifer still asleep, Luke drives the pickup to the church, images of the accident replaying in his mind. When Father Paul finds him in the pickup, Luke says he wants to receive the Eucharist, but does not confess; not that morning, not ever. Luke and Jennifer must perform to keep their secret: that she had killed a nineteen year old CETA worker who had been walking home from a friend's house. Only God

227. Ibid., 468.
228. Ibid.
229. Ibid., 469.
230. Ibid., 470.
231. Ibid., 471.
232. Ibid., 472.
233. Ibid.

knows Luke's secret, and Luke "felt Him watching from the wind and the night as I knelt over the dying boy."[234]

Dubus's preconciliar Catholic characters might use the language of mortal sin here, but Luke has been established as cultivating an idiosyncratic sense of prayer and relationship with the divine. He continues to talk to God in the morning, but God does not respond, and "that is not something I require . . . I know Him, as I know the part of myself that knows Him."[235] That is why Luke can say he has been "arguing" with God: his prayers and own rejections give layers to the self-dialogue.[236] Luke knows his sins. He has failed to save a life, and to provide small comfort to a grieving family, even "deepening their pain at the chance and mystery of death by giving them nothing—no one—to hate."[237] He feels God's rejection of his receipt of the Eucharist the morning after the accident, how "He [was] watching me, even from my tongue, intestines, blood, as I have watched my sons at times in their young lives when I was able to judge but without anger, and so keep silent while they, in the agony of their youth, decided how they must act."[238] Though Luke is no child, he fits his own definition of sin: "Their reasons were never as good or as bad as their actions, but they needed to find them, to believe they were living by them, instead of the awful solitude of the heart."[239]

Yet Luke is living that awful solitude now. Gone is the peace of his past. He does not live a life of penance; he has become steadfast, telling God "I would do it again."[240] The reason fits with the splintered narrative of "A Father's Story": when Jennifer came to him that night, "what rose from the bed was not a stable owner or a Catholic or any other Luke Ripley I had lived with for a long time, but the father of a girl."[241] God finally speaks to him here, reminding Luke that he is also a father. Luke qualifies that he would have called the police if one of his sons had hit the man. God wonders if Luke loves them any less; Luke explains: "I tell Him no, it is not that I love them less, but that I could bear the pain of watching and knowing my sons' pain, could bear it with pride as they took the whip and

234. Ibid., 474–5.
235. Ibid., 474.
236. Ibid., 475.
237. Ibid.
238. Ibid.
239. Ibid.
240. Ibid.
241. Ibid.

nails. But You never had a daughter and, if You had, You could not have borne her passion."[242] God responds with a statement, that Luke loves his daughter "more than you love Me," to which Luke responds that he loves Jennifer "more than I love truth."[243]

God says that Luke loves in weakness, to which Luke agrees, "As You love me."[244] "A Father's Story" is about this most difficult love of weakness. Dubus admitted his shortcomings as a father, and "A Father's Story" reads as an apology on the page. For Dubus the writer and man, the connections of earthly love complicated the relation between man and the divine. He never tipped the scale in favor of man, but he does offer insight into why Catholics live in paradox through continual sin. In *Townie*, Andre remembers Dubus praying the rosary to his "real father," not God.[245] He tells his sons, who are working on Suzanne's home, that they are doing "holy work."[246] During one of their late night talks that became more frequent closer to Dubus's death, Andre remembers one particular anecdote from his father's youth. He sat with his friends in a car outside of a brothel. His friends went inside, but Dubus remained in the car. He had gone to Mass that morning, and felt "holy."[247]

It is perhaps this proximity to sin, and the occasional but sweet decision not to sin, that best identifies Dubus's Catholic core. When Dubus died, his sons fulfilled a promise: they built his coffin in one night, and even dug the plot for his grave. Their actions seem necessary, as "Pop had eaten life, and his death had left a cavernous, gnawing hole in the air we moved through."[248] In *Townie*, Andre learns how to become a better father and man from Dubus, but those lessons are often not of imitation, but critique. Dubus, it seems, would have been fine with that distinction.

242. Ibid., 475–6.

243. Ibid., 476.

244. Ibid.

245. Dubus III, *Townie*, 365.

246. Ibid., 366.

247. Ibid., 374.

248. Ibid., 383.

Chapter Four

Hopkins Channeled

The Essays and Poetry of Paul Mariani

"If I had not discovered Hopkins," Paul Mariani reflects, "I would have had to invent him."[1] Mariani first discovered Hopkins as a final-semester senior at Manhattan College, where he'd been assigned a presentation on William Butler Yeats. Mariani traded with his fraternity brother, who had been charged with researching Hopkins. The rest is literary-biographical history: "Of the actual presentation I remember nothing beyond a sense of delight."[2] Although Mariani would later publish *Commentary on the Complete Poems of Gerard Manley Hopkins* and *Gerard Manley Hopkins: A Life*, his writings about Hopkins have never lost that sense of delight. Mariani's embrace of Hopkins parallels his own poetic paradoxes: his content mirrors Dubus, but he shares Hansen's literary fidelity to the Church.

Mariani's poetic approach to Catholicism can be broken into three periods: a young narrator's complicated maturation; a narrator's composite experiences during middle age, where the divine reaches into the daily; and that narrator's spiritual maturation, where the weight of the divine mystery nearly overwhelms the prosaic. His cumulative *Epitaphs for the Journey* (2012) revisits and revises earlier work, while offering a complete whole. The identity of the priest—particularly the Jesuit tradition—connects his poetic periods, and anchors his critical writing, explaining his thematic tendency to sacramentalize the mundane. Mariani spent ten months in 1956 and 1957 "at the Marianist Preparatory School in Beacon,

1. Mariani, *God*, 30.
2. Ibid., 33.

New York, as a postulant seeking entrance into the priesthood."[3] Although his "religious calling . . . died or . . . underwent a transformation into something else," Mariani remained fascinated with the role of a priest.[4] The clerical identity becomes critically malleable for him, as James Joyce is labeled a "spoiled priest whose portrait of Irish Catholicism seemed so cold, so aloof, so analytical."[5] Mariani's intimation that Joyce's intellect and talent smeared the same Catholicism that cultivated his cultural sense is delivered with the sting of disappointment. Even Ralph Waldo Emerson, a lapsed Unitarian, is labeled in similar terms.

Mariani "tried to make myself into a priest / and failed," but still finds worth in the connection between poetry and priesthood.[6] Hopkins is Mariani's true exemplar of literary priesthood. Mariani finds Hopkins's prosody arising "through long reflection on the nature and evolution of language structures, especially Greek and Latin and the Anglo-Saxon roots of English."[7] Hopkins's investigations into etymology and language likely led him to prescient questions, often articulated within Mariani's work: "if the Word became incarnate, enfleshed itself in the matter of the world, in the matter of humankind, how could we find it? How witness to it?"[8] In quoting Hopkins's "God's Grandeur," Mariani wonders if "words themselves be charged with that grandeur. But it would have to be instressed on the poet as witness, who in turn would witness for us."[9] Mariani, as a Catholic literary critic, fills the next step in that progression. If the Catholic poet offers a supplementary imaginative liturgy of experience and vision, the Catholic literary critic must negotiate the tendency to ascribe importance based on doctrinal fidelity with the need to make all things new, in the literary sense.

The danger in any religiously influenced poetry is allowing one particular poet to cross the line from necessary to absolute, a poetic deity in whose even "lagging lines" adherents find the power of gospel. Hopkins is the perfect candidate: he is adored by secular writers for his linguistic prowess, and to readers unaware of his time period he might even appear postmodern. He is the religious writer who wrote with religious passion,

3. Ibid., 3.
4. Ibid., 5.
5. Ibid., 32.
6. Mariani, *Epitaphs*, 64.
7. "Interview with Paul Mariani," para. 4.
8. Ibid.
9. Ibid.

and yet remains largely unassailable because of his idiosyncrasies, and his well-documented struggles with faith and focus. Postconciliar Catholic writers find Hopkins a literary exemplar: here was an Oxford-educated convert who plied his trade in near-secret, who was poorly published in his lifetime, who garnered the praise of the future laureate of Britain, and who toiled in near-obscurity as an instructor of elementary Latin. Contemporary poet-teachers of composition might consider him their patron saint.

Whether or not Mariani critically allows Hopkins to reach similar height, Mariani's representations of priests in his own poetry are refreshingly varied. Priests appear in both foreground and background, performing Mass and other clerical duties. His reflections on the profession reveal men equally wrapped in ritual and intelligence, as the "little German priest reciting Virgil and the amniotic rhythms of the Latin" at the Beacon seminary.[10] That "puffy, froglike [eyed]" priest "whose name I have forgotten" returns in "Light Streaming Into the Head": "a gentle, self-effacing presence / whose liver-mottled hands had once brushed light / across the dusty shelves which housed, he said, / his Virgil and his Ovid."[11] Those unflatteringly introduced eyes "flared, brightening / the dusty room, and I had stared, wondering / where all the light was streaming from."[12] In "Winter 1956," another reflection of the narrator's time at Beacon, the German priest is "framed in the chapel light, shaking / as he lifted up the bread and cup, / so much in love with God he was."[13]

"As oldest son," the narrator of "Saying Goodbye" follows the "signal from the undertaker's / young assistant."[14] The narrator is quietly accepting: "So this is how / it ends. With a backhoe idling / behind a row of maples, its driver / impatient to be home for dinner."[15] The ritual of profession and practicality are contrasted with another rite: "a green tent sighing high above a pit, / words about the Resurrection choking / the claustrophobic air."[16] Even the narrator's assurances to his mother as his

---

10. Mariani, *God*, 19.
11. Mariani, *Epitaphs*, 64.
12. Ibid.
13. Ibid., 48.
14. Ibid., 130.
15. Ibid.
16. Ibid.

"right hand / strokes the bronze side of her casket" feel even-handed, not definite: "Everything is going to be just fine."[17]

"Saying Goodbye" does not contain the polarities of belief often present in the work of Hopkins, but is a useful example of how Mariani constructs the natural Catholic tendency to question faith. The priest's homily is given no syntactic importance, and the green tent's sighs are almost a reaction to the unimportance of his words. In fact, the priest is the only man intimated in the poem who is not directly described; even the "impatient" driver is given more linguistic space. Such is the strength of Mariani's poetry: it would be mistaken to label "Saying Goodbye" simply a poem of the mind during grief. Mariani's subtle movements and observations resound, as that "idling" backhoe overwhelms all other sounds of the poem, even the words of faith. The narrator is merely an actor in a performance, however real: a member of the cast whose only words are to his mother's coffin. Mariani's poems craft a particular space, and they unfold with Catholicism as a backdrop, but not a crutch.

"The Cistern" is a reflection on Psalm 88, read by a priest while the narrator and others listen "beneath St. Peter Gallicantu / in Jerusalem," the believed location of the house of Caiaphas.[18] Reproduced lines from the psalm, such as "*I am a man gone down into the pit*" and "*one more among the dead, / among those You have forgotten*" again reflect a speaker troubled by the disconnect between God and man, faith and action.[19] Yet this narrator turns from anger to curiosity, wondering if Christ "call[ed] upon the psalms / to warn him in his need?"[20] He reflects upon Christ's Passion, noting "they dragged him here to try him" but "his quizzers grew tired / and impatient."[21] The narrative fluidly shifts from reported action to direct narration of events: "Let others try him / in the morning. Enough for now / to knot a rope across his chest / and drop him into darkness."[22] The shift might explain why the narrator, earlier in the poem, "could not keep from weeping."[23] The first result of this pilgrimage is that the narrator feels communal guilt for the punishment of Christ, though he later identifies with Christ himself. The final stanza includes a truncated version of

17. Ibid.
18. Ibid., 136.
19. Ibid.
20. Ibid.
21. Ibid.
22. Ibid.
23. Ibid.

Matthew 27:46. The narrator, referencing the Matthean excerpt, notes that the onlookers "misread him, thinking / he was calling on Elijah."[24] The narrator connects with Christ again, that this scene is "As each of us will be: alone, / friends scattered to the winds," before again settling into direct narration, "Except for one out in the courtyard / growing cold, poised now to deny him."[25] This indictment of Peter is given typological precedent, as the psalmist ends with "*The one companion left me.*"[26]

"Solar Ice" begins with a priest raising the Eucharist, "a small white sun around which everything / seemed to coalesce, cohere & choir."[27] The narrator, in the congregation, has a moment of rejection, and "in that instant the arctic / hatred flared, shutting out my world / & spring."[28] Mariani's Catholic worldview creates the context for this moment: the common duality and intersection between moments of religious jubilation and dissatisfaction. The shift in perspective results in the Eucharist "diminished to a tiny o: / an empty cipher, like some solar disc / imploding on itself."[29] The narrator is not devaluing the Eucharist, rather, projecting "some old wound rubbed raw again, / a jagged O at the center of my world."[30] The narrative never rights itself: the narrator wonders "if this is hell," with his final lines reflecting the style of Hopkins's "The Golden Echo": "& ice & ice / & ice & more ice on the way, and this / sweet abyss between myself & You."[31]

Those final lines also intimate Hopkins's "To R. B." While Hopkins's verse is a lament for lost creativity intoned to Robert Bridges, the second person in "Solar Ice" is Christ. Mariani locates this spiritual distance during Mass, but there is a distinctly preconciliar milieu to his structuring of the narrative. A clear demarcation of place and hierarchy exists between the priest, who is titled the equivalent of God rather than his profession, and the lay congregation. While Mariani does not suggest that the priest is responsible for the narrator's skepticism, a marked contrast exists between

24. Ibid.
25. Ibid., 137.
26. Ibid.
27. Ibid., 181.
28. Ibid.
29. Ibid.
30. Ibid.
31. Ibid.

the natural rebirth outside—"All about swelling buds on beech & ash / & maples"—and the "self-salt taste" of the narrator at Mass.[32]

The narrator's spiritual "winter world" makes ritual feel rote, turning the Eucharist into a "cipher." Mariani is most likely using the connotation of cipher as unworthy or unimportant object, and yet another connotation is possible: the Eucharist, as a tangible message of Christ, is hidden from the narrator because of his shift in perspective. The "ice" surrounding him is of his own creation, and that narcissism results in not a rejection, but a temporary rebuffing of the sacrament before him.

Mariani's usage of an epigraph from St. Augustine's *Confessions* for another poem continues these considerations of narcissistic spirituality. Augustine's secular literary stock has been cemented as an early exemplar of the memoir genre, but Ben Yagoda reminds that Augustine's work was part of the reemergence of autobiography in Christian Europe, where the genre had become a religiously oriented text. Augustine's dual appeal to secular memoirists and Christian theologians feels appropriate to Mariani, whose excerpt from *Confessions* deals with a search for memory that appears "at last, fresh from the depths." Memoir presupposes personal importance: even the memoir that locates the writer as a secondary character, a recipient and observer rather than the focus, validates the writer as one qualified to document. The contemporary Catholic narrative poet resides in a similar world, yet the precedence exists, of course, in Hopkins. "To R. B.," delivered as an apology and lament, would not exist if the narrator—if the poet—did not think greatness previously existed, or at least was attainable.

Another nod toward "To R. B." is found in "Making Capital," prefaced by a quote by Hopkins voicing his usual poetic hesitance. Mariani's poem begins with a lament, that "For six weeks I've tried lassoing the wind" with no success.[33] He has been moved before by "sweet whisperings to the mind," though "God knows I've tried" by attending Mass. The scene is not inspiring: "Congealed light on the pews, cold as Fate, / candles guttering, half the parishioners half asleep. / And the priest up at the pulpit, embellishing a story taken / from one of those Chicken Soup series for the soul."[34] Mariani's postconciliar Catholic world is one where "the papers had been screaming now / of scandal," and while that "poor priest" cannot be faulted for the congregation's drifting minds, the Church contains im-

32. Ibid.
33. Ibid., 193.
34. Ibid.

perfections.[35] The narrator's mind wanders into daydream, and he thinks of Isaac, and then Christ, before returning to a similar refrain: "But what / had this to do with where I found myself? Everything, / you'd think. Or nothing. Depending on the view."[36] As in "Solar Ice," that view is tenuous. Concurrent thoughts follow of Isaac and Christ: "as the one went on to populate / a nation, while the other—nailed to that wood—rose from the stink / of death, promising to lift us with him."[37]

That death of Christ, "a good man going under," was a necessary theological and salvific precedent to "struggling to raise himself again, bent on doing what he had to do."[38] Clearly the narrator is finding strength in Christ as man, and while he finds that peace in church, it does not exactly arise from the machinations of Mass. The priest is not mentioned as a conduit, and neither are the other parishioners, who nearly form a vision of death. Rather, it was that "loop in time," that "blip of light" of the resurrection that changes everything.[39] Mariani seems intent on the same theological ambiguity present in the final pages of Walker Percy's *The Moviegoer*: is salvation always direct, or sometimes by proxy?

Similar indirect grace occurs in "Pietà," where "it took three martinis before / she could bring herself to say it."[40] The woman's son "lay alone there / in the ward," HIV-positive, "a dozen years ago."[41] The narrator's statements that follow, "Consider Martha. Consider Lazarus," are as much spoken to the woman as they are delivered to the reader.[42] The woman's grief went without consolation, "except this priest . . . an old / friend who'd stood beside them through the dark / night of it all."[43] She continues her recollection after her son has died: "to see [the priest] lift her son, light as a baby / with the changes death had wrought, and cradle him / like that, then sing him on his way, a cross / between a lullaby & blues, *mmm hmmm*, while / the nurses, still not understanding what they saw, / stayed outside and watched them from the door."[44]

35. Ibid.
36. Ibid., 193–4.
37. Ibid., 194.
38. Ibid.
39. Ibid.
40. Ibid., 133.
41. Ibid.
42. Ibid.
43. Ibid.
44. Ibid., 134.

The image is a marked change from the priests in "Solar Ice" and "Saying Goodbye." Earlier in the poem those same nurses stood "masked & huddled in the doorway, afraid / to cross over into a world no one seemed / to understand."[45] That the priest is the only one "willing to walk across death's threshold" reveals a lack of concern for self that enables the narrator to widen his own understanding of the world.[46] The priest is the synthesis of masculine and feminine, so that gender becomes irrelevant: the allusion to Mary, rather than Christ, widens the pastoral scope. Because the narrator is the recipient of the impromptu confession, he is a metaphorical stand-in for the priest, whose office in the poem rises above the clerical. By using a party as an entry point to this difficult confession, Mariani shows how the tangible world can blur into memory, and how memory can lead to grace, even in the midst of "Hats, favors."[47]

The laity's metaphorical priesthood is more complicated in "The Gospel According to Walter" and "Smoke Rings," poems representative of an earlier aesthetic. More recently, Mariani has been interested in "the model of Christ on the road—to Cana or Capernaum or Jericho or Jerusalem or Emmaus—that is what I am looking for" in contemporary Catholic writing.[48] "The Gospel According to Walter" begins with an "open Bible" passed around during a game.[49] Next up is the narrator's brother, who "grunted" before reading excerpts from the second chapter of Luke.[50] The angel's call for the shepherds to "*not be afraid*" is upended by Walter: "Who the fuck's *he* kidding? Didn't you figure / them guys would blow their cookies when they saw that?"[51] The immaturity is placed within the age of the game's participants, characterizing the angels as "hoverin' over 'em like fuckin' / Huey gunships" followed by "some fuckin' floodlight / saying: Go thou *now* & catch the stable action / in yonder Bethlehem."[52] Walter finally "stopped to catch his breath, his impromptu exegesis / of the Sacred Text & the Sublime fulfilled."[53] He spins the Bible for the next turn,

45. Ibid., 133.
46. Ibid., 134.
47. Ibid.
48. "Interview with Paul Mariani," para. 6.
49. Mariani, *Salvage*, 37.
50. Ibid.
51. Ibid.
52. Ibid.
53. Ibid.

and the narrator gives him the last word: a refrain that the angels had a wingspan of "at *least* eleven fuckin' feet."[54]

Such language employed in even satirical exegesis might sound crass, particularly in the preconciliar world of the poem, but the expansive and associative "Smoke Rings" shows how deeply the youth of these poems have appropriated and concurrently subverted elements of Mass and the priesthood. A pastiche of images, "Smoke Rings" includes Walter "genuflecting on his / right knee before the stack / of Fifties records."[55] Walter "mulls, meditates, / takes a deep drag on his *Lucky Strike* / arabesquing between his teeth" before putting a record on the turntable.[56] His "priestly / eyes aglint," Walter enters a "hypnotic trance" of "half chanting, / half mocking his own ground bass / antiphonal to those disembodied / voices flooding through the twin speakers."[57] Mariani channels the sweeping descriptions of Joyce's Buck Mulligan as he transitions into a memory of "Father Hagen, in purple / chasuble and stole, ascending the seven / steps up the imitation Gothic altar, face / forward, handing me the biretta as we / mumbled the strange polysyllables as best / we could."[58]

In this preconciliar world of Mass, unusual language is ritualized with music and smoke. The priest is clearly an artificer: though he rises up a faux-ornate altar, he is graced with the power of the moment, leading "a plain chant pale against the stained / glass windows."[59] The words and power of that Mass drift "out through cracks / to mingle with the early morning traffic / like ordinary water mixed with wine."[60] The narrator is shocked out of this preconciliar memory by his brother's smoke-induced cough. They recall the "balding horsetrader" who first sold them cigarettes: "O we watched / the poor bastard trembling jack off daily / from the moted loft above in golden light / sublime."[61] Here Mariani sounds like the "spoiled priest" Joyce, from the subversive "O" to the baseness of action. Even the pitiful old man is Joycean, "who watched it all go up in smoke": his money and cigarettes.[62] The smoke is made analogous to when "the

54. Ibid., 38.
55. Ibid., 123.
56. Ibid.
57. Ibid.
58. Ibid.
59. Ibid., 124.
60. Ibid.
61. Ibid.
62. Ibid.

priest, lighting the magnesium flare / at the Pope's crowning: *Sic transit Gloria mundi.*"[63]

The only pause between the base and the celebratory is the space of a stanza break. Later in the poem the narrator remembers a Holy Thursday midnight at the seminary, when "strange urge came upon me there" to kneel and face the moon, "remembering / the Man himself beheld, kneeling in an olive / grove while all the others slept."[64] That monastic thought is undermined by the narrator's contrast to his brother, who he imagines "lay or lie / (or both) in the tricky web of the Perfect Woman."[65] Those "nine long chaste months" were worsened by letters from Walter who, "although he knew the mails / were checked," boasted of conquests real and imagined.[66] The narrator prayed for Walter while fantasizing: "contemplating deft fingers [undoing] the buttons / of her blouse, exposing both those goodies creamy / sweet. And harder did I pray as I witnessed / exploring hands go south to moist mysteries beyond / any my fondest wayward dreams should cross, / until I trembled in my Passion while black hooded /cretins howled."[67] Again, a bounty of loaded Joycean imagery. Prayer juxtaposed with lust, "mysteries" compatible with divinity and sexuality. Even the line-breaks feel deliberate and heavy. Mariani's treatment of sexuality in "Smoke Rings" reflects Hansen's deconstruction of ecstasy.

The final stanzas of the poem return to its psychotropic beginning: "as in a vision, a polyphonic chant drifted up / and out the high dustspattered windows to mingle / with the evening scents."[68] These secular brothers accomplish similar results as the priest; that the earlier associative imagery was tied to the act of transubstantiation feels less heretical than complicating. Mariani is not positing that these boys fulfill the roles of priests, but he is dramatizing that the boys, so steeped in Catholic ritual, are almost "playing" priests. The poem ends with Walter's continued "mouthing," almost in tongues, "caught up / as smoke issued from his troubled visionary lips."[69] The narrator wonders if, like during preconciliar Mass, "by singing we could somehow / slow the thin incessant drift of things."[70]

63. Ibid.
64. Ibid., 127.
65. Ibid.
66. Ibid., 128.
67. Ibid.
68. Ibid., 130.
69. Ibid.
70. Ibid.

Walter might seem bombastic, but he is the narrator's "doppleganging / brother," never far from some unspoken Id.[71] The narrator is the subject of "Betty: September 1957," placing it directly after the Beacon Prep months. That time period has been used by Mariani as a locus of not only his early intellectualization of Catholicism, but also his marriage of the faith with more secular concerns. The poem begins with an already cracked "moral Code" now "breaking into ice floes."[72] Outside the walls of Beacon Prep, the narrator revels in the sounds and images of nature, all beneath the "glow of a single humming / streetlight," helping the secular become saintly: "black cathedral-high arched elms awash / with the benediction of the present."[73] Walter, a friend named Grippie, and the narrator sit with girls in a Ford. The friend calls the narrator "priest" and asks "ain't this better / than the stuff they fed you at the Sem?"[74] The ensuing scene mirrors Stephen Dedalus's first encounter in *A Portrait of the Artist as a Young Man*. His "fingers touch in utter disbelief" the girl's neck, sees her "plumdark / lips uplifted toward me."[75] Those lips are compared to the "silver tinking tintinnabulation" of Easter bells.[76] The young narrator previously "crooned" to Mary; now he has "vowed" to "defend" this girl in a white sweater.[77]

Mariani uses sexuality as a friction point of Catholicism during youth, using the word *mystery* in both sexual and religious connotations. The same boy in the Ford in "Betty" was placing a marker in his physics textbook "beside the picture / of the lovely in the arm-length cashmere sweater" in "Goodnight Irene."[78] At Beacon it was Brother Clyde's "injunction" to stop; years earlier, in the world of the poem, the male influence is the narrator's father in a mechanic garage. The preteen narrator is listening to his father sing "Goodnight Irene" "beneath the row of fan belts."[79] The narrator only sees "part" of his father's face "down in the grease pit, / the wrench in his clenched right fist, / his hooded lamp throwing fitful

71. Ibid., 123.
72. Mariani, *Epitaphs*, 53.
73. Ibid.
74. Ibid., 54.
75. Ibid.
76. Ibid.
77. Ibid.
78. Ibid., 30.
79. Ibid.

shadows / all across the wall."[80] It is with that phantasmagoric image his father "performs / whatever mysteries it is he does to cars," a priest of the mundane.[81] The narrator feels "useless," so he drifts around the garage, reaching a nude calendar. Only "cellophane with the nightie / painted on it" covers the "mystery of the lady kneeling there / who smiles frankly at me."[82]

Mariani stresses the masculinity of place with the "warm smell of leaking / kerosene," a radio that reports Marines fighting in Korea, and the Ford pickup.[83] There, working below the car, the father's next refrain of the song leads the narrator to an innocent question: "But my mother's name is not Irene / her name is Harriet and I wonder why / my father wants to see this other lady / in his dreams."[84]

Mariani's long poem, "The Eastern Point Meditations," might further explain the earlier representations of sexuality. The poem is a confession of the narrator's affair, voiced to the reader, the narrator's son, and to a priest "under the low lamp waiting."[85] The narrator desires "a little summer with a girl" and not "the bills, the frets, / the daily round of things."[86] The narrator finds penance for those sins through distance and meditation, in a "cell" with a "silent crucifix," where he realizes the only way toward salvation, and possible saving of his marriage is the same Catholic architecture that first birthed his conceptions of sexuality years prior.[87] He thinks of the words of a priest, who explains the salient difference between *schola intellecta* and *schola affecta*, stressing the kenotic elements of the latter. The final sections of the poem reach near-reverie, the clarity of a man clearly impassioned in life and on the page: "In this the poem / the prayer and love are one."[88]

While Mariani might intersect with Joyce in representations of sexuality, he differs from his predecessor in representing the clergy involved in Catholic schooling. "Soldiers of Christ" is a nostalgic reflection of the

80. Ibid., 31.
81. Ibid.
82. Ibid.
83. Ibid.
84. Ibid., 32–33.
85. Ibid., 116.
86. Ibid.
87. Ibid., 117.
88. Ibid., 120.

"gaggle of German nuns who fed us" and an arthritic Brother Frank.[89]
The poem's highest point is when Brother Ed, "standing in the doorway,"
warns the narrator and the rest of the Beacon Marching Band about "local
rowdies" who will attempt to distract the procession.[90] Those rowdies are
presented in typical fashion, "black leather jackets . . . toothpicks dan-
gling Brando-like," but the narrator's reflection on the brother's warnings
is telling: "still we / stumbled on, Christ's soldiers and me . . . to the heady
music only we could hear."[91] The poem complicates "Class," a considered
essay that traces Mariani's "disbelief" at "becoming one of them, one of the
new breed of college professors from the working class."[92] The "rowdies"
of "Soldiers of Christ" are displaced from the narrator less because of an
economic status they largely shared and more a lack of appreciation for
Catholicism.

In "Class," Mariani writes of constant fear of not having enough
money, leading him to a succession of jobs: "pumping gas and cleaning
toilets," dishwashing, "shredding classified government documents with
byzantine numerical formulas into the early hours of the morning in a
small office room behind the local movie house," farm hand, painter, and
more.[93] Although Mariani has long since moved to more academic pur-
suits for remuneration, "many of my poems still take as their subject my
first world."[94] An early reviewer, Christine Stenstrom, placed Mariani "in
the vein" of poets with the "penchant for mythologizing their personal
lives in the sometimes mistaken belief that the public exposure of private
trauma can elevate mere biographical detail from the mundane to the
universal."[95] The reviewer claims that Mariani "relentlessly mines chapters
from his family history," and is thankful for the "few poems where the poet
restrains rather than unleashes his ego."[96] Citing his biographical interest in Williams and Berryman, Mariani's "inflated personal mythmaking"
results in poetic solipsism.[97]

---

89. Ibid., 51.
90. Ibid.
91. Ibid., 52.
92. Mariani, *God*, 19.
93. Ibid., 23.
94. Ibid., 24.
95. Stenstrom, "Mariani," 113.
96. Ibid.
97. Ibid.

Stenstrom's criticisms feel overshot. Mariani's work is far less solipsistic than conflicted: an academic, poet-priest remembering his more meager origins in a "cape cod . . . across from the high-school football stadium."[98] Mariani is aware of the potential for criticism, noting how "difficult to speak of what presses one most closely without overly investing in the I."[99] He continues: "in trying to deal with one's past in mock-epic strains, or in a skittery, polysyllabic discourse replete with mythic overtones that quickly—one sees now—crossed over into the Cambodia of the mannerist and the baroque."[100] Mariani wonders if he can write about his mother's attempted suicide: he says it is so "easy to slide off into the unreal, consolatory dream world of language,"[101] and yet surreal language paints the most powerful representation of that moment: "In the cage of kitchen light, in his long johns, my father stands in the hallway, his voice low and cracking. Go out and get her, he tells me, and I go. Outside, it's Mineola. There's fog everywhere, and fumes, and in the shadow of the kitchen light I can see drizzle swirling. There's the eerie Bessemer-like glow from the plastics factories a block away, just beyond the empty stands of the football field."[102]

In criticism, Mariani is attracted to biography; in poetry, he is attracted to autobiography. That focus does not require apology; in fact, the tendency to connect all things large and small might be considered a trope of literary Catholicism, one certainly shared by Dubus. Mariani writes of his daily ritual of "ris[ing] and driv[ing] up country roads to make the 7:00 A.M. Mass."[103] Prosaic actions—waking, washing, eating, driving—in order to attend a building made of base materials. Yet belief in the grace of God enhances all of those elements for the Catholic writer. The tendency to dismiss as poetic narcissism all connections between daily life and divine sound like the assumption that only fabricated, high-minded moments are worthy of God's attention.

"Toward a Sacramental Language" allows Mariani to elucidate his poetic positioning of the divine next to the mundane. He sees that action as part of a tradition—with his closest contemporary being Richard Wilbur—of "a language that pays homage to the splendid grittiness of the

98. Mariani, *God*, 24.
99. Ibid., 25.
100. Ibid., 27.
101. Ibid.
102. Ibid., 27–28.
103. Ibid., 36.

physical as well as to the splendor and consolation of the spiritual."[104] Such language is "sacramental"; in fact, the act of poetry might serve a nearly liturgical role in revealing "God's immanent presence" daily, "if we only know what to look and listen for."[105] Poets whose words "[proclaim] the splendid luminosity of things" include "Whitman, Williams, and Stevens . . . Bill Heyen and Charles Wright and Philip Levine," none of whom are Catholic.[106] He concludes the essay: "There are moments when we are graced with a creative insight into the mysterious, awe-filled world we did not create. And isn't it a matter, after all, of raising the quotidian to the level of spirit, of correcting an imbalance by learning to see the Spirit as it lifts everything into the light."[107]

Mariani is not only aware of the fine poetic line between engagement and narcissism, he is aware that poets have often strayed, pointing the contradiction of William Carlos Williams's self-questioning "why even speak of *I*, which interests me not at all" when Williams's "diagnostician's eye" was trained on his home in *Paterson*, including himself.[108] Contrastingly, Mariani listens to the silence of everyday for whispers of the divine and eternal. That awareness is a Catholic trait; Ross Labrie finds the Catholic perception of "the world in a sacramental manner, as a place charged with the creative and providential activity of God" as consistent with the tendency of many Catholic writers to juxtapose the mundane with the divine.[109] Mariani's poem "The Music of Desire," about a young man stocking a sparsely-visited grocery store, examples similar juxtaposition. The narrator listens to a radio and thinks about a lost crush. He recognizes that loss is as ubiquitous as the consecration of the Eucharist. The comparison of young love lost and the Eucharist feels more in the tradition of John Donne than contemporary poetics, but Mariani is clear to establish a Catholic architecture to his poems and narrators. His shifts might seem abrupt to a secular reader, but the progression is clear: this boy's day is coaxed by the ritual of dusting and sweeping, of fingers drumming on a counter and register with the continuous melody of a trumpet in the background. The symbolism of Mass is not forced, but is complicated by those final lines. Mariani brings the reader along with the metaphor, but

104. Ibid., 234.
105. Ibid.
106. Ibid., 257.
107. Ibid.
108. Ibid., 25.
109. Labrie, *The Catholic*, 2.

he allows it to unfold: the narrator is making a connection of communality, while also upending his own analogy to return to the individual.

Rather than arising from narcissism, connection between the mundane and the divine is a Catholic movement, one comfortably preconciliar. An American family could transition from Saturday night episodes of *The Honeymooners* to the exalted register of Latin Mass. In much the same way that Robert Alter finds Old Testament linguistic genealogy in the juxtaposing registers of William Faulkner, the American preconciliar Catholics of Mariani's poetry find the language of faith transforming everyday diction. In "Mairzy Doats," Mariani again uses the Ford as cultural referent, and this time the words of the Andrews Sisters, that "trinity of sisters," are "floating" to the backseat, where "They make / no sense, the syllables that sing *liddle lambsey divey*."[110] Despite the misunderstanding, "they terrify and comfort," much like the misunderstood Latin of Mariani's preconciliar youth.[111]

Mariani's poetry consistently engages that problem of narcissism in the first-person narrative voice. These occurrences range from the minor, in "Manhattan," to the stubborn, in "Quid Pro Quo." "Manhattan" begins with a college night spent drinking at a few bars, where drunk conversation leads to "how Aquinas avers / means can be said to justify the ends."[112] Those means become the narrator's reaction to a man staring at his college jacket, which results in his "fists knotted in his greasy hair, / smashing his head against the blacktop border."[113] The rest of the night speeds in "some phosphor glare" with the narrator slicing his leg on barbed wire in a drunken attempt to steal a sign.[114]

The poem careens forward, but the final stanza returns to Aquinas. The narrator is taking an exam and looks at his "bloody cor-duroys" before turning to "Self-Loathing & old friend Fear."[115] The poem ends without lesson or instruction, and the Thomist allusion is almost too direct to be absolute. "Quid Pro Quo" takes the problem of narrative narcissism to another level. The context is his "wife's miscarriage (her second / in four months)," and the setting is an empty college classroom with a "budding

---

110. Mariani, *Epitaphs*, 15.

111. Ibid.

112. Ibid., 58.

113. Ibid.

114. Ibid.

115. Ibid., 59.

Joyce scholar" who was a "lapsed Irish Catholic."[116] The professor "surprised" the narrator "by asking what I thought now / of God's ways toward man."[117] Mariani presents no other subjects beyond the miscarriage, so the friend's jab is certainly meant to question the narrator's faith. Mariani appears to craft the setting of divine defense—"the room's pinewood panels / all but swallow[ed] the gelid light"—but the narrator instead raises his "middle finger up to heaven, *quid / pro quo*."[118] The gesture is more than the questioning of Job: this narrator "was sure / I'd seen enough of God's erstwhile ways toward man."[119]

The narrator has appropriated the language of his skeptic questioner, using "toward" as a pointed action, a God less caring than deterministic. Mariani's choice to set the narcissistic action within a classroom reflects his decision to stress the "lapsed" identity of his questioner: the skeptic captures the believer in a moment of pragmatism tinged by anger. He likely expected the narrator to smirk, but the defiance speaks of the narrator's narcissistic faith, wondering why God hasn't responded to his prayers, expecting that faith and fidelity guarantee some individual attention.

The skepticism of the classroom is contrasted with "a creaking, / cedar-scented cabin off Lake George," where "my wife and I made love."[120] On a "sagging mattress" beneath "the great black Adirondack stillness," the couple looks through the broken cabin roof "into a sky that seemed / somehow to look back down on us."[121] It is a "holy place," made holy by the love of the couple and the much gentler God above.[122] Nine months later, the narrator's son is born, and "the fact of his being there / both terrifying & lifting me at once."[123] When that son later becomes a priest and "knelt before a marble altar to vow / everything he had to the same God," the narrator wonders: "How does one bargain / with a God like this, who *quid pro quo*, ups / the ante each time He answers one sign with another?"[124]

Considered together, "Manhattan" and "Quid Pro Quo" debunk their own narcissistic narratives without becoming pedantic. Rather, the

116. Ibid., 81.
117. Ibid.
118. Ibid.
119. Ibid.
120. Ibid., 81–82.
121. Ibid., 82.
122. Ibid.
123. Ibid.
124. Ibid.

poems dramatize a poet clearly interested in investigating the elements of questioning God, of engaging the divine in dialogue, a conversation that is controlled by one participant. Divine control might undercut the attempts to bargain, but the signs offered reveal a God capable of surprise. Mariani revisited "Quid Pro Quo" for a 1996 anthology, noting the poem "still haunts me."[125] Mariani admits the difficulty of the poem's glue of narcissism: "the relationship of the speaker to his God, the same one he has underestimated more than once, trying to make the Lord of subatomic particles and the Lord of exploding new galaxies over into *his* own sorry image."[126]

Mariani's honest self-effacement returns in an even more prosaic sitting in "Landscape With Dog," an unusual elegy. The dog's life is cataloged through "bearing gifts: frozen squirrels, / sodden links of sausage, garter / snakes, the odd sneaker" and his scratches on "doors & tables."[127] Sparky ages as "Ice storms, wakes, elections came & went. / And always he was there, like air."[128] Mariani turns the poem with a qualification: "But then there's this / to think about & think about again."[129] The narrator remembers "trying to get / the stubborn mower started, June blazing / & grease & six-inch grass & sweat, / & no time then to stop to pet a dog."[130] The narrator's choice to refer to the dog as animal and not pet undermines the earlier, sentimental presentation. Reflecting "Saying Goodbye," mundane concerns flatten emotions and distract focus. Mariani's mixture of qualifiers and ampersands clutter the narrative, which then turns: "Sparky simply lifted off those / cog-wheel scrawny legs of his . . . and lay down / somewhere in the woods to die."[131] The narrator's guilt is palpable: his focus has been on the inanimate rather than the animate, treating his dog as one of the indiscriminate objects brought "up the back steps."[132] "Landscape With Dog" documents a loving owner's moment of mistake and ignorance, and yet those seconds of disinterest result in longstanding guilt. Mariani's midcareer poems hinge on a similar theme: individual

---

125. Mariani, *God*, 40.

126. Ibid., 44.

127. Mariani, *Epitaphs*, 104.

128. Ibid.

129. Ibid., 104–5

130. Ibid., 105.

131. Ibid.

132. Ibid., 104.

decisions and moments in the mundane world contain gravity not found in the immediate moment.

His newer poems further refine that theme into an operating principle, and are his creative work, particularly in their biblical breadth, that best reaches the pathos and aesthetics of Hopkins. In these poems, recognition of the impersonal, of the wider faith moment, allows Mariani to transition into poems that decenter the narrator, even if that speaker remains a necessary element. The ending of "Casualty Report" might summarize the tone of these poems: the narrator, thinking about a car accident, ends his reflection rinsing "silverware / in the kitchen sink," that metonym of the domestic in the foreground of his "wondering whether to try and get / the right words right this time, or simply let it go."[133]

This decentering of the personal allows Mariani's narrator's to reach other layers of depth and breadth. In "Mother of Consolation," "What you look hard at looks back hard at you": the focus is on the Christ child, who is "his mother's son, and hers alone, / in any way one's DNA supplies."[134] An interesting theological statement that Mariani continues: "If too he is his Father's Son, how can you know / but by what burns behind the gaze, or in / the innocence of blessing? And even then there's no / way to know until you touch the mystery within."[135] The narrator explains that an understanding of Christ is only achieved by gazing into his eyes: seeing him, accepting him, and moving forward guided by his grace. And yet it is Mary, his "mother's doe-brown eyes turning to gaze back at you," that is an integral element.[136]

Mary's husband, Joseph, is the subject of "Shadow of the Father," which reads with the cadence of a prayer. The narrative begins with a question: "How shall I approach you, Joseph, you, the shadow / of the Father?"[137] Joseph's complex personage is excellent poetic fodder, and Mariani pays sufficient homage, even likening contemporary violence— "where Palestinian gunman roamed the Church / of the Nativity, while Israeli snipers watched / from the adjoining rooftops"—to "Herod's horsemen hunting down a baby."[138] He is also able to return to more domestic concerns: "How difficult it must have been, standing in, as every father /

133. Ibid., 183.
134. Ibid., 173.
135. Ibid.
136. Ibid.
137. Ibid., 196.
138. Ibid.

must sometimes feel."[139] Christ must have found "his courage and outrage against injustice" from Joseph, though the narrator notes the unflattering lines from Luke 2:49, delivered in the KJV translation: *"Didn't you know / I had to be about my father's business?"*[140] After those words, "which must have wounded . . . you drop / from history."[141]

Saint Joseph, "Saint of happy deaths," is the subject of daily prayers by the narrator's wife, whose father, now dying, is "thinking of a future he no longer / has."[142] The narrator's plea is simple: "Joseph, be with her now, and with her father, as he faces / the great mystery, as we all must at the end, alone . . . Be there, / as once you were in Bethlehem and Nazareth and Queens. / You, good man, dreamer, the shadow of the Father."[143] Joseph, no longer operating in the shadow of Christ, is now messenger and helper.

In "The Father," a mere ellipsis is enough to connect the narrator and his grandson with Joseph, who has pledged to care for the infant Messiah "knowing it is that other Father / who keeps him grounded in the presence of so much arcing light."[144] Mariani's son, Paul Jr., is a Jesuit. Mariani writes: "the electric moment came for me when he lay supine on the church floor in Los Angeles, arms outspread in the shape of a cross, along with four other men, and offered himself freely to the Lord . . . something happened—something of a very serious nature—which meant a renewed sense of surrender for me as well."[145] Mariani's 2003 memoir, *Thirty Days*, reveals his own rejuvenating retreat into living the Ignatian Spiritual Exercises that his son practices daily. The trend of narrator as enabling a form of sacrament through humility continues in "Passage," where the narrator reads to his mother-in-law. He "half-shouted" the passage because "she didn't have her hearing aids plugged in."[146] He reflects on the moment because / she was fast approaching the threshold / now of some great mystery. She wanted / to be fed and I had fed her as / I could, with the words I witnessed / turn to bread before us on the table."[147]

139. Ibid.
140. Ibid.
141. Ibid., 196–7.
142. Ibid., 197.
143. Ibid., 196–7.
144. Ibid., 199.
145. "Interview with Paul Mariani," para. 8.
146. Mariani, *Epitaphs*, 179.
147. Ibid., 179.

Lay narrator as priest, words as bread, and love as a transubstantiating force. The result is a narrator, and poet, becoming fully subsumed within the sacramental tradition. "Death and Transfiguration" is the end point of this evolution. The poem begins with speed: "Down the precipitous switchbacks at eighty / the pokerfaced Palestinian cabby aims his Mercedes / while the three of us, ersatz pilgrims, blank-eyed, lurch/ and the droll Franciscan goes on about the Art Deco Church / of the Transfiguration crowning the summit of the Mount."[148] In a reflection of Raphael's "final work," a commissioned painting of the Transfiguration, Mariani includes one of his few corporeal representations of Christ: "For those who only dream / of some vertiginous, longed-for transfiguration, he would seem / to hold out something magnanimous and large: the benzine brightness / of the Christ, eyes upraised in the atom flash of whiteness, / that body lifted up, cloud-suspended feet above the earth."[149] An ekphrastic representation, yet Mariani's poetry is largely devoid of direct representations of the body of Christ, instead relying on the metonym of sacrament. The narrative scans the rest of the scene, including "fear-bedazzled friends" and an "epileptic youth, whose eyes, like Christ's, are wide."[150] The youth "has been bound / round with fear," and only Christ can bring him solace in this "prologue to the resurrection."[151] In true Mariani fashion, the conclusion speaks to both the present and eternal, the mundane and divine: "first the old fears descending, then dejection / and the dunning sameness in the daily going round and round of things. / Then a light like ten thousand suns that flames the brain and brings / another kind of death with it, and then—once more—the daily round / again. But changed now by what the blind beseeching eye has found."[152] These displacements of the personal, applied in hindsight to Mariani's earlier, more personal poems, help elucidate his aesthetic: for Mariani, of most importance "is the sense of experience . . . as a way of suggesting that we human beings are all in this together."[153] Mariani's ability to renew biblical narratives, while also building more personal ones, reveals a continual self-questioning, a reflection certainly in the Jesuit spiritual tradition.

---

148. Ibid., 137.
149. Ibid., 138.
150. Ibid.
151. Ibid.
152. Ibid., 138–9.
153. Paul Mariani, 2012.

Mariani offers a unique nexus of the contemporary Catholic literary experience. He is a Catholic writer whose scholarship has analyzed work by Catholic and secular poets, allowing the concerns of those independent spheres to be complimentary rather than stifling. Mariani was the poetry editor of *America* between 2000 and 2006, publishing both Catholic and non-Catholic writers. Mariani speaks to a postconciliar breadth of catholicity, adding to Catholic and Christian writers "poets who have borrowed from the Christian tradition—from Chaucer and Marlowe and Shakespeare and Spencer and Milton to Thomas Hardy and Hart Crane and William Carlos Williams and Wallace Stevens and Theodore Roethke and Marianne Moore,"[154] or putting it in other words: "Many have been ransacking Catholic edifices for centuries for durable stone and stained glass."[155] Yet he also remembers and appreciates the universality of Latin Mass, noting "it felt good be included" in an international liturgical celebration.[156] Mariani recognizes the most recent translation's goal of returning to "the original meanings," but misses particular, more idiomatic expressions, including the previous phrasing at Communion.[157] The new language that precedes receipt of the Eucharist makes Mariani think "of a bad pun on roof as shelter, and the roof of the mouth, and so the word sticks every time I have said it."[158] For Mariani, the new translation arises out of good theological intention, but results in poor poetry. He will "respond as everyone else in our dwindling parish responds" by using the new language, but thinks the retranslation "doesn't seem like a particularly creative solution to the problematics of our protean languages."[159]

Mariani's thoughts introduce a curious paradox: the Church's attempt to produce a translation closer to the accuracy of the Latin Rite has resulted in a movement away from the same poetics of ritual that defined that earlier translation. Granted, writers like Hansen, Dubus, and Mariani have experienced both preconciliar and postconciliar liturgical traditions, so the new translation must seem like a half-hearted return to the romanticized earlier Latin, but their hesitations speak to another concern: what is the active role of the Catholic writer in the liturgy of culture and experience? Mariani's canon offers the possibility that the Catholic writer might

154. "Interview with Paul Mariani," para. 17.

155. Mariani, *God*, 228.

156. Paul Mariani, 2012.

157. Ibid.

158. Ibid.

159. Ibid.

exist in fidelity to the Church while simultaneously mining the personal and the domestic to extend the moment of Mass beyond the rows of pews. A synthesis of these three writers has become the prototype for the rising generation of writers working from the Catholic tradition.

Chapter Five

Interrogating Tradition
Contemporary Catholic Voices

SANDRA M. GILBERT'S FOREWORD to the anthology *Reconciling Feminism and Catholicism* includes an anaphoric litany of reasons why "I am and am not a Catholic."[1] Her praises and laments are common among postconciliar Catholics who have lapsed: she attended Catholic schools, admired the physicality of beautiful churches that are "stone forests of yearning, emblems of our human desire for something we don't have here and now in the flesh,"[2] appreciated "the solemn liturgy of the mass," and respected the "brilliant argumentation of the Church fathers."[3] Yet she critiques the subordination of women that upends any of her intellectual or emotional attempts to return to the Church.

Gilbert's prose reveals the tendency toward hyperbole in preconciliar memoir and memory by postconciliar writers. Recalling Ash Wednesday, where the "priest, in liturgical purple signifying death and grief, loomed mysteriously behind the railing," she "remember[ed] the ferocity, or so it seemed to me, with which his thumb dug into my forehead" and "the grim satisfaction, so it seemed to me, with which he muttered his sacred Latin phrases more *at* me than *to* me."[4] Gilbert's appositive hedging, though, could be lost on a reader. Her imagery is consistent with the stereotypical

---

1. Gilbert, "Foreword," xi.
2. Ibid.
3. Ibid., xii.
4. Ibid., xiv.

presentation of religious characters in literature as living projections of all ecclesiastical criticisms.

Gilbert's anthology moves these simplifications, and in comparison Hopkins's "To R. B." feels quite applicable to the paradoxical feminist relationship to the Church: the pull of origin and ritual, and yet the push of "resistance."[5] The wide boundaries of feminism continue a common theme in postconciliar Catholic literature: the paradox of faith and critique, resulting in sustained interrogation of tradition. The writers in Gilbert's volume share traits observed by Ross Labrie as applying to many postconciliar writers: "Less concerned about their transgressions from ecclesiastical practice and authority and considerably less focused on the church's role in transforming society, they are instead self-conscious about their upbringing as Catholic and tenuous about their beliefs as adults in a society inclined to scoff at the persistence of religious belief."[6] The contrast with Anita Gandolfo's previously mentioned observation of the classic form of the Catholic novel—"a product of the preconciliar Church, which measured the worth of fiction by its literary fidelity to doctrine and dogma and its value as an evangelizing force"—is sharp.[7] Gandolfo notes that postconciliar Catholic literature often "challenges the Church, for [the literature and theology] asks that the experience of people be the focus of ministry."[8] Although acknowledging the usefulness of Catholic contemporary literature to "[express] the unique situation of the Church in the United States at this particular historical moment," Gandolfo concludes that "From the evidence of fiction, postconciliar Catholicism seems mired in the residual ethos of the old paradigm while unable to effectively envision the emergent culture of the new."[9] Her now decades-old assessment needs updating.

The writers already profiled in *The Fine Delight* have shown varieties of postconciliar Catholic culture, and their similarities and differences should reinforce the continual fragmentation of Catholic experience. It would be incorrect, though, to mistake a lack of uniformity for a lack of vision. Peggy Rosenthal, in *The Poets' Jesus*, shows that literary splintering is to be expected. Rosenthal's expansive study moves beyond Catholic poets, but her points are applicable in this narrow context. Rosenthal

5. Ibid., xxxvi.
6. Labrie, *The Catholic*, 277.
7. Gandolfo, *Testing*, xi.
8. Ibid., 209.
9. Ibid., 206.

finds that "theological" interest in Christ's "status as truly divine and truly human" is what "charges" the imagination of contemporary poets in the same way it inspired "the Johannine writers, like Clement of Alexandria, like Ephrem."[10] Contemporary poets are inspired by "finding in the Word made flesh a figure in whom to situation the inherently mysterious human condition of living two natures at once, flesh and spirit."[11] The Christ paradox becomes a way to embrace the beautiful complexity of existence, and is at once a means toward poetic and life freedom, as well as a call to concerted reflection. Rosenthal tracks the poetic evolution of Jesus in previous centuries, from his Romantic-era elevation to postmodern undermining, to identify the particular formation of Christ on the current page: writers comfortable dramatizing the humanity of Jesus. The result is a literary paradox that sounds similar to the experience of Catholic writers in this volume. These Christian writers might document their personal struggles with faith, but those interrogations are largely framed through contextual and cultural lenses, rather than deep critiques of the entire Christian faith. These writers are "stimulated by the creative tension of carrying on this probing enterprise in a culture that is often fearful of even touching on the questions, [and] they can confidently explore where and how transcendence might be in our world through the figure of Jesus Present."[12] Contemporary writers form their own peculiar literary subculture, marked more by shared experiences, dogmatic interrogation, and idiosyncratic appreciation of ritual and belief than steadfast allegiance to an institution.

The "transcendence" shown by contemporary Catholic writers comes in diverse forms, and sometimes uses Catholicism as a pivot point. Essayist Patrick Madden converted from Catholicism to Mormonism as an undergraduate at Notre Dame, though the shift was "not really a rejection of Catholicism or its fundamental tenets."[13] Madden's spiritual sense is framed by an acceptance of mystery, of humility in the face of divinity, and it is "likely that the Catholic tradition is more deeply engrained in me than the Mormon tradition."[14] Madden often speaks of "wonder," and the essays in *Quotidiana* (2010) reinforce the desire to pursue the breadth and depth of associations. Madden finds his chosen form of the essay as Cath-

---

10. Rosenthal, *Jesus*, 166.

11. Ibid.

12. Ibid., 167.

13. "Interview with Patrick Madden," para. 6.

14. Ibid.

olic, identifying Montaigne's precedent as "a believer who was unafraid of doubt . . . [who] could entertain contrary notions without losing his core faith."[15] Montaigne's form of the essay is essential, since the medium "[gets] us closer to the naked individual spinning through the dizzying world, naked and honest, trying to make sense of things."[16]

Madden's essays channel the wonder and joy of Catholic intellectual thought noted by Rev. James Martin. Madden whirls through laughter, Rush lyrics, and death with verve. The more he discovers, the more he wishes to know. In "The Infinite Suggestiveness of Common Things," Madden wonders at "authors who wrote from seemingly insignificant, overlooked, transient things, experiences, and ideas, who were able to find within their everyday, unexceptional lives inspiration for essaying."[17] Madden sounds like he might have Hopkins's notebooks in front of him as he lauds the quotidian, the everyday, further revealing his Catholic tendency to see the prosaic world in new light.

Perhaps Madden's most Catholic literary trait is his concurrent love for, and subversion of, litanies of words. In "Garlic" he playfully includes "A List, in Spanish, of the Various Fruits and Vegetables Available in Different Times of the Year at Mercado Modelo, as Given Me by My Father-in-Law Some Months after Our Visit to the Market."[18] Readers conditioned to the joys of the essay form will navigate through the list and find beauty in the letters and the connecting story. Like other writers in *The Fine Delight*, Madden finds transcendence in lower gears, an observation of a world made of words.

The life of Montaigne has convinced Madden that "it's a firmer faith that's weathered some resistance."[19] Madden's maxim applies to, if not enlightens, the writing of Hansen, Dubus, and Mariani, all writers who transitioned from preconciliar to postconciliar thought and writing. Yet some artists in this final section were born after Vatican II, so their tensions of liturgy and language are different. While it might be tempting to identify the period between Vatican II and 2011's retranslation as a viable Catholic literary period, the variations of Catholicism practiced, and retreated from, resist singular definition. Yet the following writers share personal and liturgical tensions with the Church, while also implicitly and explic-

15. Ibid., para. 10.
16. Ibid., para. 14.
17. Madden, *Quotidiana*, 2.
18. Ibid., 65.
19. "Interview with Patrick Madden," para. 19.

itly voicing appreciation for certain ecclesiastical elements, and remaining fascinated with the life of Christ.

Unlike Hansen, Dubus, and Mariani—all lifelong, practicing Catholics—these contemporary writers are diverse in their Catholic identities: some still practice, others are lapsed, while others waver between faith and skepticism. They share common experiences and language, though they reveal a literary and personal rejection of superficial Catholicism, and their writing and ideas reveal further nuance and quality in new Catholic writing.

Paul Lisicky

As Waldmeir and others have shown, Catholic literary ritual is subsumed with the importance of the physical form: the body as artifice, as expression of emotion and intellect. Joanne Pierce notes the transition of the body from the traditionally scriptural focus on the body of Christ—both in life and in resurrection—toward the body as Christian object, one marked by "purification" and "ordeal": "both of these rituals focus on the body, and the use of physical elements as mediatorial elements of God's presence with the self-communication to human beings."[20] The human body becomes a locus of conflict: it is necessary that we all have bodies, that we act with those bodies, and yet the biological and physiological needs of those bodies might become incongruous with the doctrinal beliefs of Catholics. Jennifer Knust continues Pierce's inquiry, identifying the particular theological strain that results from the conception of the body: "there is a tension in much of early Christian discourse between an affirmation of the human body, its privileged place in salvation, and a deeply felt ambivalence about the possibility that our bodies, especially our bodily desires, will betray us."[21]

Granted, the focus of Knust and Pierce is on early and medieval Christianity, but the grounding in Pauline discourse makes the discussion necessary for modern theological considerations of body. Knust's observation that "Paul longed for a resurrection body that could replace these limited, corrupted bodies subject to sin and death, yet he insisted that the body and creation were to be included in the redemption to come" is prescient: the body is not simply to be discarded, but rather transformed,

20. Pierce, "Marginal," 59.
21. Knust, "Body–Critical," 68.

reformed, and made better.[22] The material, physical body is more than simply a location of conflict and tension. The body is an organic theology in and of itself: "the lush sensuality of the body is capable of steering the gaze away from the transcendental God back toward earthly realms, where the human being's 'fallen' nature is drawn as apple is to ground."[23]

Inquires into particularly Catholic conceptions of sexuality, then, inevitably arise from constructions of the body. John Paul II's *Theology of the Body*, his encyclopedic attempt to articulate a Catholic theology of sexuality, reveals the complications of sexual inquiry within a Catholic framework. Poet Donora Hillard's 2010 volume shares the work's title, but attempts a feminist response through fragmentation of form and memory. Yet even earlier, Luke Timothy Johnson reacted with skepticism to the lectures; even if a theology of the body must intersect a theology of sexuality, "Do not the sins of gluttony and drunkenness and sloth have as much to do with the body as fornication, and are not all the forms of avarice also dispositions of the body?"[24] Johnson calls for more breadth, "a more generous appreciation of the way sexual energy pervades our interpersonal relations and creativity—including the life of prayer! —and a fuller understanding of covenanted love as life-giving and sustaining in multiple modes of parenting, community building, and world enhancement."[25] A theology of the body does not dismiss sexuality. Rather, theology of the body recognizes the complexity of sexuality. Johnson ultimately concludes that while John Paul's work is necessary, "it reveals the same deep disinterest in the ways the experience of married people, and especially women . . . might inform theology and the decision-making process of the church."[26] Johnson's call echoes much lay Catholic sentiment: can a theology of sexuality truly be honest and pragmatic unless that theology is grounded in the realities and experiences of actual sexual practice?

To be certain, Johnson's focus in his reaction to *Theology of the Body* is not grounded in a Catholic redefinition of sexuality to encapsulate homosexuality, though that content is an unavoidable evolution. A theology of sexuality, of the body, will likely only be pastorally successful if it is observant rather than prescriptive, focused on detailing the varieties of sexual experience and then, once cataloged, constructing a response. The

22. Ibid.
23. Ziegler, "Medieval," 11.
24. Johnson, "Disembodied," 113.
25. Ibid., 118.
26. Ibid., 120

place of homosexuality within that theological canon was brought into focus with Vatican II and the subsequent *Declaration on Certain Questions Concerning Sexual Ethics,* published in 1975. Reaction from some continues to be complicated: Andrew Sullivan writes that the preconciliar position was that homosexual acts "were condemned in exactly the same way and for exactly the same reasons as premarital heterosexual sex, adultery, masturbation, or contracepted sex . . . [homosexual acts] failed to provide for the essential conjugal and procreative context for sexual expression."[27] Sullivan finds even less clarity in postconciliar positions.

Theologies of the body and sexuality are further complicated when presented in works of literature, texts of creative intent. These theologies are dramatized at the analogical level through the themes of identity formation and building in Paul Lisicky's 2002 memoir, *Famous Builder.* The collected essays are threaded by theme, location, and experience. The creative nonfiction genre affords narrative experimentation, which therefore complicates the presentation of a single identity. The Catholic memoirist, in particular, must operate on several analogical and literary levels: because the Catholic experience is so grounded in community and ritual, attempts to show an individual identity are tempered by the experiences of a whole. This theme of identity puts a particular spin on a perennial question of the genre: is memoir the true identity of the writer, or a representation of that identity? Must the Catholic postconciliar memoirist be even more deliberate with contextual detail, as to best frame the communal portion of the identity when such traits appear in flux? Might reasonable readers accept the fictionalization of narrative necessary to present a profluent story to an audience, including Lee Gutkind's concept of narrative compression? These concerns are particularly appropriate to postconciliar Catholic literature, which is already created in a moment rife with reconsiderations of language and faith identity.

Lisicky is an ideal writer to engage these tensions. An accomplished liturgical composer in his teens and early twenties, whose music "still appears in hymnals and songbooks all across the country," Lisicky interrogates the faith act through the lens of performance: where public and private faiths intersect.[28] His liturgical past occurred during a "brief, fleeting period in which there was so much hope and possibility about the church, before the institution settled back into its fearful, conservative ways."[29] Yet

27. Sullivan, *Virtually,* 7.
28. Lisicky, *Famous,* 149.
29. Ibid.

the faith remains embedded in Lisicky's worldview and prose. He recalls visiting his ailing mother, who still "insisted on making a sandwich" for him, though he could see the inherent difficulty.[30] Reflecting Dubus, he would like to call her "gesture . . . Eucharistic," noting that he "needed to let her make the sandwich," finding a certain "beauty to brokenness, to all the selves we'd been (or almost been) over time."[31] Lisicky's most consistent trope—the space of homes and buildings, present in *Lawnboy* (2006), *Famous Builder*, *The Burning House* (2011) and *Unbuilt Projects* (2012)—speaks to an awareness of positioning one's self, of localizing identity after recognizing the burden of place. In much the same way, the postconciliar Catholic writer must place himself in many "houses": the institutional Church, the house of his own body and corporeal desires, and the house of Christ. Gay Catholic postconciliar writers, in particular, have difficulty finding a sense of home: if the Church abhors the sin but not the sinner, to echo Johnson, why is homosexuality more troubling to certain Catholics than other temptations of the body, even temptations that can cause physical harm to others?

Lisicky's composing past is reflected in his focus on the performative elements of Mass, where "texts insist on being sung."[32] Lisicky extols the work "of the liberal Dutch church, the music and texts of Bernard Huijbers, Huub Oosterhuis, Antoine Oomen, and Tom Lowenthal. I've loved that work since I was a teenager, its dignity and common-sense, its lack of sentimentality, its respect for social justice."[33] A spoken Sanctus "thuds along" with "no highs and lows, no contours"; when much of Mass is already "fragmentary . . . Responses and acclamations need the emphasis of melody and harmony or else they're swallowed up."[34] Communal singing means a unity of voice and soul, becoming "part of the larger body."[35] Lisicky finds a corporeal paradox: "At the same time, it's very intimate. We get to meet our own bodies again, as well as the bodies of the people to our right and our left."[36]

That sense of bodily transformation might explain Lisicky's attraction to the work of Flannery O'Connor, a writer concerned with "disruption":

30. "Interview with Paul Lisicky," para. 4.
31. Ibid.
32. Ibid., para. 6.
33. Ibid., para. 22.
34. Ibid., para. 6.
35. Ibid., para. 7.
36. Ibid.

"Grace doesn't often happen without confrontation, especially confrontation between strangers."[37] Equally important is "the relationship between irreverence and reverence in her stories."[38] Lisicky finds another duality of "grandeur and mystery alongside its down-to-earthness" that makes Catholicism so appealing to writers. In a literary sense, Lisicky is continually "drawn to . . . [a Catholic] space for its questions, its room for contradiction."[39]

"Wisdom Has Built Herself a House," a central essay in *Famous Builder*, documents contradiction in the suburban American, postconciliar "New Catholic" experience. The essay dramatizes the period's liturgical movement toward ecumenism, the formation of Catholic identity beyond confirmation, and Catholic sexuality. The year is 1975, and the location is Lisicky's southern New Jersey church, "(Correction: Parish Center)," during the Fifth Sunday in Ordinary Time.[40] The mood is clearly relaxed: "casual behavior seems oddly in keeping with [the] surroundings" of the church, which is a "starkly modern, circular affair" with "abstract banners in every conceivable size and color—fishes, wafers, lopsided chalices— hang[ing] from the industrial black ceiling."[41] Lisicky, a gifted teenage liturgical musician, feels at home with these "fellow parishioners, [who] love to flout tradition and convention," celebrating without "a kneeling bench or a crucifix in sight."[42] The attitude is distinctly postconciliar, a time "before the deeply conservative Pope John II puts a damper on the party."[43] The play of "party" with "celebration" is important: Lisicky and his peers "are the new Catholics: rebellious, ironic, sophisticated, sexy."[44]

This "new" Catholicism is marked by "receiv[ing] Communion in the hand years before we've been given the Bishop's green light."[45] Lisicky and the other musicians "struggle through bootlegged hymns from the radical Dutch church," most notably a revision of Psalm 13, "which is entirely absent of direct references to God, the Lord, or any higher power."[46]

37. Ibid., para. 12.
38. Ibid.
39. Ibid., para. 17.
40. Lisicky, *Famous*, 108.
41. Ibid., 107–8.
42. Ibid., 108.
43. Ibid.
44. Ibid., 109.
45. Ibid., 108.
46. Ibid.

The lyrics are more reminiscent of seventies-era popular music than devotional works: "Even then I'll cling to you, cling to you, cling tight to you, whether you want me or not."[47]

Lisicky reflects from the perspective of a progressive youth, one likely thankful for the more upbeat celebration of Mass. Music becomes an identifying element, with local Jewish residents referring to the parish as a nightclub. Lisicky remembers when "Mass [was celebrated] in the chapel of the Diocesan nursing home," where "we often burst into spontaneous, hearty applause" in response to the spiritual power of music.[48] The evolution in musical performance is complemented by, and perhaps representative of, a postconciliar cultural shift, at least in this particular diocese. Even the traditional musical director is "friendly with the wildest priests in the diocese . . . she calls them Vince or Joe, something which, no matter how open-minded I am, seems delightfully transgressive."[49]

Music becomes metonymic for the new look at liturgical language prompted by that earlier translation, as well as a distinguishing element of the faith. Lisicky reinforces his Catholic identity through a negation of other denominations. One music teacher "is anything but a Roman."[50] Lisicky finds her musical catalog "a little stodgy" and "is grateful to be Catholic" while "she's so . . . *Presbyterian*."[51] Catholicism is yoked with progression: "*We* use guitars and electric basses. *We're* smart enough to know that the old forms are falling away."[52] Lisicky frames his identity in music: "I spend Saturday afternoons alone in the dank music library of the Blackwood Catholic Center, sitting cross-legged on the orange-gold carpet, where I listen to scratchy, already outdated recordings . . . while my classmates hang out at the Echelon mall, looking for dates."[53]

Lisicky's presentation of music is never far from his portrayals of sexuality, and the crux of his memoir is the recognition of his own homosexuality. One of the music directors tells Lisicky about "another composer, a former Scientologist and current lay Franciscan, who has a boyfriend on the side," and later, another former music minister who moves in with a

47. Ibid.
48. Ibid., 112.
49. Ibid., 113.
50. Ibid., 119.
51. Ibid.
52. Ibid.
53. Ibid., 114.

man.[54] Music becomes a paradox: a nod toward tradition, and yet the possibility for new expression. Lisicky publishes his original compositions, and his choir travels to Cape May to perform during the Holy Thursday Mass. He is nervous— "I must be perfect for the Bishop" —but the performance is a success: "we have become something else, something elevated and other, transcending our limitations. We're celebrating all that's good and right about the world, all that's possible."[55] Filled with the optimism that celebration brings, Lisicky admits a certain innocence, the hope that since "the church was changing," including the possibility that "priests someday could marry . . . then couldn't I be understood and loved by the world around me?"[56]

Lisicky attends a different church during the summer, where he is "stupefied by the flat-footedness of the ritual. Ancient pole fans oscillate throughout the sanctuary, working to cool us with their feeble whirr. The grim monsignor trudges through the Mass."[57] Again, music is integral: "the *other* can only be embodied through the agency of art."[58] Later, Lisicky attends a workshop at a Catholic college in Wisconsin. There is no mention of a priest at Mass; rather, folk composers "trade guitar riffs, sing reedy, gender-bending harmonies" while "light cascades through the stained-glass windows of the saints, pooling blue, red, and yellow on the floor."[59] Lisicky concludes that this was "the most engaging, innovative Mass I've ever been to in my life."[60]

The wide publication of his compositions ensures that Lisicky will never forget his Catholic youth; "more than once, wandering into church while visiting my parents, I've heard a choir struggling through one of my responsorial psalms."[61] Lisicky admits that he has "kept this side of my personality hidden from my friends, some of my very closest friends, for reasons that are not quite clear to me."[62] He hesitates to "[work] on

54. Ibid., 113.
55. Ibid., 123–4.
56. Ibid., 131.
57. Ibid., 133.
58. Ibid.
59. Ibid., 138.
60. Ibid.
61. Ibid., 149.
62. Ibid.

new music" for fear of hearing "charges about colluding with the enemy," a Church with complicated positions regarding homosexuality.[63]

Lisicky concludes the essay wondering whether "my decision to turn away from music has come at a cost."[64] The lost opportunities include the possibility of "nam[ing] what we'd *want* God to be, even if He or She remains elusive and intractable, resisting our definitions."[65] Nearly a decade after that essay's original publication, Lisicky remains cautiously optimistic. He now attends Mass "at an urban parish, where progressive politics and progressive theology are very much alive. Lay people of all colors, income levels, and sexual orientations are involved in the liturgy."[66] Lisicky prefers talking about the Church at the local, parish level, where "the story's more complicated": "the parish is where grace is actually transacted, especially in the liturgy. There are good people out there, very quietly, very humbly, doing their part to change things."[67] Like many Catholics who hold deep doctrinal disagreements with the Church, Lisicky "felt a terrible pang whenever I walked by a church and heard singing coming from inside. It's home to me . . . The rhythm of the liturgy is really intrinsic to how I think, to how I make art. I miss it when I'm away from it for too long. It's exile."[68]

Lisicky laments "when we hear people talking too easily, too certainly, about the divine," fearing that those "overworked phrases . . . are expected to stand in for the hard work of seeing, naming."[69] He echoes O'Connor's critical calls for fiction that upsets and disrupts, and his growing work furthers the necessary conversation about contemporary Catholic sexuality, localizing that conversation in the powerful regions of home: body, song, and soul.

Joe Bonomo

Joe Bonomo's creative non-fiction reconstitutes postconciliar Catholic memory, finding the sacrament of confession an apt analogy. Bonomo does not remember the content of his youthful confessions: "mostly I

63. Ibid.
64. Ibid.
65. Ibid.
66. "Interview with Paul Lisicky," para. 9.
67. Ibid., para. 10.
68. Ibid., para. 20.
69. Ibid., para. 23.

remember talking toward a silhouette. And that process of conversation, of muttering toward a vaguely recognizable human figure, is a crucial connection to writing."[70] The physical space of the traditional confessional was perfect for "finding the right words through trial and error, coming in prepared but also being open to digression and, ideally, for epiphany of a sort," as in the essayistic act.[71] In "After Cornell," Bonomo reflects on these early experiences in opening one's self for that silhouette. His entry was a "grope in the darkness."[72] That absence of light allows the penitent to "depart from the corpus"; the inability to see the priest is necessary since "the confessor must shed anatomy's garment."[73] Bonomo, in reflection, found the process imperfect, partially because of setting: "the small, enormous dark box behind the plum-velvet curtain, where whispers strayed like incense, and where the body threatened to dissipate."[74]

The postconciliar, face-to-face confessional style "introduced a newer ... fearful prospect: intimacy."[75] The traditional darkness and lack of a body was comforting, but now Bonomo had "to thrust myself, flesh, bones, and pounding blood at once, toward the vulnerability of repenting frailties," and that "seemed at odds with the liberating casualness surrounding the church's new policy."[76] Although students at his Catholic school are given the choice, Bonomo felt the confessional box "seemed akin to stepping into the Old Age, of black, black, black," and opts for the new style with "genial" Father Paul.[77] That confession was held in a softly lit room, where "I was not conceding my sins on my knees as had been the custom; rather, I was a casual supplicant, sitting with my legs crossed, as was the Father."[78] It was less confession and more dialogue; most importantly, there "was no mystery."[79] Now an "informal discussion in the light," the previously solemn sacrament had been "robbed . . . of its sacred unknowns."[80]

70. "Interview with Joe Bonomo," para. 3.
71. Ibid.
72. Bonomo, "After," 162.
73. Ibid.
74. Ibid., 163.
75. Ibid., 164.
76. Ibid.
77. Ibid., 165.
78. Ibid., 166.
79. Ibid.
80. Ibid., 167.

The trope of space is an essential one for Bonomo, whose first book, *Installations* (2008), collected poetic meditations on rooms. Bonomo conceives the collection as "rooms in [an] imagined museum [that] become sacramental places, places where mystery and the mystifying occur, or can occur."[81] In "Occasional Prayer," Bonomo returns to the trope of space when invoking the Matthean words of Christ to pray in private. His early prayer was admittedly self-centered, much like the hurried, misguided prayers of Jake Barnes in *The Sun Also Rises*. When Bonomo later returned to the deliberate practice of prayer, the act created a sense of weightlessness and dislocation: "after Eucharist when I'd return to the pew and kneel in silence, press my hands together so tight that they'd whiten, and focus so intensely on saying the Lord's Prayer . . . I felt as if I'd become invisible to myself."[82] The essay examines the paradox of prayer: an act equally predisposed to selfish and unselfish motives. Prayer can be deep and focused on family, friends, and community, or, "more frequently," it is prosaic: "that the White Sox will bring the tying runner home from third. That the DVD + R disks will format."[83] Bonomo is able to create a new private space for himself in prayer, and yet he realizes it is often "too easy to simply close the door behind me after praying, the thrown light switch a darkened synapse gap that widens, stranding me further from prayer as a daily necessity."[84] He wonders if, post-prayer, "am I really in the same house?"[85] Bonomo even appropriates the space trope when discussing his process in non-fiction: "writing an essay is like building a house without knowing in advance how many rooms or floors you'll put in."[86]

In "Swooning at St. Andrew's," Bonomo returns to the connection between Catholicism and memoir, writing about a girl who faints during daily Mass in Catholic school. Bonomo is clear that the particulars of the moment are hazy, just as "the mustiness of the church . . . confounded her small body."[87] That fall was "shocking" because usually the only sound is faith, "the music of wishing to believe."[88] The sound when her "head slammed into the pew" was one of the few times "in church

81. "Interview with Joe Bonomo," para. 8.

82. Bonomo, "Occasional," 18.

83. Ibid., 21.

84. Ibid., 20.

85. Ibid.

86. "Interview with Joe Bonomo," para. 10.

87. Bonomo, "Swooning," 7.

88. Ibid.

when body became body."[89] Catherine's fallen form is sketched with the gravity of martyrdom: "Beneath the nuns and a single giving girl waving missalettes and handkerchiefs at Catherine's sweaty face, there beamed from the now-conscious girl a look of simple but absolute contentment, of dazed and absorbed peace, and pleasure."[90] Her face held the "gaze of ecstasy."[91] The complexity of that countenance remained with Bonomo, and, thematically, placement of this scene within the church is essential. While this daily Mass is characterized elsewhere in the essay as pedestrian in its repetition for these children, this event blurs the lines between real and unreal, acceptable and unacceptable.

"The God Blurred World" continues this postconciliar shading. The Stations of the Cross were "cinematic drama" for students stuck in boring classrooms.[92] Sunday services blended into each other, but Holy Days "arch[ed] into a kind of cohesion: the pantomime of Easter; the stripping down of the altar during Lent; the slender green palms we brought home to hang, drooping and ignored, in the kitchen."[93] The Stations of the Cross even quieted the "tense playground politics," since students knew they had been "lifted into something grand."[94] The only school experience that came close was when Sister Nena "would ask us to lay our heads down on our desktops" while she read to them, creating the same feeling of bodiless haze Bonomo experienced when Catherine collapsed in the church.[95]

That similar awareness of body is another reason Bonomo was attracted to the Stations. He recalls the simple "Sixties-style generic reliefs of dark brown wood and shiny, gold-tinted metal" that became powerful through the accompanying narrative.[96] "Thin," his "head hung in anguish . . . [and] forced to carry a cross," Christ captivated the children.[97] Bonomo embeds the words of Ingmar Bergman, whose own father was a Lutheran pastor; the inclusion is consistent with Bonomo's perception of the Mass as a performance, but one inevitably under deliberate control. Much as the young narrator might experience an overwhelming film, he

89. Ibid.

90. Ibid., 8.

91. Ibid.

92. Bonomo, "God," 93.

93. Ibid.

94. Ibid.

95. Ibid.

96. Ibid., 94.

97. Ibid.

left the Stations charged with the "wholeness" of that fragmented Passion narrative.[98]

Bonomo's adoration for the ritual was tempered by the "bureaucracy and backstage machinations" of being an altar server.[99] He expected an "exotic portal of sacred vessels and vestments," but instead discovered "a flimsy calendar . . . fluorescent tubes and cardboard boxes stacked unceremoniously onto wobbling, cramped shelves," not to mention "Communion wafers, pre-Consecration, wait[ing] in drab plastic bags."[100] The reflective indictment is complicated, though, by the admitted naivety of the narrator. That Mass needs to be celebrated with human hands and populated by human misgivings should not debunk its content; rather, it should uplift it, enhance the fragmented beauty of the ceremony, and appeal to the same interest in the marginalized Bonomo discusses elsewhere in the essay.

"The God Blurred World" is certainly written by a memoirist who finds the material and method for his non-fiction formed by his childhood Catholicism, even if he has since moved from practice. Mass "was a magnificent introduction for me to a fundamental aspiration, the translation of the untranslatable" through a "panorama of the aural, the written, the theatrical, the visual, the plastic arts, which all nearly overwhelmed my nascent senses."[101] This "Spirit of Story"[102] replaced a daily belief in the dogma of the Church, yet Bonomo admits that "Steeples cast long shadows."[103] The cultural tattoo of Catholicism, specifically the act and pleasure of prayer, is "what's driven me back into church the several odd, if intense times," since prayer satisfies the "need to run away from myself, that desire itself feeling more and more as the preening of egotism."[104] And the material of Catholicism, "sin, and forgiveness, and benevolent treatment of fellow humans, of compassion and, maybe above all, of humility" are "bedrocks upon which a writer can create, engage, and essay his or her self and place"; writers like Bonomo, whose lyric lines make skepticism an act of linguistic reverence.[105]

98. Ibid., 95.

99. Ibid., 96.

100. Ibid.

101. Ibid., 94.

102. Ibid.

103. Bonomo, "Seams," 146.

104. Bonomo, "Occasional," 22.

105. "Interview with Joe Bonomo," para. 15.

Mary Biddinger

Mary Biddinger's 2011 chapbook, *Saint Monica*, connects sexuality with the postconciliar tendency to reconsider the personage of saints. Iconographic representations of saints occur in numerous forms, from mass-produced figurines and images to biographies steeped in legend, making them especially rich fodder for postconciliar writers. Biddinger's subject, the mother of St. Augustine, is projected into the present. The chapbook is a unique take on the communion of saints: these women *become* St. Monica because they are likely recipients of her patronage. In "Saint Monica Burns It Down" and other poems, Biddinger brings Monica to the present Midwest, with images of "a warm Budweiser in each pocket," two terriers "holed up / in ruts beneath the shed" and "reflections / of his white undershirt illuminating / the window frame."[106] Biddinger's collection resists allegory, yet rightfully so: since Augustine's writings are our prime source of information about Monica, her mythology has created a malleable persona. "Saint Monica Stays the Course," one of the collection's prose poems, dramatizes the May Crowning procession at a Catholic school. Sister Cathleen has instructed the girls "in the correct way to proceed" and warns them to "Keep your eyes on the Virgin" and to "not stop marching."[107] Monica is part of this procession; her mother "had stayed up all night stitching an empire-waist smock with puff sleeves that were perky but not bulbous."[108] The poem includes expected practical instructions—look straight, not into the pews; do not become nervous and sick; clasp "your bunch of daffodils"—but is augmented by imagined, absurd admonitions for the event, as well as the probable later experiences of these women as adults.[109] Monica and the girls are to ignore everything from concussion to menstruation, with the nun's only advice to say "two Hail Marys and one Glory Be, and get over it."[110] That same advice is given when the girls might "feel like [they] will die after ten-hour shifts waiting tables, stray husbands pinching your ass and snapping your bra strap," or if "your fiancé slams you against a wall and you suffer a concussion upon impact, breaking your glasses, keep marching to the bathroom with a bottle of Windex and a roll

106. Biddinger, *Saint*, 36.
107. Ibid., 13.
108. Ibid.
109. Ibid.
110. Ibid.

of paper towels and make that crooked mirror shine."[111] The girls will be ready because they "have done this before."[112]

Biddinger ends the poem without a return to the Marian procession, a clever move to blur the reality of that Monica's future. Other older Monicas, though, are less lucky. In "Saint Monica of the Gauze," her "room is red with iodine" from apparent spousal abuse.[113] Monica needs to help the police "find the bones" of a murdered childhood friend in "Saint Monica of the Woods."[114] Yet Biddinger returns to her jocular treatment of post-conciliar Catholic school milieu in "Saint Monica and the Devil's Place," a euphemism for the Hell warned by Sister Rita. This particular Monica would tempt eternal damnation "if it meant one hour alone with Kevin McMillan in the falling-down barn."[115] Yet a later poem, "Saint Monica Gives It Up," is more complicated. The unnamed plurality of "They say chastity is a gift" are the nuns at the school, but they "have never seen / Kevin McMillan bare / to the waist in an apple tree."[116] Tempted, Monica's hair "nearly / unraveled itself," but she grabbed her Saint Christopher medal and found other diversions to temper her desire.[117] Twenty years later, she still dreams of Kevin, intimating that fantasy never became a reality. Monica did not "give it up."[118]

A theological curiosity in the collection is "Saint Monica Takes Communion Twice," where Monica "just got back in line and did it all over again."[119] The poem is a metaphor for the malleability of Monica's identity within the collection, as well as traditional tendency to blur the lives of saints through elegies. "The first time it was the girl with hair tucked behind her ears. The second time it was the girl with hair in her face, hands unfolded, bra strap peeking out from the neckline of her sweater":[120] these two identities unfold through the rest of the prose poem, living conditional lives until the more likely conclusion: "could it be some Sunday in Ordinary Time, the Eucharistic minister with hair tucked behind her ears,

111. Ibid., 14.
112. Ibid.
113. Ibid., 11.
114. Ibid., 34.
115. Ibid., 17.
116. Ibid., 19.
117. Ibid.
118. Ibid.
119. Ibid., 30.
120. Ibid.

the Monica with hair in her face taking that long walk down the aisle, destined to turn around and do it all over again."[121]

Biddinger's Catholic themes in *O Holy Insurgency* (2012) are subtler, but build toward a new, distinct literary Catholicism through image. As in *Saint Monica*, there are moments of youthful reflection, when a narrator "had dreams of becoming a Carmelite / nun, spending every day with my onionskin / dyes and stitchery."[122] In this world, "There were wonders, but we didn't know / they were wonders, or that they belonged / to us."[123] The entire collection is written in that Johannine mode of wonder. In "A Singularity," "Sometimes there were common doves / that looked spectacular from far away."[124] Even imagery that arrives blurred becomes clear, as in "A Very Hard Time," when "in bed, / the headlights of an ancient / station wagon slashed across / my body, like a reverse fever."[125] Biddinger's narratives stretch beyond their inciting concreteness, reaching the paradoxically soft precision of prayer, no matter the winding narrative road.

The collective voice is present in many of these poems, as if the narrator is whispering shared memories to the reader, but often the narrator seems to be speaking to a specific other, likely "the man I love."[126] The cumulative result of the book's image and tone is a folk Catholicism in poetic form. In "A Diorama," a baby or form of a baby arrives, kept "quiet on my tiny breast."[127] The sign of a child is "strapped to your chest / with a frill of blue elastic from stray / underpants. *A second coming*, they said."[128] The collective voice makes even prosaic moments folkloric. In this imaginative Midwest one finds "all the trailer hitches gleaming like sins."[129] Faith arrives like a silent breeze, and is often misunderstood: "Was that *amen* you were saying? Or only / the shutters readying themselves for rain, / children steaming indoors from mines / they dug into the hillside. No, you said / *amend*. The alleluia was just imaginary."[130] A line from the title poem summarizes this Catholicism of the earthly flesh: "Every night we remake us /

121. Ibid., 31.
122. Biddinger, *Holy*, 6.
123. Ibid., 9.
124. Ibid., 43.
125. Ibid., 27.
126. Ibid., 61.
127. Ibid., 48.
128. Ibid., 49.
129. Ibid., 52.
130. Ibid., 54.

as our skin transubstantiates."[131] Biddinger's two Catholic themed collections reveal a writer lifting postconciliar language and texture from Mass in order to lift the tactile moments of relationships. The displacement is a careful interrogation, a poetic desire to let faith permeate spaces it might never reach.

Amanda Auchter

Amanda Auchter's sequence of saint poems in *The Glass Crib* offers another form of reverence for the canonized. While Biddinger is focused on reinvention, Auchter remains tied to the original lives and perceptions of the saints, but with particular focus on the corporeal. Auchter places herself in the Christian artistic tradition of the body as "a house for God," one that is "life-giving, but also one that is feared, desirous, and, above all, holy in both the ways it is fallible (human) and infallible (divine)."[132]

"Bring Splendor," the final section of the book, is the most infused with religious iconography and emotion. A woman considers adultery, but ultimately chooses to remain faithful. A mother implores her frustrated daughter to "offer it up," and she does, her "knees to the floor / [to] give it all back to the God / who asked me to bear it."[133] These characters struggle to remain faithful to God and family, and yet find salvation in those same places. "Bring Splendor" transitions from everyday flashes of faith to the travails of those later canonized into legend. Auchter's saints suffer, and they document this pain in first-person narratives. While Biddinger's Saint Monica becomes contemporary, Auchter's saints are "grit-pressed, obedient," aware of pain's marriage to penance.[134] Auchter wrote the saint sequence separately, but wanted to "bring across" the "larger themes" of the collection through these narratives."[135] She felt it was "essential" to include these saint-themed poems in the collection to "break" the "misconceptions" about the modern Catholic, both layperson and artist.[136] Another Catholic Texan, Mary Karr, has influenced Auchter, both in terms of Karr's charged personality and their shared liberal Catholicism.

131. Ibid., 41.
132. Amanda Auchter, 2012.
133. Auchter, *Glass*, 58–59.
134. Ibid., 60.
135. Amanda Auchter, 2012.
136. Ibid.

Auchter diverges from Karr with her sustained focus on the paradoxes of the Catholic body; particularly the forms of those who encapsulate polarities of the faith: "the blood, and the body, and the deaths, and the drama, and the opulence."[137] Saint Agatha's "flesh / spooled in [a knife's] rusted light."[138] She was "buried tasting / the earth" because she "would / not open" herself to the men requesting sex.[139] Agatha's virgin marriage to Christ is punished on secular Earth with torture, leading Auchter to end with a startling image, showing her awareness of Orazio Riminaldi's visual of the saint: "My breasts held up like loaves of bread, like two / cakes that stopped rising."[140] Motherhood becomes a Eucharistic action, a sacrament of giving now taken from Agatha.

Saint Cecilia, later incorrupt, remained with "roped hands" in a room with "no window, / but stone walls" for days until her death.[141] Like Agatha, Cecilia "died / looking into the earth," continuing the confluence of saint with nature, yet identifying a break in the metaphor, as her "body / that would not grow / back into moss and ash, my refusal / of rot."[142] Her incorruption is a testament to the metaphysical permanence of the body. Auchter's narrative about Saint Theresa is direct in this dislocation between form and soul: "There is no pain but the bodily."[143] Though her lungs are "ember-stung," and she sees her own face in the "bright approach" of an arrow, she speaks the language of acceptance: "Leave me now to breathe / the white embers. Leave me all on fire."[144] Saint Catherine of Alexandria's pain is even worse: "how my bones break, how the sling- / shot twangs and splits / my lip."[145] Auchter's taut language is populated with the language of the Passion: body, blood, bones. When Catherine "ask[s] of death," she does so not to stop the torture, but to embrace the beyond of her belief.[146]

These poems are not mere documentation of bodily suffering. "St. Bernadette Visits Our Lady of Lourdes" is suffused with gravity but not violence. Bernadette, in present tense, moves with simple actions but

137. Ibid.
138. Auchter, *Glass*, 61.
139. Ibid.
140. Ibid.
141. Ibid., 62.
142. Ibid.
143. Ibid., 66.
144. Ibid.
145. Ibid., 63.
146. Ibid.

addresses a second-person God: "Map my palm and I will find the water-course, / the floating moon. I will say there was a woman, / a cave's blue light. How far away was the darkness, / how each stone held the shape of your face."[147]

Auchter's saint personas feel designed to, as she writes elsewhere, "light the dark wick, / give this offering a name."[148] She does so in the powerful "Glossolalia," originally the titular poem of the book, where the lines "Let me speak of belief, / its small sounds in the distance, its ear / its tongue, the quiet murmur of flood and field" reveal the saintly in the common.[149] The poem is, in part, an apology: "If inside of me you find there are no vaulted / ceilings, no bright stained glass, but thimbles, buttons, a flask, let the illuminate still find me / as I thread and mend."[150] The poem contains whispers of Hopkins's tendency toward the lament: in "these past years / of hazards, wildfires, high winds," the speaker might "have lost track of you," but wishes to find God again through the "heat flicker of your voice, / a sign, the echo of apparition, the difficult / matter of flesh rising from thin air."[151] Nearing that "winter world" of Hopkins, this narrator recognizes that the word and grace of God is often seen in sideways moments, intangible reflections. While the narrator recognizes that she has "lost track" of God, the poem's complexities hinge on a dialogue with the divine. When she wonders if God has "lost your way of speaking," if he has "slid / inside my folded palms and slept," the words are not meant to be a complaint, but rather a continued admission of "my failure."[152] Auchter's most clever move is to phrase questions as statements, with each of the early sentences of the poem beginning with "if" but ending without a question mark. Prayer has that double-sided delivery: talking to God is an absolute act of faith, an audacious moment of humility and confidence.

Anthony Carelli

Anthony Carelli finds "the 'act' (or creation or reading or recitation) of poetry and prayer as different than the 'form' of poetry and prayer."[153] While

147. Ibid., 65.
148. Ibid., 69.
149. Ibid., 67.
150. Ibid.
151. Ibid.
152. Ibid.
153. Anthony Carelli, 2012.

their forms might overlap, "prayer seems to be a much more exclusive category than poetry."[154] Yet both poetry and prayer "are acts of humility, a subjugation of self in the service of a text."[155] For Carelli, "the poetic act is predisposed to emotions and thoughts in general but no more predisposed to the emotions and thoughts of theology or liturgy than the emotions or thoughts of any other sphere into whose mysteries we might try to peek."[156]

Carelli's *Carnations* (2011) brings the ecclesiastical and biblical to Brooklyn, with conceits worthy of the metaphysics. In "The Muse," the narrator is "shopping for fish" and meets an older woman who has read his poetry.[157] They stand together "in the great tabernacle quiet / that is the smallest supermarket," staring at "a part of salmon."[158] The fish's body has been "netted, penned, / hosed, thrown, bludgeoned, flayed, / quartered, boarded, wrapped and frozen" so that "we might glimpse, it seems / —by what it lacks so profoundly / yet precisely—its divinity."[159] After sharing that observation, the woman notes that "*the Lord* has never appeared" in his poems.[160]

Her words are wonderfully ironic: few contemporary collections from secular publishers such as Princeton University Press hinge so fully on ecclesiastical and biblical elements. Nearly all of Carelli's titles are explicitly Catholic or theological, and yet *Carnations* further redefines the concept of a Catholic book of poetry. Consider "The Sabbath," a poem about a couple who "fought until dark."[161] The narrator admits an imperfect memory, doubling-back on statements, but the poem presents eccentrically Eucharistic symbolism. On this cold night, among snow, they "weren't speaking," nearly as solemn as Mass.[162] They play Frisbee, and thought it "banked / and hissed in the sky"; consistent with the poem's tone, the Frisbee might be the Host.[163] Elsewhere the narrator of "Lectio Divina," a rare contemporary poem about joy that does not slip into irony,

154. Ibid.
155. Ibid.
156. Ibid.
157. Carelli, *Carnations*, 7.
158. Ibid., 8.
159. Ibid.
160. Ibid.
161. Ibid., 2.
162. Ibid., 1.
163. Ibid.

states "If the item presented is a chicken pie / I will see the lord."[164] God, it seems, in all things.

In "Glass Work Song," "my best friend's father would speak of the lord."[165] The narrator begins the poem with the near-apology that the man "was no theologian."[166] The man needs to be prompted, but once questioned "his cantos were carried by a foreman's voice / so unlike our own."[167] Queried about Christ, the man's "great voice slowed, faltered, / bent, and broke finally" in praise, that high song "gathered / in dinnertime steam."[168] The elevated words create a "fellowship" of men, but were less an elucidation of the divine than a hymn-like appreciation.[169] Carelli finds comparison with his own "very disciplined and devout Catholic, church-going father."[170] Similar to the man in the poem, if "the occasion comes to apply language to his faith it seems his humility trumps his righteousness and the result is silence."[171]

Language might be fallible for some of these narrators, but "The Muse" ends with a final stanza that posits poetry's role in relation to faith. The narrator's inquisitor, Mrs. Otto, left their conversation, "shepherding her squeaky cart / to the end of the line, where / a poem extends a broken silence."[172] That poem reaches a place "where faith resounds and finds / no end."[173] Carelli's willingness to appropriate religious language without repeating dogma reflects his agency in deciding his Catholic identity. Carelli, who was baptized but not confirmed Catholic, "never heard [his father] attribute any of his moral positions to Biblical or ecclesiastical law."[174] The decision to not become confirmed was his, not his parents, and though "I have attended Mass less frequently" afterward, "the foundational vocabulary . . . has clearly stayed with me."[175]

164. Ibid., 28.
165. Ibid., 3.
166. Ibid.
167. Ibid.
168. Ibid.
169. Ibid., 5.
170. Anthony Carelli, 2012.
171. Ibid.
172. Carelli, *Carnations*, 9.
173. Ibid.
174. Anthony Carelli, 2012.
175. Ibid.

Carnations was written "very much out of both my frustration with absolutist engagement and co-opting of scripture and my conflicting belief that scripture is holy only in so far as it excites and incites our imagination to everyday re-engage the text and the world anew."[176] The book certainly reads as written by a Catholic formed by the language and ritual of faith more than the office of the Church. While some poets might hesitate to separate the two, Carelli's offerings posit the lay participant as priest, and churches are more enabling edifices than absolute locations of belief. The narrator of "The Begats," flanked by "Grand stone castles growing on the avenues / wings and additions" and surrounded by "more churches here than / people I know," wonders why there couldn't be simply "one church."[177]

The narrator does not need a church to pray, instead choosing the pie shop. He asks God to grant him another day suffused with daily mysteries, where "I see the same pies become flesh / as I heat them, swaddle them, hand them to commuters."[178] As with the glass worker father who had to sing when simple words were not sufficient, the narrator admits that "All these images I tend tend to diminish."[179] He, apologetically, asks for silence, and also speaks with penitence within "In Ordinary Time." A new employee then, he has to speak a litany of apologies, though "Never before have I been so forgiven."[180]

The dislocation of belief from within the walls of a church continues in "The Lord's Prayer," where two boyhood friends hurl frogs while standing in a creek. The narrator is concurrently aware of the violence and linguistic sanctity of the ritual. The thrown frog will "fly stone-like to the skylight" in this "nameless ceremony."[181] Success "sends the critter shattering / for an instant, beyond fog, into the invisible."[182] The narrator realizes they "are cruel, inscrutable, indefensible, / yet holy."[183] The frogs are "bodies of praise" that the men "send up" into the air "only to gather eventual elegies."[184] In this poem, and others in *Carnations*, "the center of

---

176. Ibid.
177. Carelli, *Carnations*, 25.
178. Ibid., 26.
179. Ibid.
180. Ibid., 20.
181. Ibid., 52.
182. Ibid.
183. Ibid.
184. Ibid., 53.

the heavens / is earth," and yet also they might "glimpse for seconds at a time / earth as it is in heaven."[185] Two sinners, "eyes uplifted," participate in a violently dual theology, yet Carelli describes it straight, knowing "You can't fake it."[186]

Carelli's talent for engaging the divine in the odd continues in "The Crucifixion," prefaced with an exasperated newsman's consonance. The poem begins with a question, "What now?" which applies to most of the narrators in the collection.[187] Here a dead sperm whale has "washed a question ashore: *once given, how do you go about giving god back?*"[188] Carelli's penchant for titles is most complicated in this poem. Is the whale Christ? He resists allegory but embraces analogy. The collective narrator of the poem wonders if it is "shameful" that they, "still unknowing, will answer with dynamite?"[189]

Those theological questions are a "Monkish distraction" from the real work of digging pits, followed by relaxation.[190] "New questions flock" as "Spirals of terns and gulls / collapse from the sky to pick at the carcass staunch as a church."[191] They recognize that a "god / has come," but wonder: "What will make it matter? Fire, nails, camera, action. As if / we make the unimaginable more: we plant the charge, we run the cables."[192] "The Crucifixion" resists simple analogical decoding, and fits Carelli's sentiment that "Poetry is a way of gesturing not altogether stupidly at the mysteries, complexities, and confusions of our lives in relation to each other and the world or the universe or a god."[193] The poem is certainly more gesture than posit, and *Carnations* offers these mysteries with a smirk, but not sarcasm. "Sure" would not exist in a collection focused on mere subversion. This later poem at Rowan Creek is calmer than the former, but no less in awe of temporary majesty. There "Two thousand years / made slow as glass," the eye focused on "a rainbow trout / glimmering off."[194] The trout is gone from sight, but the water, "so full of glimmer," now "becomes sky / wob-

185. Ibid.

186. Ibid., 52.

187. Ibid., 51.

188. Ibid.

189. Ibid.

190. Ibid.

191. Ibid.

192. Ibid.

193. Anthony Carelli, 2012.

194. Carelli, *Carnations*, 55.

bling branches."[195] The poem ends: "That glimmer there / was not the lord, / but still the lord / may be the glimmer."[196]

David Yezzi thinks that "poems and prayers have different ends: the end of a poem is aesthetic communication, the end of a prayer is God. Liturgy works to tune the soul; poetry works to tune the emotions."[197] Yet the "two become almost indistinguishable, however, when the experience conveyed by the poem is the poet's experience of God."[198] Carelli's poetry is a marriage of both forms and acts; that such spiritual wealth is crafted by a lapsed Catholic speaks to the faith's reach.

Brian Doyle

Brian Doyle, in *Leaping: Revelations and Epiphanies* (2003), thinks that all writers must be "enormously" curious, aware that the "facts and details" they encounter are the "visible ends of long invisible stories."[199] Doyle finds stories in all things, and the role of the writer is to "drape words on experience" in hopes that "words give some hint of the shape of the moment, and pray that our attentiveness matters in a way we will never know."[200]

Doyle's mantra is true for all writers, but is particularly descriptive of the Catholic aesthetic. If the Catholic worldview is to find God in all things, then a closer attention to those things reveals unusual complexities that can best be presented through narrative. Story becomes an internally Catholic action: mystery and layering is valued over directness, and hope, in varying permutations, remains. *Mink River*, Doyle's inventive 2011 novel about a fictional Oregon town, is less driven by linear progression of plot and more grounded in the deepening of personal and community story. Populated by eccentric and complicated characters, *Mink River* begins with an overview of this hilly, coastal town, where there "are so many more stories, all changing by the minute, all swirling and braiding and weaving and spinning and stitching themselves one to another and to the stories of creatures in that place, both the quick sharp-eyed ones and the

195. Ibid.
196. Ibid., 56.
197. Yezzi, "Power," para. 20.
198. Ibid.
199. Doyle, *Leaping*, xix.
200. Doyle, *Grace*, 94.

rooted green ones and the ones underground and the ones too small to see."[201]

Mink River, with a talking crow and a generous amount of names that sound like kenning (Maple Head, No Horses, Worried Man), could only be written by someone with a narrative sense of humor and playfulness. Late in the novel, Moses, the talking crow, offers a speech from on top of a football helmet: "Human people . . . think that stories have beginnings and middles and ends, but we crow people know that stories just wander on and on and change form and are reborn again and again."[202] Doyle's essays and the characters of *Mink River* intimate a particularly Irish tinge to this predilection toward story. In this sense, and from a linguistic standpoint, Doyle finds a curious ancestor in James Joyce. Joyce's disdain for organized Catholicism is clear, but he must be considered a profoundly Catholic writer for several reasons. Baptized and raised Catholic, Joyce was taught by Jesuits, and his theological and cultural Catholic representations in *Dubliners* and *Ulysses* are not the work of an uninformed religious student. The anecdote that Joyce attended Good Friday and Holy Saturday services throughout his life is legendary, but, as R. J. Schork notes, the reason was "not some residual trace of personal piety, but an abiding appreciation for the music and hymns."[203] Joyce thought Catholicism, its clergy, and ritual were worthy fodder for his fiction, despite his personal divergence. As Umberto Eco summarizes, the "entire Joycean project might thus be seen as the development of a poetics . . . the dialectical movement of various opposite and complementary poetics."[204] Joyce's melding of critical sources, ranging from his imperfect readings of Aquinas to his idiosyncratic take on James Clarence Mangan, coalesced in the Jesuit-influenced, "radical opposition between the medieval man, nostalgic for an ordered world of clear signs, and the modern man, seeking a new habitat but unable to find the elusive rules and thus burning continually in the nostalgia of a lost infancy."[205] In the Joycean schema, the answer is not the Church, and yet Eco formulates Joyce's central considerations in the language of almost ritual paradox: "Art and life, symbolism and realism, classical world and contemporary world, aesthetic life and daily life, Stephen Dedalus and

---

201. Doyle, *Mink*, 13.
202. Ibid., 315.
203. Schork, "Joyce," 108.
204. Eco, "Artist," 329–330.
205. Ibid., 331.

Leopold Bloom."[206] Eco ultimately qualifies that it is the influence of Giordano Bruno, not the Jesuits, that finalize this aesthetic, but the Catholic reader might notice Hopkinsesque cadences in these secular oppositions.

Doyle, a practicing Catholic, diverges from Joyce in his identity within the Church, but retains some hints of Joyce's folk Irish Catholicism. Joyce, who appropriated Irish myth while claiming that W. B. Yeats's interest in Sligo County folktales was provincial, represented Catholicism in hyperbolic images, allowing the symbolism and performative nature of Mass to undercut, rather than support, Catholic theology. Doyle even reflects Joyce in minor linguistic tics, including repetitive usage of the exclamatory "yes" at the end of sentences—used by Joyce in a far different way in *Ulysses*—and the eschewing of quotation marks. Yet the true connection between the two writers can be found in the sprawling, associate freedom of sentences in Doyle's *Mink River*, and their resulting Catholic atmosphere. An anaphoric section of the novel documents a priest's anointing of "the sick and the dying and the dead," including the local bishop.[207] The death of a beloved nun leads to a funeral ceremony held, as she wished, in her school auditorium, with the reading from Acts of the Apostles delivered one sentence per person, "so that many members of the community might thus weave their voices together in prayer for the unimaginable voyage of her spirit."[208] Doyle's characters are compassionately constructed, including this nun, who "carried her worn wooden prayer beads everywhere, and knocked on doors with both hands at once, and wore only red hats."[209] These characters are folkloric, including a priest who "steps down into a beam of buttery light from the shadowed altar" during daily Mass.[210] Doyle interweaves the priest's colloquial sermon with description of the church, leading into notes of how each parishioner departs from the service. As with the fiction of Dubus, Doyle's characters live Catholic lives without introduction or qualification. A character kenned as "the man who beats his son" goes to confession, delivering a long-winded ramble ending with "Can you help me?"[211] The priest "wants to say something wise" but "can bring no words to his lips" other than "Yes."[212]

206. Ibid., 330.
207. Doyle, *Mink*, 95.
208. Ibid., 117.
209. Ibid., 118.
210. Ibid., 151.
211. Ibid., 187.
212. Ibid.

Doyle's Catholicism is most thoroughly explored in his non-fiction, and is characterized by a connection between language and ritual, self-effacement, and the synthesis of joy, wonder, and love in daily acts of faith. Doyle's wistful storytelling, the relation between the personal, mystical moments of faith and the familial or communal system, and both a love for and questioning of the efficacy of language—and therefore the doctrinal complexity of Catholicism in document form—create a nuanced literary approach to the faith. Doyle's work is optimistic without being naïve, and linguistic without allowing his words to overwhelm the signs of the faith.

In public readings and written prefaces, Doyle mentions the brevity of human interaction, how most lives remain parallel without intersecting. Yet he sustains a faith in the connection created by words, the silent enjoyment and experience of reading work by a stranger. Reflecting on his sister's silence pledge, Doyle remembers her saying that silence is at first difficult, but then "becomes a prayer."[213] He has come to appreciate silence more as he wakes "earlier and earlier."[214] Stories, spoken and written, still "wash over me all day like tides," but his words are channeled onto the page, an act of silence.[215] Such reflection might connect to his call, or question, for Catholic artists: how will they "elevate and energize and shove and rebuild and resurrect the Catholic idea?"[216] Success seems to hinge on a responsible approach to Catholic language, a language absolutely wedded to ritual, sign, and tradition.

Doyle's own language is wedded to the roll and rise of the essay form, allowing him to deliver melodic moments of sermon. Doyle's Catholicism is grounded in empathy and humility, where "we turn again and again to one another, and bow, and ask forgiveness, and mill what mercy we can muster from the muddle of our hearts."[217] Christ is found in the Catholic community, a group of believers who mark death with "thin naked white crosses" as a way of bridging the gap between the momentary and eternal.[218] Those markers are "holier than any church, because those sweet bellies and those roasted holes in the grass are where souls entered and left this intricate realm; they are places of mercy and mystery; they are the

213. Doyle, *Grace*, 29.
214. Ibid., 33.
215. Ibid.
216. Ibid., 11.
217. Ibid., 20.
218. Ibid., 60.

portals from which the created emerges and through which the created departs."[219]

The origin of Doyle's variety of literary Catholicism appears to be his mother, who taught him that epiphanies and miracles were possible "pretty much every minute if you are paying attention."[220] Catholicism is readymade for optimism and openness to the sacred in the daily. While Doyle finds much to praise in other faith beliefs, "Catholicism seems far more joyous, far more celebratory, far more invitation to partnership, far more expectation of responsibility in creating the wonder of the future than mere acceptance of Mastery."[221] The latter trait—lay and religious responsibility to be progressive, to not only believe in and revere Christ, but to translate that belief into action—makes the faith "not Master and Servant—it is Father asking children to rise to their best selves, to accept responsibility, to use their holy tools to create what can be."[222]

Doyle's essays are a way for him to contribute, and his work is simultaneously optimistic and realistic. His writing is continually focused on renewal: of faith ritual, of perception, of overlooked sign or representation. "Litany of the Blessed Mother" is a series of Marian devotions delivered as vignettes, ending with the epistrophic "pray for us." The mothers of these vignettes are, in the tradition of Mary Biddinger's refiguring of Saint Monica, women who are comforters and providers, but also human and prone to frustrations and confusion. Yet still, these are mothers are "to whom we will run sobbing and laughing when our chapter closes and the path to your arms opens wide."[223]

Doyle extends this sense of renewal to Mass and the person of Christ. In "Glory Bee," a bee buzzes in a residence hall room where a priest says private Mass. That bee was "cutting steps in the air" as the priest "sang and chewed the words as if they were poems."[224] Doyle, in that small, unusual space, made even more singular by the buzzing insect, heard the words "as if for the first time," feeling "the Mass washing over me like a sea of sound."[225] It is in this most unusual Mass, "stripped to its bones," that Doyle realizes the ceremony "is a fiercely persistent memoir, a naked meal

---

219. Ibid.
220. Ibid., 28.
221. Ibid., 13.
222. Ibid.
223. Ibid., 101.
224. Doyle, *Leaping*, 113.
225. Ibid.

for a naked carpenter, an act of exuberant joy that he lived and died and lived."[226] Doyle further investigates the nakedness, or absolute honesty, of the Christ body elsewhere. In "Christ's Elbows," Doyle examines the tradition of discussing the body of Christ, and reaches a telling conclusion: the term has become absolutely focused on the symbolic and metaphorical import, rather than the physical, real human form. Doyle wonders what the result has been for the Church and the faith; might Catholics benefit from even more attention toward the tactile physicality of Christ?

Because Christ's adult, public life was so brief, and the literary form of the Gospels are less concerned with eyewitness observation and more with metaphor and narrative, they are largely devoid of physical description of Christ. Doyle finds no attention toward "carriage, bearing, bounciness of stride, height, weight, injuries; the strength of his handshake, the length of his fingers (Did his hand swallow the hand of the girl he raised from the dead? Could he palm the heads of the children who followed him like puppies?), the weight of his hand on the shoulders and faces of the men and women he healed with his touch."[227] Doyle finds much pastoral worth in contemporary consideration of what lies behind the scriptural Christ. If Catholics more fully reflect on the physicality of Christ, they will better understand his itinerary, his references, and why an action such as the washing of feet "was such a momentous ritual at the time."[228] Doyle wonders if Christ "must have sighed many a night when he stared down at the worn and dusty pins that carried him so far so fast."[229] Ironically, the great amount of Catholic religious iconography has possibly dulled Catholic observation of such physicality when it should accomplish the opposite. Doyle ponders a crucifix nailed to his university office wall. He researches the life of the object, from a Massachusetts company to an Oregon devotional store, to how it now "elevates our room," reminding Doyle "that once upon a time there was a man who so loved men and women and children" that he underwent the Passion.[230] The crucifix also makes Doyle think "of all the millions of men and women and children who have given their bodies and lives for others . . . so many of them silent in their

226. Ibid., 114.
227. Ibid., 54.
228. Ibid., 55.
229. Ibid.
230. Ibid., 49.

struggles and never to be celebrated or sainted after their difficult lives and obscure deaths."[231]

Doyle's devotion to joy gives voice to those silent souls on the periphery, if only by showing how words can coax hope. "Grace Notes" examples Doyle's vignette approach, a staple of creative non-fiction writers from Edward Hoagland to Gary Fincke, which allows Doyle to jump between physical manifestations of grace, biblical representations, and the paradoxical grace of everyday life. Grace can be said at the table, or it can be a verb, as Doyle feels graced with his children. For Doyle, grace is a state of being that some can achieve without explicit recognition, while others, including religious, can never attain: "Every Catholic at some point sighs for the church in which he lives, such a wonderful and cruel entity, such a brilliant and idiotic and lurching-gracelessly-toward-grace enterprise."[232]

Doyle uses the same loose structure for "Altar Boy." He remembers that the most important element of his role was "to be where you needed to be without seeming to get there."[233] Doyle "was the key" to his priest's "famous twenty-two minute Mass."[234] He is appreciative of the dynamic of this "artist," whose sense of performance was essential to the liturgical celebration. The mystery of Mass is sometimes brought to youthful reality by the altar boys, who knew that the "way to make money was to work the banks of candles on either side of the altar," where parishioners handed the boys money instead of slipping a folded bill into the steel box.[235] Curious altar boys "gobbled" communion wafers, but those sneaked tastes were disappointing: they had the texture of "typing paper," and became even less appetizing and mysterious when Doyle discovered they "came wholesale from a convent in New Jersey."[236]

Doyle's altar serving experience is of the preconciliar variety. He had to know the twenty-two rites of the Mass, as well as the thirteen distinctive Masses. The solemnity of this preconcilar world is almost represented as restrictive. Under the "dense purple light," among lingering "smells of incense and cigars and dust," he hears the "dry shuffling of shoes" as the congregation moves toward the Host.[237] Despite the lull of the "groaning

231. Ibid.
232. Ibid., 33.
233. Ibid., 67.
234. Ibid.
235. Ibid., 69.
236. Ibid.
237. Ibid., 78.

organ," Doyle felt the rarefied air was necessary: "I remember the stiff black cloth under which you hid all desire and personality as you prepared to assist at a miracle that you did not and could never understand but that you watched for ravenously."[238]

Part of his fascination with the able priest is due to the more reverential, rather than collegial, relationship between priest and altar server. When a visiting Franciscan performs Mass and then sits in the locker room with the altar boys, they are confused by "his hooded brown robe and bare feet in enormous sandals."[239] Their spheres are well defined and separate. Their separation reinforces the high nature of Mass; as he echoes elsewhere, Doyle feels unsatisfied at other faith services, since "being dipped in miracles every day inoculates you against the mundane."[240]

Although Doyle lived a young life entrenched in Mass, he did not pursue a religious life. His vocation is fatherhood, and his words in the penultimate section of the essay summarize the lasting effect of his personal participation in Mass: "I believe so strongly, so viscerally, in a wisdom and vast joy under the tangled weave of the world, under the tattered blanket of our evil and tragedy and illness and brokenness and sadness and loss, that I cannot speak it, cannot articulate it, but can only hold onto religion like a drowning man to a sturdy ship."[241]

Doyle's reflection on working as a summer camp counselor, "The Meteorites," might be the best implicit reflection of such a worldview. Only eighteen, Doyle already saw his work as "ministering" to the four to six year-olds on his watch. They are a predictably rowdy bunch, and yet Doyle also "learned to love that summer."[242] Doyle has to clean a boy who has soiled himself, and now believes "that when we stood together many years ago in a sweltering dirty toilet, on a brilliant August morning, amid fat buttery bars of morning light, Daniel sobbing convulsively as I washed him with a moist cloth, we were engaged in a gentle sacrament: Daniel learning that he must confess to be cleansed, me understanding dimly that my silence with this weeping child was the first wise word I had ever spoken."[243] It was that sense of compassionate love that Doyle learned, a love first begun by another boy, David, who said "*Counselor, Danny needs*

238. Ibid.
239. Ibid., 72.
240. Ibid., 74.
241. Ibid., 79.
242. Ibid., 173.
243. Ibid., 161–62.

you.[244] Doyle writes that those "four words fell from his mouth and were scattered by the four winds: but they have been a storm in me."[245] Doyle, more than most, has presented this postconciliar storm in a pastorally ripe, realistically applicable manner.

Kaya Oakes

Radical Reinvention, a 2012 memoir by Kaya Oakes, is a pastorally instructive testament to authentic religious reconsideration. Oakes's memoir represents the direction of postconciliar Catholic literature: writers struggling to reconcile doctrine with social and cultural evolutions, ultimately rediscovering the worth of the Church's core tenets. Oakes's honest and approachable prose makes her spiritual progression believable, creating a work applicable to both progressive and conservative ideological sections of the Church. Her memoir is less a story of polar reversal than a representation of how religious devotion is cyclical.

Unlike most writers profiled in *The Fine Delight*, Oakes's faith experiences are fully postconciliar, yet her book reveals the difficulties of both ideological and social transitions. The nuns at her elementary school "were pleased to be walking around out of habits, [but] they were awkward in normal clothes."[246] Appearance was not the only struggle: because of a "lack of instructions from the Vatican about new forms of catechism," the children complete hokey crafts in lieu of elementary reflection: "we made endless God's eyes, wrapping yarns around popsicle sticks and carrying them home to mothers" who already had quite the collection.[247] No one expects children to be theologically aware, but the point is obvious: sometimes no entity seemed less prepared to fully engage the complicated revisions of Vatican II than the actual Church.

This "mostly entertaining and slightly absurd" youthful Catholicism was enhanced, upon reflection, by "service to others, liberation theology, and the legacy of scholarship used to enlighten the present day."[248] Throughout *Radical Reinvention*, Oakes is careful to make qualifications of criticisms, revealing a writer authentically torn between personal preference and deference to tradition. The resulting tension creates far more nu-

244. Ibid., 173.
245. Ibid.
246. Oakes, *Radical*, 4.
247. Ibid.
248. Ibid.

anced representation of early postconciliar life than the typical complaints about overbearing nuns. Even open confession, a progressive moment of her childhood, "totally failed" in her own experience.[249]

Oakes, though, did not remain in the Catholic school system. At the public school, "Nobody ever talked about God," and that silence seems more powerful than direct criticism.[250] Oakes drifted from the Church. After her father's funeral Mass, she did not attend services for almost a decade. She never quite becomes an atheist, but her staunch skepticism of the Church leads her to transform religious gestures, like crossing herself, into cultural responses. She has to defend her youthful Catholicism to her non-believing friends, who mistakenly associate Catholicism with Rush Limbaugh. *Radical Reinvention* offers much pastoral worth in distinguishing Catholicism from the more general Protestantism that occupies most uninformed discussions of Christianity in America. Even her spiritual advisors join the act, reiterating that "Jesus doesn't say unbelievers are going to Hell . . . That's what fundamentalists think."[251]

These misinterpretations of Catholicism, ironically, are part of the force that drives Oakes back to the Church. In finding the need to constantly define and redefine her Catholic faith, she is framing and polishing arguments, becoming an apologist. She wonders if "[the Church had] any hope of changing if people like me bailed on it."[252] Leaving proves difficult for reasons connected to her ethnicity: "There's something appealing about the idea that my ancestors were not tea-sipping Episcopalian Wasps, but broke-as-hell, ghetto-dwelling, hard-swearing, garbage-truck-driving, potato-famine-escaping, gallon-o'-whiskey-drinking, short-lifespan living Catholics."[253] Echoing Brian Doyle's laments about other faith beliefs, Oakes never feels fully comfortable except at Catholic services. She admits that a certain "arcane part of me pined for Catholicism even as I ground my teeth every time another horrible story about it emerged in the news."[254]

Oakes subsequently enters the RCIA program, and that experience serves as a convenient structure for the first half of the book. The experience is a complicated reminder of why she is attracted to the faith, but also frustrated by certain elements of the infrastructure. Oakes is most

249. Ibid., 5.
250. Ibid., 3.
251. Ibid., 99.
252. Ibid., 11.
253. Ibid.
254. Ibid., 12.

interested in the elements of Catholicism that differentiate the faith from other celebrations. She describes with care when "catechumens shuffled up to the altar, their sponsors blessed their heads, shoulders, hands, and feet softly [making] the sign of the cross on each one. You don't see people kneeling down to bless one another's feet all that often in contemporary culture, and the gesture is startling."[255]

Oakes's particular appreciations further reveal her idiosyncratic Catholicism. She is less interested in the miraculous events of the New Testament and more attracted to "the stories of Jesus and people, particularly when he's talking to women."[256] Although Oakes is clearly interested in the intellectual tradition of Catholicism, her reconnection with faith is also an emotional one. During the RCIA period, she begins crying in church. She's "not used to" open emotions, but is unable to control herself: tears flow during a hymn, prayers, homily, and even the "sun arcing through the clerestory windows above the altar."[257] Oakes, to her credit, accepts these mysteries and moves forward.

Oakes's perception of the Church is bottom-heavy: her interactions with priests and nuns at the local level are overwhelmingly positive, and only when she begins to think of the Vatican as an autocratic force does her voice sour on the Church. The curiously named Father Godot is especially useful to both Oakes's spiritual development and the reader's pastoral appreciation. Self-described as "not a Passionist," Father Godot assures that there are many ways of "relating to Christ," including a focus on salvation, healing, social justice, and, in Oakes's instance, writing and sharing the faith.[258]

Oakes, more than most contemporary religious memoirists, is up to the task. It is no surprise that she is asked to give biblical reflections at local churches; she is continually finding ways to renew considerations of often told tales, such as the washing of the feet. She notes how our contemporary aversion to feet made "Jesus performing the act even more revolutionary" on those "who trekked miles and miles through the deserts of the Middle East."[259] This interest in reflection enables Oakes to move beyond her confirmation to become an active Catholic in the pastoral sphere. Oakes certainly voices her doctrinal disagreements with the Church, and most of

255. Ibid., 23.
256. Ibid., 34.
257. Ibid., 96.
258. Ibid., 130.
259. Ibid., 69.

these are related to the decisions made about a woman's body, including abortion. Yet her activism is not merely criticism; she never does her own version of proselytizing, instead focusing on good works and emulation of Christ.

She realizes, though, that certain elements of the faith do not come easy. When she does not "hear" God at a spiritual retreat, she becomes frustrated. She has begun to master the intellectual component of her faith, but that component has made her keep part of her faith "at a distance," prompting one spiritual advisor to quip "You like to read about [your faith], but you don't like to feel it."[260] Oakes considers an arbitrary but useful duality of Catholics: the Thomas Merton variety, whose life is more insular and intellectual, and those who follow the steps of Dorothy Day in social activism. Oakes's vocation is a combination of both approaches: she begins volunteering, but she also joins what has been deemed a "pray and bitch" group: Catholic women who meet to discuss the Bible, faith, the Church, along with silent meditation and a concluding discussion of grievances. Oakes, whose spiritual development was largely formed by male priests, is now coming to terms with the role of women in the Church, and she learns that role and identity is complicated: "you can be Catholic and feminist. You can be Catholic and lesbian. You can be Catholic and a straight female and not have kids. You can be Catholic and have children but wonder if they should be Catholic. You can be Catholic and believe in better access to birth control, especially in impoverished and AIDS-ravage communities. You can be Catholic and female and not be a nun and still be a leader in the church."[261] These meetings help cement Oakes's interests in silent reflection and social change. She considers the ordination of women, looking back to the important role of women in the New Testament, as well as the Roman Catholic Womenpriests movement. She is troubled by recent Vatican criticisms of American nuns: though *Radical Reinvention* was released before the Vatican's reprimand of The Leadership Conference of Women Religious, her discussion is applicable to that report. Her concern with women evolves into a general reconsideration of sexuality in the Church, and her expressed confusion that homosexuality, about which "there are seven lines in the entire Bible," is of more concern than "caring for the poor and outcast," of which "there are hundreds, maybe thousands" of lines.[262]

260. Ibid., 104.
261. Ibid., 141.
262. Ibid., 173.

In all of these criticisms, Oakes is idealistic while being realistic, and continually returns to Vatican II as the opportunity for ideological reconsideration. She is careful to recognize that changes are slow and not universal. Even those skeptical of some of Oakes's assertions will likely listen to her overall argument because she does not reside simply in critique. Oakes, and other lay Catholics like her, remain committed to the Christ-like consideration of the poor and outcast, and that shift in perspective is another form of Catholic social activism. This is the personal line she has drawn: the Church is exemplary in "ministering to the poor, caring for the sick, educating people in forgotten communities . . . encouraging the flock to stand up to injustice and fight oppression."[263] Oakes, clearly, loves and values Christ not merely for his identity, but for his actions. She feels that the Church, though, is "awful at understanding what it means to be a woman, or to be gay, or to want to express your sexuality without catching a disease."[264] Oakes, whose husband sometimes attends Mass with her but is not Catholic, becomes a useful contrast in the memoir: even within the skeptical community, Oakes reveals an interest in educating others, while recognizing that her criticisms might never be reflected in institutional change.

The only moment in the memoir that Oakes seems to oversimplify the Church is her disdain for Latin Mass, which she thinks is "a terrible thing."[265] Her criticism is likely grounded in her postconciliar youth, but a larger, and more reasonable origin becomes clear: Oakes is interested in a communal, participatory Church, and she finds a prototype in the early Church, "when Catholics prayed in underground churches and Catholicism was something small, humble, free-form, and new."[266] Her criticism reaches an apex during a trip to Italy, when, echoing Dubus's Luke Ripley, she feels that the "Vatican is admittedly beautiful and majestic, but it's not about the real hard work of belief."[267]

Yet Oakes, for all her criticisms of the institutional Church, would not choose any other faith belief. In fact, rather than simply being around other progressive Catholics, her "spiritual soul mates . . . aren't necessarily people exactly like me; rather, they're people I want to learn from."[268]

263. Ibid., 186.
264. Ibid.
265. Ibid., 208.
266. Ibid., 216–7.
267. Ibid., 224.
268. Ibid., 237.

In this way, the more doctrinally conservative ends of the Church are a necessary comparison point for Oakes to further craft and refine her own theology. She ends *Radical Reinvention* with a sequence of useful analogies, both for her own experience and other progressive Catholics. She reflects that the Psalms "don't take the form of praise but the form of a lament or even a curse," finding a sense of catharsis in the action of "[taking] our negative sentiments and [giving] them to God, so we're less likely to act on them."[269] For Oakes, the essential element of prayer is not the complaint, but the faith "that God still won't turn you away," and that recognition "becomes an act of confidence and a real transformation."[270] This "change of heart," or metanoia, is the "realization that God will not reject you," and that though "you may curse and bewail your state and the state of the world around you . . . [through that action] you may also get closer to God."[271] For that reason, *Radical Reinvention* might be considered a template for postconciliar Catholic memoir. Additionally, Oakes's complicated spiritual journey offers another wrinkle in the postconciliar Catholic aesthetic: interrogation and skepticism might ultimately lead to a more realistic, world-ready faith. Oakes's perception of Catholicism was aided by genuinely engaged priests and nuns whose honest faith gave her confidence to express her own beliefs. The fragmented identity of the contemporary priest—reviled for the sins of few, praised for the grace of many—becomes the final, and perhaps best, vehicle for the postconciliar Catholic literary paradox.

269. Ibid., 238.
270. Ibid., 239.
271. Ibid.

Chapter Six

Priest, Writer, Catholic

The New Postconciliar Trinity

J. F. Powers haunts this book. The preeminent fictional chronicler of American parishes straddles conciliar lines, though his work, in form, content, and reference leans toward those earlier years. In his final novel, *Wheat That Springeth Green* (1988), former track star Joe Hackett dreams of being a saint, but first learns he must simply "get on with his job" as a parish priest.[1] That job is not easy or glamorous: "Frequently reported, of course, like flying saucers, were parishes where priests and people were doing great things together. 'But I've never seen one myself, if it's any consolation to you guys,' Joe said, and paused."[2] While usage of the term flying saucers is not the ultimate demarcation between conciliar periods, Powers's cultural cues reveal a writer more comfortable with an earlier aesthetic.

Flannery O'Connor appreciated that aesthetic, although she was a picky admirer, only enjoying his fiction about clergy. The two occasionally corresponded, their regionally disparate wit resulting in mutual appreciation. An even more effusive admirer of Powers was William Gass. His essay-review of *Morte D'Urban*, Powers's 1963 National Book Award winning novel, is glowing at points, praising Powers's "rare richness of theme and perception . . . [and] gentleness of tone."[3] Powers's stories had

---

1. Powers, *Wheat*, 200.
2. Ibid.
3. Gass, *Fiction*, 134.

been appearing in *Accent*, a publication that had also showcased Gass and O'Connor.

Gass is a keen reader of Powers's Catholicism, summarizing his central thematic question as "how can the spirit express itself in nature without compromise, without debasement, since one is so distant from the other, and each is obedient to different laws?"[4] In language that prefigures Waldmeir's later postconciliar analysis, Gass wonders "can a mind manipulate its body without becoming its body first," leading him to question if it is "possible for the church to do its work in the world without becoming worldly itself?"[5] This particular form of "spiritual corruption" is dramatized in Powers's fiction at the local, parish level, but Gass extends the inquiry wider.[6] He quotes Powers who, in "Lions, Harts, Leaping Does," presents Father Didymus, who arrives at the recognition that even saints are "beset by the grossest distractions."[7]

Didymus remembers "on Good Friday carrying the crucifix along the communion rail for the people to kiss, giving them the indulgence, and afterwards in the sacristy wiping the lipstick of the faithful from the image of Christ crucified."[8] Gass recognizes that the "mystic, for example, forgets his fellows in his flight toward the divine," and uses the word "paradox" to identify the "obligation laid upon those who follow the Ideal to yield themselves to practice."[9] The secular, prosaic world is felt through the knees of saints. For Gass, that lipstick on the crucifix is not "continuing love."[10] God is here, but he is more misunderstood than ever.

As a secular Protestant, Gass explains that "the position of the priest has always struck many people . . . as curious."[11] Priests deny the physical; they are "celibate as though to celebrate it."[12] The preconciliar priest "[incants] an ancient tongue" making him "a figure altogether strange to this world."[13] Despite those intellectually ascetic movements, priests "smoke cigars, prefer martinis, improve [their golf] game, accept personal gifts,

4. Ibid., 136.
5. Ibid.
6. Ibid., 135.
7. Powers, *Stories*, 53.
8. Ibid.
9. Gass, *Fiction*, 136.
10. Ibid.
11. Ibid., 137.
12. Ibid.
13. Ibid.

and drive about in large cars."[14] Gass's suburban priesthood sounds cut from the cloth of Cheever, but his endpoint is reasonable: "If the Catholic Church is to survive and grow and do its work, it must attract wealth, acquire political power, advertise itself, build, train bright ambitious men for the priesthood."[15] The Catholic Church must "energetically compete, and to compete it must be heard, it must be chic, it must seem glamorous to the crowd, right up to date."[16] The pragmatist will find acceptable truth in such sentiment; the cynic will smirk. Gass, it seems, can do both; after all, meanwhile the "Protestants are building bowling alleys."[17]

This paradox of the narrow Catholic moment filtered through the priest, acting as Christ but fully human, establishes the final evolution of postconciliar interrogation. That this interrogation is whispered rather than shouted enhances its effectiveness. Conciliar liturgical changes affected the laity, but they also profoundly redefined the personage of the priest. He is no longer mime; he moves through the rows, shakes hands, faces the flock. Performance has ceded to celebration; the altar is no longer a stage, but a gathering point. For a cultural Protestant like Gass, the priest is pure Catholic literature: actor, dramatist, counselor, symbol. Similar appreciators include postconciliar Catholic writers, who have found the priesthood an important nexus of the progressive and conservative, the daily and weekend face of the Church.

Graham Greene's whiskey priest was a grand sinner, the heights of his gravitas inversely connected to the depths of his dogmatic ruptures. Powers brought the priest back to the rectory. Postconciliar writers follow him out the door, down the street, and then back into his private room. Erin McGraw, John Reimringer, and Tom Bailey, an Episcopalian, continue the postconcilar traditions of paradox and interrogation, but soften their edges. Their fictions dramatize a priesthood that, despite cultural attempts to generalize the whole based on the terrible sins of the few, has become an effective metaphor for the changing Church.

Erin McGraw's postconciliar representations of the priesthood are tempered by her own vacillations of faith, articulated in "True Believer." McGraw began attending daily Mass after her divorce, an experience that "often drives Catholics from the church, [but] instead threaded me into

14. Ibid.
15. Ibid.
16. Ibid.
17. Ibid.

the tight fabric of daily observance."[18] McGraw "never intended to become a person who might be mistaken for a true believer."[19] After overzealous years in Catholic school, McGraw distances herself from religion as a public school student, but retains an acute sense of faith and, in true postconciliar fashion, deliberately separates the two modes. As a teenager, McGraw struggled to identify reasons for the evil and pain she viewed in the world, finally arriving at a fragmented conception of the divine: "If this world reflected God's purpose, then the divine way of doing things had very little to do with rewarding goodness or even providing goodness with a little decent protection. Jesus, I could not help remembering, had been crucified. The divine way of doing things seemed indifferent to safety, the one quality I craved. If God could not keep me safe, who could?"[20]

Her Mass attendance during college was less as an active member of a faith community, and more to achieve the "desirable status of nonconformist,"[21] which she would later trade for "intellectual."[22] After reading Nietzsche, McGraw realizes that she had been attending "Mass merely in order to be counted among the faithful, to check in with the home office, to keep alive a relationship that I might need one of these days. A spiritual insurance policy, for which I paid one hour every Sunday, and about which I thought, willfully, nothing."[23] Although she recognizes that her confident philosophy professor was delivering another form of sermon, she is attracted to the strength of his rhetorical flourish, unlike the tepid delivery of the campus priest, who almost seemed afraid to turn away his flock.

McGraw soon learns that she has taken a far too personal approach to reading the German philosopher. She need not abandon her faith to understand his ideas, that are ones couched in the same rhetoric as her professor, who consoles her toward the recognition that her faith has been strengthened by navigating unwelcome territory. As an academic, McGraw might avoid some public pronouncements of faith, like a crucifix in her office, but she knows her faith is implicitly revealed. She has become purer in that faith: "Once I finally accepted the stubborn presence of my faith, I began to attend Mass mindfully. Once I began to attend Mass mindfully, I

18. McGraw, "True," para. 3.
19. Ibid., para. 11.
20. Ibid., para. 26.
21. Ibid., para. 28.
22. Ibid., para. 29.
23. Ibid., para. 44.

began to pray. Way leads on to way. Without ever intending to, I now find myself living in a world that is filled, every day, with the shadow of God's hand. In normal human decisions I see supernatural implications, what might be the movement of grace. I am no kind of mystic, and most of the time I do not pay close attention to those movements. Still, I feel them in place around me, making the world shimmer with promise."[24] McGraw has learned to find comfort in complexity and mystery rather than her earlier longing for prescribed reason. Her conclusion is one of freedom: "In place of my lifelong, highly polished fears now exists the conviction that all life, in ways I cannot begin to predict, will pass through sorrow and pain into joy."[25]

McGraw's favorite literary representation of Catholicism is the parish priest. In "Punchline," Father Phil Castor is by turns blunt and coarse, lately taken to "on-the-spot additions" to his sermons that are quoted and misinterpreted by parishioners in equal turns.[26] Father Phil's litany of weekly events is delivered by McGraw with juxtaposition reflective of O'Connor: at his Wednesday night lock-in with at-risk youth, one boy dies after shooting speed before arriving; Thursday is the aftermath, with police and the hospital; Thursday night is a wedding rehearsal and dinner; and on Friday he visits a nursing home. Father Phil practically bilocates his way through the story, before finally arriving at his desk to revise an upcoming sermon.

McGraw's delivery is wry, but the comparisons with O'Connor might be too superficial: whereas her southern predecessor was building an architectonic criticism of fundamentalist ilk with Catholicism only arriving in whisper, McGraw's interests are religiously insular. Father Phil realizes, after mediocre grades in philosophy, that he would have been better-suited learning accounting than Aquinas. Yet, for all of McGraw's winking, her eyes are wide open when dealing with Father Phil's increasingly honest introspection, which is labeled by his brother as nearing solipsism: he blames himself for the boy's overdose. He is unfit to talk, although he "was expected to talk to committees, talk to engaged couples or kids in trouble, talk to the sick and bereaved, talk from the pulpit, talk on the phone."[27] He concludes that "existential angst" is acceptable, but tears during Mass

24. Ibid., para. 65.
25. Ibid., para. 75.
26. McGraw, "Punchline," 37.
27. Ibid., 42.

and his asides during homilies were worse sins.[28] When his brother Gary barely survives a hit-and-run, Father Phil loses control, returning to one of his parishioner's misheard sermon excerpts that now appears accurate to reality: God is a trickster, and Father Phil's life is the punchline.

The punchlines of "The Penance Practicum" are softer, and top-heavy. McGraw begins the story with a light-hearted admonition of the seminary Halloween party from an overzealous seminarian, one of "Rome's hall monitors" who "ran every five minutes to look something up in one of John Paul II's encyclicals."[29] Father Dom, a faculty member of the admissions committee at Saint Boniface, is annoyed by the ironically conservative seminarians of the postconciliar class. Yet his attention is focused on Joe, an earnest seminarian with little talent for counseling, who defers to dogmatic pronouncements instead of consoling an HIV positive penitent during a practicum confession. Father Dom is disappointed, but unlike Father Phil of "Punchline," he is more critical of his own contribution to this cosmic joke, where he "was left holding the bag for the Infinite."[30]

Father Dom, for reasons connected to pity, tries every possible intervention to sustain Joe's enrollment and hopeful success, finally agreeing to the seminarian helping at a facility for terminal children. The idea seems doomed from the start, but Father Dom's capacity for perpetual forgiveness seems less a discipleship of Christ and more a willingness to overlook the obvious. Joe, as to be expected, fails to console a patient who requests he modify a prayer on her behalf. He becomes flustered, more concerned with his nervousness than the patient's needs, and begs for "guidance" from Father Dom.[31] The priest, though, has fallen ill and vomits. The scene concludes with McGraw's trademark reversal: Father Dom, who began the story concerned with his costume for the Halloween party, realizes that sometimes his vestments as a priest are only cloth deep.

Father Benni, another faculty member, had voiced the opinion that Joe was unfit for the priesthood, concluding "Calls can be misheard."[32] John Reimringer's 2010 novel, *Vestments*, is an honest dramatization of such an occurrence. A devout Catholic during his youth, as Reimringer "got older [he] drifted to the left and the Church drifted to the right."[33]

28. Ibid., 43.
29. McGraw, "Penance," 18.
30. Ibid., 23.
31. Ibid., 34.
32. Ibid., 26.
33. Forbes, "Reimringer," para. 17.

He wrote *Vestments* in Joycean "exile from the Catholic Church, which I deeply loved as a child, and whose rituals and people I still deeply love."[34] Reimringer's postconciliar sentiment is with the "average Catholic, parishioner or priest, [who] is ill-served by the Church's leadership these days. The novel is an elegy for what the Church could be and still occasionally is."[35]

That elegy is dramatized through Father James Dressler, a thirty year-old priest whose upcoming celebration of his brother's wedding will be his last clerical duty for a year. Unofficially, James is on sabbatical to teach theology at a local university, but his relocation was for another reason: "There'd been, briefly, a woman."[36] Reimringer's novel engages that transgression with care, and sufficient back story. The novel opens in St. Paul, Minnesota, where church bells announce the hour. The location is the dining room of his childhood home, where he is celebrating Mass for his mother until his father arrives to "drop off his alimony."[37] The domestic meets the divine as the Host rests on a paten set on the dining room table. Dressler offers the Eucharist to his mother, but refuses his father, who has since remarried before divorcing again.

Dressler's power as a priest might be his only masculine edge against his father and brother, Jacky, who both consider him nothing more than a man. The particulars of Dressler's Catholicism are distant from his father's sharply preconciliar, more fundamentalist polarities. As a child Dressler would sneak to morning Mass, where his fingers "[broke] a thin film of ice" in the holy water."[38] Although he goes to church to escape, the sounds and smells of his strained home blur his prayers. He only is able to find "refuge in the litanies of the Mass."[39] Now, Dressler attends Mass in his "civvies," and goes elsewhere to avoid questions from his mentor: Reimringer uses the trope of vestments to redefine Dressler's identity throughout the novel.[40] He attends Mass at a Mexican church, where Reimringer juxtaposes Dressler's ritual dedication—"a rosary twisted so that the beads dug into the tendons and flesh," lit votives, cool air, a time "for those who went to bed early or slept badly or woke alone"—with Betty García, Dressler's

34. Ibid.
35. Ibid.
36. Reimringer, *Vestments*, 14.
37. Ibid., 5.
38. Ibid., 29.
39. Ibid., 30.
40. Ibid., 31.

high school love.[41] In Joycean fashion, the sensory images of his faith are juxtaposed with the "deep scent of her body, twisted sheets, the squeaks and rattles of the different beds and couches and backseats where we made love."[42] Young Dressler wanted "to use the rhythm method, while Betty called that Vatican roulette and insisted on rubbers."[43] No planning works: Betty becomes pregnant, and her lawyer uncle convinces her to get an abortion. Even Dressler's preconciliar mother, in a moment of dogma ceding to practicality, agrees. Dressler is silent, and not present for the procedure, though he never lets the memory pass.

His distant acceptance of the abortion finds its lineage in his father's absolutes now tempered by the realities of daily life. After Dressler "[thumbed] a cross into the foam on [a] Guinness with the same motion" as applying Ash Wednesday ashes, the father and son begin one of their theological conversations.[44] His father critiques priests for being "obsessed with sex," and a local priest for caring more about food at a funeral reception than paying respects to the dead; when Dressler responds by citing Aquinas, his father concludes that "You think too much."[45] Dressler's blue-collar aesthetic has been complicated by the "locker room full of knowledge and power" at seminary.[46] That learned faith is in contrast to his sister's domestic Catholicism. Anne's liberalism has transformed into a life with a vegetable garden, where "Ceramic deer and rabbits grazed about [the Virgin] Mary's feet or looked up adoringly."[47] Anne's newfound faith is a descendent of their grandfather's pray-at-the-bed piety; a man who flunked theology but had memorized Butler's *Lives of the Saints*.

Even Dressler's view on abortion has evolved: good and evil is now replaced with "wrenching decisions between bad and worse outcomes."[48] His faith has become an amalgam of the conceptual and the "unexpectedly sensual fabric of Catholicism, made up of rosary beads and silver crucifixes, the weight of altar robes on my shoulders, incense and candlelight, the red and blue cloth markers in my grandparents' black leather missals and the old-paper smell of the gilt-edged pages, the ritual rhythms of the

41. Ibid.
42. Ibid., 31–32.
43. Ibid., 54.
44. Ibid., 105.
45. Ibid., 106.
46. Ibid., 131.
47. Ibid., 108.
48. Ibid., 127.

Mass, the hymns of the Christmas season that promised more reason to the world than we could see."[49] For all his lyric thoughts, Dressler realizes the daily minutia of the job makes mundane the meaning of the word "clerical." Out of vestments during his leave, he worries about holding eye contact with a priest, who was probably afraid that Dressler might "bother him after Mass, disturb his routine."[50] Dressler remembers that those "Sunday afternoons are sacred": watching sports, drinking beer, talking with friends from seminary.[51]

During his youth, Dressler had worked in the rectory office of Father Phil, a mentor. He witnessed the layers of priestly identity, observing Father Phil hang his vestments while Dressler "sealed the plastic baggie of unconsecrated Hosts and carefully rinsed the chalice and cruets and made sure the markers were in place for the readings at noon Mass."[52] God was present, but man needed to make him visible. Father Phil's feet, and mind, are on the ground. He does "God's work," while contemplation is the stuff of monks.[53] He later advises Dressler to keep his "hands busy" to avoid sin, sounding more like a joking father than a spiritual guide.[54] Dressler appreciates this blue-collar Catholicism, seeing a softer version of his own father, who, when he finishes praying in front of votive candles, turns to his son and asks, "The fuck you want?"[55] The shifts, in a finer way, show that one's vestments make and remake identity; when Dressler identifies himself as "out of habit," he is also showing that his faith has been redressed.[56]

Dressler's break of celibacy and subsequent fall occur within the novel's two convoluted subplots, which include kissing a woman whose own father was a priest, and Dressler's first-hand view of a felon's suicide by shotgun. The storyline later reroutes toward its stronger, narrower precedent. At a time when American dioceses felt the reverberations of pedophilia, Dressler's sins are different, and when superiors explain that they are "too short of priests to stand on principle for too long," the reader

49. Ibid., 157–8.
50. Ibid., 32.
51. Ibid.
52. Ibid., 54–55.
53. Ibid., 55.
54. Ibid., 135.
55. Ibid., 357.
56. Ibid., 88.

pauses.[57] Such perception of rarity can lead to perception of grandeur, but Anne brings Dressler down to reality: "Why do priests . . . think God pays so much attention to them?"[58] One fellow priest who feels charged with significance is Mick, a conceited man whose dallies with women, including trips abroad, go institutionally unpunished because he knows that, in the Church, "There's room for men like me."[59] Mick allows Reimringer to portray a hierarchy of sin, leading the reader to consider that Dressler is truly a good man, the type who might spur reconsideration of priestly celibacy.

Dressler reunites with Betty, now separated from her husband, and explains his status in layman's terms: "my wife's kicked me out, and I'm living at my mom's house because she—the Church—is also my employer. It's not just losing a job or having a relationship on the rocks. It's both at once."[60] Dressler and Betty begin having sex again during his leave from ministry, in part because Dressler admits "What God wanted was no longer obvious to me."[61] This fracturing is Reimringer's preferred method of interrogation: as an elegy and not a polemic, *Vestments* arrives at real critique within a work of fiction. The critique climaxes with the death of Dressler's grandfather, and his celebration of Jacky's wedding, which becomes his final official duties as a priest. He gives the Host to his father, ceding power to self rather than Church Law. After the celebration, prayer escapes Dressler in the empty church. He crosses himself, and concludes that he must leave his vestments behind: "At the altar, I opened my eyes. Betty was my first lover, and longest and deepest, and when I took my vows, her face was the face of the world that I turned my back on."[62] He can now pray, but his plea is different: "*Lord God, forgive me for what I'm about to do. Forgive me for wanting communion with one woman over that with the people you called me to serve. And forgive me most of all for wanting a son of my own, for not finding your Son to be enough.*"[63]

Vestments does not accumulate to an indictment of the Church, or even a damning critique of priestly celibacy. Reimringer is an honest writer of fiction, willing to allow any critiques to reside in the world of his

57. Ibid., 311–2.
58. Ibid., 315.
59. Ibid., 319.
60. Ibid., 345.
61. Ibid., 375.
62. Ibid., 404.
63. Ibid., 404–5.

character, a man who has changed his vocation. The book does not posit that the postconciliar world sped Dressler's divergence; rather, that the postconciliar world has given him more power to move from the Church but remain suffused with faith.

Reimringer's novel leads toward Tom Bailey's 2005 work, *The Grace That Keeps This World*, where Father Anthony's character encapsulates the close-knit Catholicism that gives hope to the town of Lost Lake, New York. Bailey uses a Faulknerian structure of multiple narrators, with some sections delivered in the labeled first-person, others filtered in a malleable third-person, to reveal the communal experience of the town. In this Adirondack country, the ritual of seasons dictates life. Wood is needed for fire, venison for eating: all must be stockpiled, like faith in waiting, to combat the heavy winters. For Gary Hazen, life is survival: "there's no difference between the two."[64] He thinks that his family knows "all about the cold," but they will soon experience a metaphorical cold beyond their imagining.[65]

The Hazens are Catholic, but each member carries idiosyncrasies of faith. Gary's wife Susan makes a "cross at my heart, fingering the air in an endless rosary of ways that grants me the will . . . [to] step out into the now of days."[66] Susan's first narrative appears in the present, but that tense, grieving moment is reflected at every step of Bailey's elegiac novel. Her son Kevin is comfortably postconciliar. He considers himself a good Catholic because he attends Mass and confesses his sins, but he "wasn't crazy," and could make his own decision to use condoms when having sex with his girlfriend, Jeanie.[67] Gary David, the other son, also attends Mass, but harbors his own secret. While his father is "stumbling blindly down the stairs to plug in the coffeepot" before early morning Mass, Gary David is sneaking home from late night trysts with Josephine Roy, the new local conservation officer.[68] Gary does not appreciate Josephine's new ways: he is used to not being bothered, but Josephine gives parking violations, requires gun licenses, and confronts Gary about bending the truth regarding buck tags.

Josephine's sins might seem minor, but Lost Lake is a hunting community. The annual Hunter's Mass fills St. Pius church. The church is small,

64. Bailey, *Grace*, 13.

65. Ibid.

66. Ibid., 7.

67. Ibid., 24.

68. Ibid., 133.

but Father Anthony personally offers peace to each congregant. Gary and his family sit in the front row, but that is expected: even during daily Mass Gary is front and center because "he liked to witness the mystery" up close.[69] Bailey chooses Father Anthony as the narratalogical axis of Gary's faith. The two are close friends, but most importantly, Gary's theology is nebulous, unfinished, and Father Anthony is given the responsibility to shape his friend's soul, both in life and on the page. Father Anthony celebrates the daily morning Mass in Latin, during which Gary "would go away from himself into the sound of the Word," only exiting that ecstatic state during the Lord's Prayer.[70] In the language of Dubus, Father Anthony considers that those "moments for Gary seemed to hold out the promise that as practical as he felt himself to be, one day he might actually be able to give himself completely over to the sacrament."[71] Father Anthony uses similar kenotic language elsewhere, but Gary is the locus: a man committed to bodily and familial preparation, who simultaneously recognizes his vessel is temporary.

A Lutheran convert, Gary was particularly drawn to the sacrament of confession. He "liked to declare his penance out loud while cruising timber in the woods: stopping to lay his hand on a hundred-foot white pine, measuring it by eye against the blue sky."[72] Gary's pastoral piety is not sentimental, but it is critiqued by Father Anthony, who fears the narcissistic strand present in Gary's faith. Gary thought the sacrament of confession was imperfect, largely because he was imperfect: he thought "forgiveness could only extend so far before it became false, even wrong, to forgive."[73] Father Anthony chides personal theology, noting that Gary "did not recognize the danger of blasphemy inherent in his thinking: *There was only so much God could do.*"[74] Recognizing that Gary's hold on faith is tenuous even drives Father Anthony to reach through the confessional curtain and offer his hand, as a way of reaffirming bodily presence and connection.

Father Anthony sees the Hazens off on what will become the final hunt of the novel. Afterward, in the dark forest, Gary narrates: "Gary David passes me the cup, and I take another sip and glance at my sons."[75] Eu-

---

69. Ibid., 137.
70. Ibid., 136.
71. Ibid., 137.
72. Ibid., 138.
73. Ibid., 139.
74. Ibid.
75. Ibid., 222.

charistic language extends to the hunt, to the entire novel's juxtaposition of flesh and feeling. Even Susan, thinking of the distant summer, fantasizes in similar terms: "the sting of the black flies taking back a bite of blood for their own . . . In this conception I can rise, reborn into the day, each day, given reason through faith."[76]

The novel's tragedies occur during this hunt. Gary accidently shoots and kills Gary David. Kevin's third-person narrated sequence reveals the other son's discovery of "his father scraping and groveling. He was on his knees, bowing low, inchwormed up as if he were praying in the snow" until Kevin "saw the rifle barrel choked off in his father's mouth."[77] Gary miraculously survives the suicide attempt, and since Kevin's narration is filtered and not direct, Bailey can remain long enough in the moment for Kevin to consider how his father had "given in to the *feeling* of what to do."[78] Gary's narcissistic faith makes him subvert the kenotic action of Christ, using the same language as Father Anthony earlier in the novel. In a scene reminiscent of Leo Tolstoy's *Master and Man*, Kevin spreads across his father's injured body while snow falls; unlike the novella, both men survive.

In the face of tragedy, Susan Hazen is helped out of Gary David's funeral Mass by both her husband and Father Anthony, whose "white-robed arms [wing] over us, his purple stole flapping."[79] In this world, faith is equal parts salve and burden. Gary admits that the "Blood burns a bit going down."[80] He is given the novel's final section, where he explains his continued dedication to confession, recognizing that his "penance is to *live* with the knowledge that I killed my son."[81] He knows, consistent with his seasonal return to the forest, *"The work we live to do is work we'll never see completed."*[82] The snow, and the geese, will return, and for that he has "faith. The strength of belief."[83]

In *The Grace That Keeps This World*, faith does not eliminate evil and suffering; it offers a way to survive them. Father Anthony's kenotic model influences his lay congregants, who repeat, and perhaps perfect, that

76. Ibid., 8.
77. Ibid., 240.
78. Ibid., 254.
79. Ibid., 267.
80. Ibid., 194.
81. Ibid., 275.
82. Ibid.
83. Ibid.

model. The model is postconciliar. Waldmeir's Pauline metaphor of the traditional Church as hierarchical body, with the laity ruled by priests, is changed. Literature is the liturgy from the laity, and these "writers encourage the Church to accept the assistance offered by those who speak from within a broader history and wider culture."[84]

Postconciliar Catholic literature is not a replacement for faith. The contemporary Catholic canon is an extension, an imaginative illumination of a Word that, for many, might simply become words. Catholic convert Franz Wright echoes similar worry: that the "words of Jesus . . . are so familiar that I am constantly in danger of becoming insensitive to their power."[85] Channeling his personal experiences, Wright calls for a literary reconsideration of Christ's language, hoping for the addition of a "sacrament of words" to the existing Catholic sacraments.[86] He begins with the orality of Christ's parables, the orality of Catholic receipt of the Eucharist, and then the best attempts to mold Christ's words into narrative: the Gospels, literature. Wright preaches an active poetics of Christ: writer as participant, contributor to meaning. A pastoral vision of literary Catholicism.

Wright acknowledges that his beliefs seem like "quaint absurdity in the eyes of so many I encounter in the literary world."[87] His sentiment is shared by Ron Hansen, and by Alice McDermott, whose essay "Confessions of a Reluctant Catholic" documents a literary life in the lighting shadow of Catholicism. A cradle Catholic, McDermott's faith was never up for discussion. Mass attendance and prayer were habitual actions. When preconciliar practices evolved into postconciliar realities, her parents "accepted it all with good humor," explaining that the medium, and not the message, had changed.[88] McDermott documents, with self-effacing smirks, her drift from the Church during college, but identifies herself, at middle-age, as a "reluctant, resigned, occasionally exasperated but nevertheless practicing Catholic with no thought, or hope, of ever being otherwise."[89] McDermott shares McGraw's hesitance that tenuous Catholics seem to be the norm rather than the exception. Yet she is willing to accept the responsibility, in part because her age has allowed her to take ownership of a faith that was given to her, and the paradox of "a church we have, at various times in our

84. Waldmeir, *Cathedrals*, 14.
85. Wright, "Language," para. 1.
86. Ibid., para. 8.
87. Ibid., para. 2.
88. McDermott, "Confessions," 12.
89. Ibid., 13.

lives, seen as flawed, irrelevant, outdated, impossible, and impossible to leave behind."[90]

Like Hansen, McDermott finds that being a Catholic writer "carries certain obligations," and one of those includes reflection on the definition of how those identities might best intersect in a postconciliar world.[91] It was Faulkner, and not the Church Fathers, who brought McDermott back to Catholicism. His Nobel Prize acceptance speech reminded her that "the church, Catholicism, gave certain of my characters a language" to speak about the longing for permanence in a temporary world.[92] That Catholic language could be used to ask the questions McDermott hoped to pose as a novelist, but she "was not prepared to discover, or to rediscover . . . that they were questions for which the church also provided answers."[93] Catholicism is the "native language" of McDermott's "spirit."[94]

The writers profiled in *The Fine Delight* are practicing, lapsed, converted, ancillary, skeptical Catholics. They might be Catholic only on the page, or in the actions and words of their characters, but they are Catholic in the widest sense of the word, the only true sense of the word. The sum result of postconciliar Catholic literature is this paradoxical living liturgy, of a deeper appreciation for faith through interrogation. This interrogation is an active process. Preconciliar Catholicism was a paradox, a world made new and often strange to the daily American eye, and postconciliar Catholicism is equally complex, with parallel lines of progressive and conservative ideologies, of sin next to sainthood. *The Fine Delight* hopes to reveal that, rather than theologically and culturally melting into the American pot, Catholicism remains a literary Other. Postconciliar Catholic writers practice a continual need to self-define, both in relation to previous Catholic traditions, but also as a way to remain a separate American cultural identity. That there are many variations or hues of Catholicism does not mean those shadings are moving toward Protestant or evangelical faiths. Rather, the splintering of Catholicism, particularly in the literary sense, might mean an evolution and refinement of what it means to be Catholic in the contemporary world. In that sense, Catholic writers offer a unique spectrum of traits most helpful to pastoral outreach, instruction, and reflection: a love for scholarship and tradition, yet continual reconsideration

90. Ibid.
91. Ibid., 14.
92. Ibid., 15.
93. Ibid.
94. Ibid.

and refinement; mediation between a personal spirituality and the desire to be a part of a larger Church community and metaphysical "body"; rejection of fundamentalist, literalist readings of the Bible in favor of more nuanced readings aware of both literary form and contextual influence; compassion for immigrants and the poor, and empathy for those who have been the recipients of prejudice. It is these traits that make postconciliar Catholicism a unique pivot point in American letters: a dynamic, diverse collection of writers who simultaneously unite under an umbrella identity while exerting passionate individualism. That tension of paradoxes creates a unique set of literature, one as worthy of sustained study as it is of continued creation. Catholic writers will never agree on everything, and that dissension, united by a fascination with Christ, is perhaps their most Catholic element of all.

Bibliography

Abbott, C. C., ed. *The Letters of Gerard Manley Hopkins to Robert Bridges*. Oxford: Oxford University Press, 1935.

Arnell, Carla A. "Wild Writing: Holy Stigmata and the Aesthetics of 'Sacred Pain' in Ron Hansen's *Mariette in Ecstasy*." *Christianity and Literature* 57 (Winter 2007) 181–206.

Auchter, Amanda. Electronic interview with author. October 9, 2012.

———. *The Glass Crib*. Clarksville, TN: Zone 3, 2011.

Bailey, Tom. *The Grace That Keeps This World*. New York: Random House, 2005.

Bell, Madison Smartt. "The Man Who Understood Horses." *The New York Times* (May 17 1992) 9 and 11.

Bonomo, Joe. "After Cornell." *Quarter After Eight* 7 (2001) 162–67.

———. "The God Blurred World." *New Ohio Review* 5 (2009) 92–98.

———. "Occasional Prayer." *Fourth Genre* 12 (2010) 15–22.

———. "Seams, Hinges, and other Disclosures." *Fourth Genre* 12 (2010) 145–50.

———. "Swooning at St. Andrew's." *River Teeth* 3 (2001) 6–8.

Biddinger, Mary. *O Holy Insurgency*. New York: Black Lawrence, 2012.

———. *Saint Monica*. New York: Black Lawrence, 2011.

Brown, Dale W. "Participating in the Divine." *Sojourners* (December 2005) 38–44.

Burns, Robert A. *Roman Catholicism After Vatican II*. Washington, DC: Georgetown University Press, 2001.

Cadegan, Una M. "How Realistic Can a Catholic Writer Be? Richard Sullivan and American Catholic Literature." *Religion and American Culture: A Journal of Interpretation* 6 (Winter 1996) 35–61.

Carelli, Anthony. *Carnations*. Princeton: Princeton University Press, 2011.

———. Electronic interview with author. May 16, 2012.

Contino, Paul J. "Andre Dubus's Eucharistic Imagination." *Religion and the Arts* 6 (2002) 52–72.

"A Conversation with Salvatore Scibona about *The End*." April 2008. No pages. Online: http://www.theendnovel.com/theendnovel/Pre-pub._Interv._The_End_Novel_Salvatore_Scibona.html.

Crouan, Denis. *The Liturgy after Vatican II*. Translated by Mark Sebanc. San Francisco: Ignatius, 2001.

DeLillo, Don. *End Zone*. 1972; reprint, New York: Penguin, 1998.

———. *Point Omega*. New York: Scribner, 2011.

Bibliography

Denard, Carolyn C., editor. *Toni Morrison: Conversations*. Jackson: University Press of Mississippi, 2008.

Doyle, Brian. *Grace Notes*. Chicago: ACTA Publications, 2011.

———. *Leaping: Revelations and Epiphanies*. Chicago: Loyola Press, 2003.

———. *Mink River*. Corvallis: Oregon State University Press, 2010.

Dubus, Andre. *Broken Vessels*. Jaffrey, NH: Godine, 1991.

———. *Dancing After Hours*. New York: Vintage, 1997.

———. *Finding a Girl in America*. Jaffrey, NH: Godine, 1993.

———. *The Last Worthless Evening*. New York: Crown, 1986.

———. *Meditations from a Moveable Chair*. New York: Vintage, 1998.

———. *Selected Stories*. New York: Vintage, 1996.

———. *The Times Are Never So Bad*. Boston: Godine, 1993.

Dubus III, Andre. *Townie*. New York: Norton, 2011.

Eco, Umberto. "The Artist and Medieval Thought in the Early Joyce." In *A Portrait of the Artist as a Young Man*, edited by John Paul Riquelme, 329–48. New York: Norton, 2007.

Elie, Paul. "The Last Catholic Writer in America." In *American Catholics, American Culture: Tradition & Resistance,* edited by Margaret O'Brien Steinfels, 119–28. Lanham, MD: Sheed & Ward, 2004

Ellsberg, Robert, ed. *Flannery O'Connor: Spiritual Writings*. Maryknoll, NY: Orbis, 2003.

Eugenides, Jeffrey. *The Marriage Plot*. New York: Macmillan, 2011.

———. *The Virgin Suicides*. New York: Picador, 1993.

Fay, Robert. "Where Have All the Catholic Writers Gone?" *The Millions* (November 2011). No pages. Online: http://www.themillions.com/2011/11/where-have-all-the-catholic-writers-gone.html.

Ferriss, Lucy. "'Never Truly Members': Andre Dubus's Patriarchal Catholicism." *South Atlantic Review* 62 (Spring 1997) 39–55.

Flannery, Austin, ed. "Dogmatic Constitution on the Church." In *Vatican Council II: The Conciliar and Post Conciliar Documents*. Northport, NY: Costello, 1975.

Forbes, Eric. "The Writing Life: John Reimringer." No pages. Online: http://goodbooksguide.blogspot.com/2009/08/writing-life-john-reimringer.html.

Frykholm, Amy. "The Risks of Writing: An Interview with Ron Hansen." *Christian Century* 125 (August 2008) 24–27.

Gandolfo, Anita. *Testing the Faith: the New Catholic Fiction in America*. Westport, CT: Greenwood, 1992.

Gardner, John. *The Art of Fiction*. New York: Random House, 1983.

———. *On Moral Fiction*. New York: Basic, 1978.

Gass, William H. *Fiction and the Figures of Life*. Boston: Godine, 2000.

———. *In the Heart of the Heart of the Country*. 1968; reprint, Boston: Godine, 1998

Gilbert, Sandra M. "Foreword." In *Reconciling Catholicism and Feminism? Personal Reflections on Tradition and Change*, edited by Ron Ebest and Sally Barr Ebest, xi–xix. Notre Dame, IN: University of Notre Dame Press, 2003.

Gordon, Mary. "Moral Fiction." *The Atlantic* (2005). No Pages. Online: http://www.theatlantic.com/magazine/archive/2005/08/moral-fiction/304128/.

Hansen, Ron. Electronic interview with author. March 7, 2012.

———. *Exiles*. New York: Picador, 2008.

———. *Mariette in Ecstasy*. New York: Harper Perennial, 1991.

———. *A Stay Against Confusion.* New York: Harper Perennial, 2002.

Hungerford, Amy. *Postmodern Belief: American Literature and Religion since 1960.* Princeton: Princeton University Press, 2010.

"Interview with Joe Bonomo." *The Fine Delight* (January 2011). No pages. Online: http://catholiclit.blogspot.com/2011/01/interview-with-joe-bonomo.html.

"Interview with Pat Madden." *The Fine Delight* (February 2011). No pages. Online: http://catholiclit.blogspot.com/2011/02/interview-with-patrick-madden.html.

"Interview with Paul Lisicky." *The Fine Delight* (December 2010). No pages. Online: http://catholiclit.blogspot.com/2010/12/interview-with-paul-lisicky.html.

"Interview with Paul Mariani." *The Fine Delight* (February 2011). No pages. Online: http://catholiclit.blogspot.com/2011/02/interview-with-paul-mariani.html.

"Interview with Ron Hansen." *The Fine Delight* (February 2011). No pages. Online: http://catholiclit.blogspot.com/2011/02/interview-with-ron-hansen.html.

"Interview with Salvatore Scibona." *The National Book Foundation.* Interview by Bret Anthony Johnston, 2008. No pages. Online: http://www.nationalbook.org/nba2008_f_scibona_interv.html.

Johnson, Luke Timothy. "A Disembodied 'Theology of the Body': John Paul II on Love, Sex, and Pleasure." In *Human Sexuality in the Catholic Tradition,* edited by Kieran Scott and Harold Daly Horell, 111–22. Lanham, MD: Rowman & Littlefield, 2007.

Kennedy, Thomas E. *Andre Dubus: A Study of the Short Fiction.* Boston: G. K. Hall, 1988.

Knust, Jennifer. "Commentary: Body–Critical Embodiment." In *Practicing Catholic: Ritual, Body, and Contestation in Catholic Faith,* edited by Bruce T. Morrill, Joanna E. Ziegler, Susan Rodgers, 68–71. New York: Palgrave Macmillan, 2006.

Labrie, Ross. *The Catholic Imagination in American Literature.* Columbia: University of Missouri Press, 1997.

LeClair, Thomas. "Deconstructing the Logos: Don DeLillo's *End Zone.*" *Modern Fiction Studies* 33:1 (1987) 105–23.

Lewis, Robert P. "Anamnesis: Andre Dubus's Catholic Imagination." *Religion and the Arts* 4 (2000) 247–59.

———. "'No More Male and Female': Bodiliness and Eucharist in Andre Dubus's Stories." *Religion and the Arts* 6 (2002) 36–51.

Lisicky, Paul. *Famous Builder.* Saint Paul, MN: Graywolf, 2002.

Madden, Patrick. *Quotidiana.* Lincoln: University of Nebraska Press, 2010.

Mariani, Paul. Electronic interview with author. May 14, 2012.

———. *Epitaphs for the Journey: New, Selected, and Revised Poems.* Eugene, OR: Wipf and Stock, 2012.

———. *Gerard Manley Hopkins: A Life.* New York: Penguin, 2008.

———. *God and the Imagination.* Athens: The University of Georgia Press, 2002.

———. *Salvage Operations: New and Selected Poems.* New York: Norton, 1990.

McDermott, Alice. "Confessions of a Reluctant Catholic." *Commonweal* 127.3 (2000) 12–16.

McGraw, Erin. "Punchline." *The Kenyon Review* 33.4 (Fall 2011) 35–48.

———. "The Penance Practicum." *The Kenyon Review* 26.1 (Winter 2004) 18–35.

———. "True Believer." *The Gettysburg Review* (Autumn 2000). No pages. Online: http://www.gettysburgreview.com/selections/past_selections.

Neary, John. *Like and Unlike God: Religious Imaginations in Modern and Contemporary Fiction.* New York: Oxford University Press, 1999.

Bibliography

Nelson, Shirley. "Stewards of the Imagination: Ron Hansen, Larry Woiwode, and Sue Miller." *Christian Century* 112 (January 1995) 82.

Oakes, Kaya. *Radical Reinvention*. Berkeley, CA: Counterpoint, 2012.

O'Malley, J. P. "A Conversation about 'The Marriage Plot.'" "Prospero: Books, Arts, and Culture." *The Economist*. No pages. Online: http://www.economist.com/blogs/prospero/2011/11/qa-jeffrey-eugenides.

Percy, Walker. *The Moviegoer*. 1961 Reprint; New York: Vintage, 1998.

Pierce, Joanne M. "Marginal Bodies: Liturgical Structures of Pain and Deliverance in the Middle Ages." In *Practicing Catholic: Ritual, Body, and Contestation in Catholic Faith*, edited by Bruce T. Morrill et al., 59–67. New York: Palgrave Macmillan, 2006.

Powers, J. F. *Wheat That Springeth Green*. New York: Knopf, 1988.

———. *The Stories of J. F. Powers*. New York: The New York Review of Books, 2000.

Reimringer, John. *Vestments*. Minneapolis: Milkweed Editions, 2010.

Rosenthal, Peggy. *The Poets' Jesus: Representations at the End of a Millennium*. New York: Oxford University Press, 2000.

Schork, R. J. "James Joyce and the Eastern Orthodox Church." *Journal of Modern Greek Studies* 17 (1999) 107–24.

Scibona, Salvatore. *The End*. Saint Paul, MN: Graywolf, 2008.

———. Review of *The Angel Esmeralda*, by Don DeLillo. *The San Francisco Chronicle* (November 13, 2011). No pages. Online: http://www.sfgate.com/books/article/The-Angel-Esmeralda-by-Don-DeLillo-review-2298183.php

Stenstrom, Christine. "Review of Paul Mariani's *Salvage Operations*." *Library Journal* 13 (1990) 113.

Stevens, Jennifer. *The Historical Jesus and the Literary Imagination 1860–1920*. Liverpool: Liverpool University Press, 2010.

Sullivan, Andrew. *Virtually Normal: An Argument About Homosexuality*. New York: Knopf, 1995.

Swindell, Larry. "Our Best Novelist: He Thinks So, Too." In *Conversations with John Gardner*, edited by Allan Richard Chavkin, 34–39. Jackson: University Press of Mississippi, 1990.

"Talk About New Books." *Catholic World* 60 (1895) 562–71.

Teilhard de Chardin, Pierre. *Letters from a Traveller*. New York: Harper & Brothers, 1962.

Waldmeir, John C. *Cathedrals of Bone: The Role of the Body in Contemporary Catholic Literature*. New York: Fordham University Press, 2009.

Ward, Bernadette Waterman. *World as Word: Philosophical Theology in Gerard Manley Hopkins*. Washington, DC: Catholic University of America Press, 2002.

Wendorf, Thomas A. "Body, Soul, and Beyond: Mystical Experience in Ron Hansen's *Mariette in Ecstasy* and Mark Salzman's *Lying Awake*." *Logos: A Journal of Catholic Thought and Culture* 7.4 (Fall 2004) 37–64.

Wright, Franz. "Language as Sacrament in the New Testament." *Image* 57 (Spring 2008) 87–95. http://www.imagejournal.org/page/journal/articles/issue-57/wright-essay.

Yezzi, David. "'Power of some sort or other': on Poems and Prayers." *The New Criterion* (April 2012). No pages. Online: http://www.newcriterion.com/articles.cfm/-Power-of-some-sort-or-other—on-poems-and-prayers-7319.

Ziegler, Joanna E. "Medieval Studies Encounter Ritual Practice." In *Practicing Catholic: Ritual, Body, and Contestation in Catholic Faith*, edited by Bruce T. Morrill et al., 10–15. New York: Palgrave Macmillan, 2006.

Index of Names and Authors

Index of Names and Authors